BIG AL

BIG AL

FIFTY YEARS OF ADVENTURES IN SPORTS BROADCASTING

AL MELTZER
WITH ROBERT S. LYONS

Camino Books, Inc.

Philadelphia

Manufactured in the United States of America

1 2 3 4 5   15 14 13 12

Library of Congress Cataloging-in-Publication Data

Meltzer, Al.
   Big Al: fifty years of adventures in sports broadcasting / Al Meltzer with Robert S.
Lyons.
      p. cm.
   ISBN 978-1-933822-41-9 (alk. paper)
   1. Meltzer, Al. 2. Sportscasters—United States—Biography. I. Lyons, Robert S.,
   1939- II. Title.
   GV742.42.M475A3 2011
   796.962092—dc23
   [B]   2011033668

      ISBN: 978-1-933822-41-9

Interior and cover design: Jerilyn Bockorick

This book is available at a special discount on bulk purchases for promotional,
business, and educational use.

Publisher
Camino Books, Inc.
P.O. Box 59026
Philadelphia, PA 19102

www.caminobooks.com

For my wife, Beverly,
without whom this book would not have been written,
and to all my family and friends along the way.
Al Meltzer

To my dear wife, Joan, who is always there for me.
Robert S. Lyons

Contents

Foreword by Jack Whitaker *ix*

Introduction *xi*

CHAPTER 1
Once Upon a Time, *Big Al* was *Little Al* *1*

CHAPTER 2
A Broadcasting Career is Delayed by War *9*

CHAPTER 3
**Back to Syracuse with
Jim Brown, Boxing, and TV** *16*

CHAPTER 4
**Basketball, Bullfights, and
Al's Big Chance in Philadelphia** *25*

CHAPTER 5
**Big 5 Basketball:
Indescribable and Unforgettable** *39*

CHAPTER 6
**Life in the NBA: Not Always
Glamorous, But Always an Adventure** *47*

CHAPTER 7
Camelot at Channel 3 Eyewitness News *64*

CHAPTER 8
Life with O.J. and the Buffalo Bills *73*

CHAPTER 9

**Covering the Broad Street Bullies,
But Missing the Parade** *80*

CHAPTER 10

**Other Towns Come Calling,
But There's No Place Like Home** *88*

CHAPTER 11

**Big Al Pulls Off the Only
Local TV Hat Trick (Plus One)** *95*

CHAPTER 12

**Keeping Up with Colorful Birds
Like Buddy, Dick, and Leonard** *109*

CHAPTER 13

**Big Al Has Mitch Williams All
to Himself as the Phillies Rise and Fall** *121*

CHAPTER 14

**A Cameo with *Rocky* and a
Final Fling at Comcast** *136*

CHAPTER 15

**Wilt Chamberlain Tells All...
for the Final Time** *143*

CHAPTER 16

**Wilt Chamberlain Tells More…
for the Final Time** *162*

CHAPTER 17

A Look Back and a Look Ahead *173*

Foreword

by Jack Whitaker

For those of us who grew up in the 1930s and '40s, radio was our great supplier of dreams. It was a free ticket to the world, an important provider of entertainment and education. The movies also entertained and instructed, but they lacked the one thing the little Emerson radio on the bedside table required of us—imagination.

With a click of the dial, we could be with the Lone Ranger in the Wild West, or attending a Broadway opening with Mr. First Nighter, and then dancing in a hotel ballroom to the music of the big bands.

We would rush home from school to catch the World Series and stare in awe at the radio set as Clem McCarthy's raspy voice described the Louis–Schmeling fight or the Kentucky Derby. We would laugh out loud at Jack Benny and Fred Allen and shiver at the sound of the creaking door on *Inner Sanctum*. And it was the radio that told us the Japanese had bombed Pearl Harbor one December Sunday.

Radio brought the real world to us, but it also fed our dreams. So it was not surprising that many of us were so enamored of this magical object that we yearned to be part of it.

In those long-ago days, only the large cities had radio stations. But that all changed near the end of World War II when the Federal Communications Commission released hundreds of AM and FM frequencies. Small towns that never had a radio station now had one or sometimes two. Towns with populations of 25,000 now had another voice besides the local newspaper.

These were not the powerful 50,000-watt stations like those in the big cities. These new frequencies were mostly of the 250 to a thousand-watt power and covered an area of 20 to 40 miles. Their studios were sparse and located over a department store or other commercial buildings. And the pay was anything but lavish.

A young announcer in those 250-watt stations received a rigorous training. He had to open the station in the morning, read the news, be a disc jockey, introduce religious leaders and politicians, and do a "man in the street" program. If you lasted two or three years in this environment, you could become a complete broadcaster. The road to the top today is far less strenuous.

Al Meltzer is a complete broadcaster. He passed the test of the 250-watt world. He could have been a successful newscaster, weatherman, or talk show host. He chose to be a sportscaster. His interest began in college at St. Lawrence University, and his journey started at a small day-time radio station in Fulton, New York, whose studio was over a drug store. His early training made the crossover into television effortless.

Like most sportscasters, Al traveled a lot with stops in his hometown of Syracuse, Buffalo, Philadelphia, Chicago, and finally back to Philadelphia where he found comfort and success. Along the way were seasons of doing play-by-play for the Buffalo Bills during the O.J. Simpson years. There is a cameo of Mr. Simpson that you will find intriguing. Al's revealing interview with Wilt Chamberlain gives insight into the man, not just the superstar. Baseball, soccer, golf, and basketball all were the provinces of Al Meltzer.

Al's career traces the sports world of America during the last half-century. It was a period of dramatic change, of amazing technology, and extraordinary expansion. Al Meltzer saw it all happen, and he lays it out in this book with enthusiasm and clarity. Big Al makes all the main events.

Introduction

Years ago, I was about to interview Kareem Abdul-Jabbar. As I walked toward him, the Milwaukee Bucks star looked at me with a big smile on his face and said, "Big Al, you know *big* is a relative term." Actually the moniker was not new. TV viewers in Philadelphia had been calling me that for years. But the name actually had its origin many years ago when I was the tallest kid in my class as a fourth-grader in Syracuse. A bunch of us went to a Saturday matinee for a double feature, and one of the films featured the characterization of Al Capone, the gangster from Chicago. As we left the movie theatre, my cousin Mort called me *Big Al*.

The nickname stuck. And so have the memories—50 years of delightful recollections covering every aspect of sports broadcasting, ranging from towns in upstate New York like Buffalo and Syracuse, to Midwestern cities like Milwaukee, to the major markets of Philadelphia and Chicago.

As that noted philosopher Yogi Berra once said: "When you come to a fork in the road, take it!" As you will see, my career included many such forks and paths that opened up along the way—some of them really beyond my control.

I was there at the beginning, recreating baseball games, sight unseen, literally out of thin air. I helped to introduce sports on that newfangled contraption called UHF television when viewers needed a special adapter and a circular antenna to pick up a frequently fuzzy, black-and-white picture. This was long before the arrival of computers and instant replay.

As I love to tell people, *we were ESPN before there even was an ESPN, and we didn't even know it.* I stood in front of the camera for the first Monday night football game ever telecast, and sat in the studio as host for the debut of cable TV's longest-running series in history, HBO's award-winning *Inside the NFL.* I've been there to watch television grow from its infancy and witness the breathtaking technological advances of satellite TV.

Come to think of it, I may be the only person in broadcasting history to have experienced *everything* in radio and television. I know that I'm the only sportscaster to have worked at *five* TV stations in the same city.

This is not just a story about sports, because early in my career I interviewed entertainers like Sammy Davis Jr., Johnny Ray, and Tony Bennett. But it's primarily a personal chronicle about the wonderful world of sportscasting and the personalities that I've had the pleasure of knowing. People like Wilt Chamberlain, who granted me his final exclusive interview. And there were many others, including Carmen Basilio, Chuck Bednarik, Tom Brookshier, Jim Brown, Bobby Clarke, Mort Crim, Mike Golic, Dallas Green, Alex Hannum, Wayne Hardin, Harry Kalas, Harry Litwack, Nancy Lopez, Arnold Palmer, Bernie Parent, Joe Paterno, Jack Ramsay, Buddy Ryan, Lou Saban, Dolph Shayes, Fred Shero, Mike Schmidt, Sylvester Stallone, Bobby Thomson, Leonard Tose, Dick Vermeil, Mitch Williams, and Pat Williams. There were the memorable events that I called, like O.J. Simpson's record-breaking game, as well as my experiences at World Series, Super Bowls, NBA Championships, Stanley Cups, Final Fours, and many Big 5 college basketball contests played in Philadelphia's venerable Palestra.

There have also been some bumps and bruises along the way. Like the time people showered me with beer after a World Series game. Or the terrifying moment following a National League baseball playoff when I was stormed by angry fans who almost overturned my remote TV truck while I was standing on top of it. And that frightening incident during one of the NFL player strikes when I was tossed around like a rag doll.

And to think that I once wanted to be a dentist—opening others' mouths to pull teeth instead of opening my mouth to talk about great and memorable fun and games. But I'm getting ahead of myself. Let's start at the beginning.

((((CHAPTER 1))))

Once Upon a Time, *Big Al* was *Little Al*

When I was born on June 26, 1928 at Crouse-Irving Hospital in Syracuse, the nation was a year away from the beginning of the Great Depression. For millions of people, it would be the worst of times. For me, even though I didn't understand what was going on, it turned out to be the best of times.

The stock market crash caused about a third of the people in America—including my dad and many of our neighbors who had been prosperous up to that point—to lose their jobs. Money was so scarce that my two older brothers, Irving and Ray, and my older sister, Harriet, had to put off college plans. They were needed to help my father, Mose, and my mother, Gertrude, with the family expenses. Harriet, who was the oldest child, never fulfilled her dream of becoming a teacher. She eventually got married and had a family. Irv, who had 13 years on me, would eventually go to St. Lawrence University on a football scholarship. Ray, who was seven years older, worked at a gas station, and then spent 30 years assembling televisions at General Electric. My younger brother, Sandy, who was born in 1933, went to Syracuse University and became an attorney.

My mom and dad had come over to this country from Russia with thousands of others in the early 1900s. They were escaping from Czar Nicholas II, who forced them to live in poverty in the Jewish settlements. It was just like *Fiddler on the Roof*. In fact, I took my father to see the hit musical show one time when he was visiting me in Philadelphia and I asked him, "What do you think?" He replied simply, "I lived there!"

1

Mose was a shoemaker by trade, just as his dad had been. He went to night school to learn English and, later on, did well enough managing a bakery to put a down payment on our first house. He was six-feet-four. My mom was five-feet-two.

My father was a very quiet man, and I remember that communication between generations was difficult. I always thought that he wasn't an outspoken person like many of my relatives. After he passed away, his youngest sister, who had a very good memory, vividly described how this gentle young man had emigrated to the United States at the age of 15. He was forced to leave because word had gotten around that the police were looking for him because he was a member of an anti-Czarist organization. He had a gun hidden in his house, and if he had still been there when the Russian Revolution broke out, he would have been one of the many young people who supported Lenin in the overthrow of the government.

Even though it caused the gravest of times for others, the Depression changed my young life. When my dad couldn't afford to make the mortgage payments on our two-story stone home, we were evicted and forced to rent the first floor of a two-family house located less than two blocks from the lush athletic fields of Syracuse University and legendary Archbold Stadium, which became my favorite place. And this is where my love of sports began. Not to mention my *hidden* broadcasting talent!

I guess I was in fourth grade at the time. I was in the hallway talking with a bunch of my buddies and my teacher, Miss Shanahan, walked by, stopped for a moment, listened to me, and then interjected, "Albert, you seem to be controlling the situation, which is not unusual. You certainly like to talk, and if you like to talk that much, maybe you ought to think about becoming a radio announcer after you graduate college." How prophetic was that?

We all laughed, but it was true. I seemed to have this ability to get involved with people, and I didn't need a forced conversation. I was the tallest guy in the class all through grammar school and high school, and I kind of stood out a little bit. All this time I was absorbing tremendous amounts of information because I loved listening to the radio, and I guess subliminally I was preparing myself for my career without knowing it.

After school, I would catch up with my cousin Mort, who lived four blocks away, and we'd head for the university with its acres and acres of green playing fields next to the ancient stadium. In the fall, we'd watch the freshmen and varsity football players practice. In the spring, it would be baseball, lacrosse, tennis, and track. In the wintertime, we'd sneak into Archbold and get our fill of basketball, boxing, wrestling, gymnastics, fencing, and indoor rowing. There'd even be action at the bowling alley. The custodian used to chase us out, but we learned how to avoid him and run to one of our hiding places. There we would shoot hoops with our own basketball. The stadium with the adjacent Hendricks Field was our playground during the summer for all kinds of games from early in the morning until the sun went down.

Almost every day, we'd watch one of the teams practicing. We just hung around, not bothering anybody, and not really understanding what was going on. Soon we became a little part of the scenery and people started noticing us. They'd give us little things to do and let us clean up after practice. Mort was the batboy for the visiting baseball team.

The Syracuse Orangemen had a pitcher named Jim Konstanty, who would later help lead the Philadelphia Phillies to the National League pennant and win the league's MVP award in 1950. The football team had a speedy halfback who also ran track and was selected for the 1936 U.S. Olympic team. He went to Berlin but wasn't permitted to compete by Avery Brundage, the president of the International Olympic Committee, because Brundage didn't want to offend Adolf Hitler. Marty Glickman, you see, was Jewish. But that didn't stop him from becoming one of the greatest sports announcers of all time and the man who invented the basketball play-by-play.

One of the other popular Syracuse athletes was Duffy Daugherty, a diminutive guard on the football team, who went on to become a great football coach at Michigan State. Then there was a very tall, handsome, blond graduate assistant by the name of Bud Wilkinson, who later became the legendary coach at the University of Oklahoma. Both Daugherty and Wilkinson won national championships and both are in the College Football Hall of Fame. And it all started with the Orangemen. We were watching and helping some of the great names in sports, and we didn't even know it!

Mort and I learned more about football than kids our age could ever dream of. Every Wednesday night in one of the university's lecture halls, head coach Ossie Solem, a kind and friendly man who had coached previously at Drake and Iowa, showed game films from the previous Saturday as we sat and watched spellbound. We learned all the variations of the single and double wing and the intricacies of playing the 6-2-2-1 defense.

We also saw firsthand one of the greatest innovations ever to hit college football—the "reversed center" play. Unfortunately, it lasted for only one year before it was outlawed. Before the 1941 season, Solem learned that the NCAA Rules Committee had passed a rule that the ball may be handed to any back or lineman, provided that the lineman is one yard back of the line of scrimmage and is facing his own goal line. Ossie then devised a play where he turned his center around, facing his own backs. The center would flip the ball to one of these backs, who could return the ball to the center, who was then eligible to throw a pass to one of the team's six eligible receivers. Solem used the play in a preseason scrimmage against Army, and it exceeded all of his expectations. It proved to be very effective in the Orangemen's second game against Cornell, but opposing coaches soon started to complain, even though Dr. Eddie Anderson, who was coaching at Holy Cross at the time, called it "one of the top three offensive ideas to ever come into the game." After the end of season, the NCAA outlawed the play.

Meanwhile, during the summer, we'd slip into Archbold Stadium when it was empty and learn about every nook and cranny. Then on Saturdays in the fall, we'd sneak into the stadium when no one was around, find our favorite hiding place, and sneak out onto the field while the band was marching before kickoff.

The university's biggest event during those years was always the last regular season game against its hated archrivals, the Red Raiders of Colgate, whose campus was located about 30 minutes to the east of Syracuse. This was a tradition that began in 1891 and would continue until 1961. Colgate dominated the rivalry in the early years, and Syracuse would end up winning only 26 of the 62 games with five contests ending in ties. The teams didn't even play for four years after a reporter ran out onto the field and tackled a Syracuse player during the game in 1897.

On the Friday night of "Colgate Weekend," a huge bonfire illuminated the practice field. What a sight! Then everyone would march through the campus where the fraternity and sorority houses were decorated with signs cheering on the Orangemen. Wild parties and daring raids on opposing campuses were commonplace. It was said that any Syracuse student caught at Colgate trying to light a bonfire, or otherwise trying to sabotage Colgate's chances of winning, would be apprehended and have a "C" shaved into his hair. A Colgate student found up to no good at Syracuse would have an "S" shaved on the top of his head. (In the interests of full disclosure, and after all these years of detesting everything that Colgate stands for, I must admit that my daughter Jordana is a Red Raider, a member of the Class of 2004!)

One of my first memories of big-time sports occurred on June 22, 1938. It was a few days before my 10th birthday—the night when Joe Louis, who had lost an earlier fight to Max Schmeling in 1936, faced the German hero in a much-awaited rematch at Yankee Stadium. Louis had won the world's heavyweight title in 1937, and the fight was broadcast not only in the United States by the immortal Clem McCarthy over the NBC radio network, but throughout Europe as well. McCarthy had the greatest voice for covering horseracing and boxing events that ever existed. His deep, gravel-like voice would always grab and hold his audience's attention.

Even though I was young, I knew that my country would likely be fighting Germany very shortly. My brother, Irv, was already talking about being drafted, and I also knew how Hitler was treating the German Jews. I found myself rooting for Joe Louis like I'd never rooted for anybody in my life.

I sat down on the front porch of my house and before I could even get settled, I heard McCarthy saying, "SCHMELING IS DOWN— ONE...TWO...THREE!" and the fight was over. And even to this day I can tell you what my feeling was when I knew Joe Louis had knocked out the Nazis' favorite in the very first round. It was absolutely wonderful. As a kid, there aren't too many things that you distinctly remember, but I will never forget that moment: McCarthy's gravel voice proclaiming, "Schmeling is down!"

It was as much political as it was athletic because everyone in America felt better. And for the "colored people," as they were known at the time, it was everything. Back then, the relationship between the races was far different than it is today.

On October 5, 1940, my cousin Mort and I, who by then had become the unofficial caretakers of Archbold Stadium, watched Northwestern's powerhouse football team open its season by trouncing our beloved Orangemen, 40-0. The big news had happened at practice the day before, however, when we saw a big group gathering around Northwestern's coach Pappy Waldorf, a former All-America tackle at Syracuse, who was proudly displaying what looked like a fish bowl. Actually, it was the latest innovation in football equipment—a plastic helmet that had been invented the previous year by employees of the John T. Riddell Company, a Chicago sporting goods manufacturer. Northwestern was located in Evanston, a nearby Illinois suburb, and was one of the first schools to try out the new helmets. I remember reading an article by one writer calling them "stronger, more durable and lighter than leather helmets," and I thought *wow, the future is now!* And it was. The era of the leather helmet was over.

What a life! That's how I grew up. I was a pretty good student in school, but my love of sports was the most important thing to me. Sports helped to carry me through some of the dramatic changes that were starting to happen quite rapidly in my life. It was 1941. I was 13 years old and had just finished grammar school when we moved to the second floor of a house on Renwick Place in Syracuse's 15th Ward. The rent was $25 a month. The house was located in the most diverse section of the city—a real melting pot of groups. There were bars on every corner and some very tough neighborhoods.

Not only was I changing schools and leaving some good friends behind, but I was now a teenager and I had my first real job—delivering the *Herald-Journal* in the surrounding neighborhoods. I had 75 customers and I made three dollars a week. But the big event in my young life was finding a lost dog of various breeds in my backyard. I named him Tiny and he became my faithful companion in the cold and very snowy winters and hot summers. Since he was always at my side, no one ever bothered me. I loved him and he returned that love.

Later, when I started Central High School, I found out just how much that love meant. I never rode the school bus back in those days and would walk a mile instead. During my first week at Central, I heard an announcement over the PA system that there was a black dog roaming the halls. It was Tiny. My best friend had followed me to school. After his third trip, we had to lock him in the house. He passed away soon after I left for college.

When I got to junior high school, I was spending most of my time at the Jewish Community Center with all the kids from my neighborhood. That's where I learned to play basketball. Day and night we ran up and down the court as basketball became *the* sport in my life. At six-feet-four, I was the big guy and by the time I got to Central High, to be honest, I was pretty good—good enough to be named to the city All-Star team my senior year. I wasn't much of a rebounder, and I didn't weigh very much (no more than about 155 pounds). In fact, when I was younger, my mother was always concerned because I was the thinnest kid in my class and my shoulder blades stuck out like wings.

Twice a year, Mother would take me to the free clinic to make sure that I didn't have tuberculosis. She also fed me a steady diet of chocolate milk with raw eggs (just like Sylvester Stallone in *Rocky*). Anyway, they pushed me around a little bit on the court, but I could score. I was a very good shooter—hook shots from the free throw line were my specialty— and I had a nice, soft touch. I averaged about 17 points per game in two varsity seasons and scored 29 in one game, which was the school record for awhile.

My biggest moment as a high school player came on the day when my brother, Irv, and my father came to one of my games. I hadn't seen Irv in four years and my father had never even seen a basketball game because he was always working. I can't recall who we played, but I do remember that we won and I performed well.

By this time I was expected to contribute a few bucks to the family's cookie jar to help with the finances. During the day, I'd ride my bike to the Drumlins Country Club. (A drumlin is a hill, and it was certainly hilly!) If you were classified as a "B" caddy (under the age of 16) and carried a bag for 18 holes, you got 25 cents for a loop, maybe a dime tip, and a hot dog at the turn. Then, at night, I pedaled to the bowling alley near the university and set pins for a dime a game.

Meanwhile, Irv had blossomed into a six-foot-four, 200-pound football star at Central High School, which had one of the best gridiron teams in the country. They played in postseason games in Tampa for two years in a row when he was in Florida. After graduation, Irv worked for a wholesale grocer lifting fruits and vegetables for a couple of years. Finally, he was offered an athletic scholarship to St. Lawrence, a little school nestled in the foothills of the Adirondacks, located near the Canadian border about four hours north of Syracuse. By then he had gained 40 pounds and excelled not only in football but also in wrestling as a heavyweight. One of his teammates was Isadore Demsky, a talented middleweight who had been born Issur Danielovitch and would be elected president of the student government. After graduating in 1939, he became an actor, moved to New York, and changed his name to Kirk Douglas.

After Irv graduated, he received a one-page letter from the Detroit Lions, inviting him to training camp. They offered to pay him $115 a game for an 11-game season in the National Football League, which was not bad money in those days. But this was in 1941. By December, shortly after Pearl Harbor, the nation would be at war. Irv was drafted into the military, never got to training camp, and never played professional football.

Our lives were about to change forever!

(((CHAPTER 2)))

A Broadcasting Career is Delayed by War

After I graduated from Central High School in 1946, my brother's alma mater, St. Lawrence University, called and offered me a small amount of scholarship aid—enough to take some of the financial burden off my family and guarantee me a chance to try out for the basketball team. I was still only about 170 pounds, and I couldn't jump that high. I could still shoot, but I wasn't strong enough or quick enough to get open.

Not only that, but I often felt victimized by the old "boys against the men" syndrome. World War II was now over and 75 percent of the student body was made up of ex-GIs, many of them older than I, and a lot of them with families. I still thought I was pretty good on the basketball court, but after getting pounded around during my freshman year and sitting on the bench the following season on the varsity, I made a decision to stick to my studies as a pre-dental major. This, of course, meant a curriculum top-heavy with science courses and lab time. And surprisingly, it also led to my start in broadcasting.

One of the first things I did was to rush the Phi Sigma Kappa Fraternity. I quickly became friends with a guy named Don Danielson, who had served as a forward artillery observer in the U.S. Army during the war. A huge New York Yankees fan, he was known as "D from New Rochelle." I was a Boston Red Sox fan because I spent my summers working near my brother's house in Gloucester, Massachusetts, so we'd argue constantly. Boy did we argue! But we also got to be the best of buddies because we'd go nonstop talking trash and sports while we washed dishes

9

together to help pay for our room and board. "D" was an English major who was taking a course in broadcasting. He also handled the sports news on KSLU, the campus radio station. One time in my junior year, he asked me if I'd do the show for him because he had a date. I said, "Sure. Why not?" I read the stories and the latest scores off the news wire, and that pretty much was it.

About a week later "D" said to me, "My teacher heard you on the air and really liked the way you handled the show." He added that Old Gold cigarettes was sponsoring a radio contest and looking for contestants. "Would you like to compete?" Again, I said, "Sure. Why not? It doesn't cost anything." So I went in and auditioned—which meant reading some copy for a commercial—and, lo and behold, not only did I end up as one of the three finalists, I won a chest of Old Gold cigarettes! I wasn't smoking at the time, so I gave them to the guys in the fraternity.

But the Old Gold incident started something clicking in my mind: *Say, what about this broadcasting thing?*

The following year, when I had a little more free time, "D" asked me if I would like to help him do baseball play-by-play. Students had never done the St. Lawrence baseball games before. But "D" thought it would be a great idea to broadcast college baseball on campus. We did a game and had a blast. Then we graduated.

Two weeks later, on June 25, 1950, North Korea invaded the south. Just like my older brother a few years earlier, my immediate plans were being curtailed. Just like Irv, I was facing the draft. I wasn't going to dental school anytime soon. One way or another, I was headed for military service. I decided to enlist in the Air Force, but they had such a backlog of new recruits that they told us it would be a few months before we finally got called up for active duty.

Then the radio bug came back and hit me hard. It was summertime, so I decided to take a bus and hitchhike around New York State to see if I could get some auditions and land a temporary job in radio. I ended up in a little town called Fulton. It had a daytime radio station, WOSC, which was located above a drugstore and was on the air only until sundown. They needed a body and asked me all kinds of questions. I stretched the truth, to say the least. I exaggerated about how much broadcasting experience I had in college. I hadn't even run a control board before. But they hired me. Of course, I know why: the job only paid 33 bucks a week. I didn't have a car, so I rented a room in a boarding house a few blocks away. I opened up the station on Saturdays and Sundays and hung around during the week to read the news and do a few other things.

Meanwhile, I had forgotten that sometime earlier I had also auditioned at a few stations in Syracuse. A few weeks after I went on the air in Fulton, I got a call from WAGE, the ABC affiliate in the city. The station manager said, "Look, I understand that you're going into the service soon, but we need some help. We need somebody to work part-time. Would you like the job?" Was he kidding? I would love the job. So here I was—back on the air in my hometown! I knew that it wasn't going to last long, but I did whatever I could do to fill in. One of my responsibilities, by the way, was to meet the elevator on the fifth floor and to greet the anchor of the six o'clock news. Then I would escort him to the studio and, when the show was over, bring him back to the elevator where his wife met him downstairs. Let's just say that he was a little bit unsteady most of the time. But let me tell you, when that light went on and he was on the air, he was absolutely brilliant. He had such a great voice and such a magnificent delivery that you'd never be able to tell that anything was wrong.

Along the way I figured, if I'm going to be in this business for a little while, I'd like to do some sports. So I talked my way into covering some games and occasionally handling the 11 o'clock sports. My mother passed away in October 1951, and the Air Force granted me a deferment until the end of that year, which gave me the opportunity to pick up even more experience. I got to do record shows and read the news. I hosted all the Sunday morning "hours"—the Jewish Hour, the Greek Hour, and the Italian Hour. The Jewish Hour was great because the guy always brought in fresh rye bread and a Hebrew National salami—just like Dave Zinkoff would do years later in Philadelphia. That was my Sunday morning breakfast. On Saturday nights, the station hosted "Duke Dixon and the Swingbillies," a live show with an audience. My job was to clean up the studio afterward, which meant opening up the windows and airing everything out. But boy, did I love that! Late at night after the news and sports, I would announce a show called "Music for Dreaming." Then I'd introduce the National Anthem and sign the station off the air. I'd also be around for the network breaks because, with only two TV stations in Syracuse, radio still ruled the airwaves.

Then came the time to leave. On New Year's Eve, 1951, I boarded a troop train headed for basic training at Lackland Air Force Base in San

Antonio, Texas. I thought my broadcasting career was over. I also learned quickly that I wasn't interested in another career.

I hadn't been in the service for a week and didn't even have a uniform yet when they sat me down and asked me what my interests were. Before I even had a chance to answer, this guy said, "I've got a great deal for you. I can send you back to your hometown." I knew what was coming next because I remembered that the Army had a Russian language school in Syracuse, housed in a couple of Quonset huts not too far down the road from Archbold Stadium. From what I understood, the Air Force students studying there never got the chance to go outside. From day one, there was nothing but Russian 24 hours a day, seven days a week, for an entire year. And I'm thinking to myself: *I could go back, but where am I going to go? They don't let you roam around town. It would be the toughest course you could possibly handle.* Then I figured: *If I get a Military Occupational Specialty (MOS) in the Russian language, there ain't no way I'm ever going to get out of the service.* This was before I even knew what I wanted to do in the Air Force. I said, "Thanks, but no thanks."

One early fall afternoon, I was hanging out in my new barracks at Bolling Air Force Base outside Washington, D.C. I turned on my little radio and picked up a major league baseball game. I hadn't been reading the newspapers recently, but I started listening to the final innings of the deciding 1951 National League Playoff Game at the Polo Grounds between the New York Giants and the Brooklyn Dodgers. Bobby Thomson came up and hit that climactic home run off Ralph Branca and the Giants won the Pennant! I thought to myself, *Wait a Minute...Bobby Thomson...Jersey City Giants...New York Giants...That's Bobby Thomson!*

My mind quickly flashed back five years. I remembered my freshman year in college and this guy that my classmates claimed could stand in the end zone and throw the ball all the way to the other end zone. He could also run faster than anybody on the track team. But he was already a professional baseball player. He had played with the New York Giants' Jersey City farm team, and he was scheduled to go to Spring Training with the big club. I mean he was a tremendous athlete. I would have loved to see him play football. His size and his speed would have made him unstoppable. I didn't know him very well, but I certainly knew who he was. His name was Bobby Thomson and he had been talked into attending St. Lawrence University for a semester by Hal Shumacher, who was known as "the Prince." Shumacher was an SLU graduate who had pitched for 13 years with the New York Giants and was highly respected in major league circles.

I was marveling about this great athlete from my alma mater. I wanted to tell everybody—friends and strangers alike: *Bobby Thomson...* *Bobby Thomson...I went to school at St. Lawrence with Bobby Thomson for a semester.* But no one really cared. It disappointed the hell out of me because I wanted the whole world to hear that I knew this guy, but people in the barracks had other things on their minds. I was proud of my alma mater, and I wanted to tell the world that St. Lawrence University was big-time! I was also proud of Bobby Thomson, who lived to the ripe old age of 86, passing away in 2010.

Most people don't realize that the SLU Saints are Division III in all sports except hockey. On the ice, they're Division I with a few interesting Philadelphia connections, I might add. The skating Saints' captain from 1983 to 1985 was a kid named Rejean (Ray) Shero, who replaced Craig Patrick as general manager of the Pittsburgh Penguins in 2006, and, like his father, was the brains behind some Stanley Cup winners. His dad, a guy named Fred Shero, coached the Flyers to both Stanley Cups and later coached the New York Rangers. Rejean was drafted by the Los Angeles Kings in 1982, but never played in the NHL.

Another name familiar to Philadelphia fans is Mike Keenan, a former Flyers coach who also did something that no one had done in New York in 54 years—he guided the Rangers to the Stanley Cup in 1994. Mike played at SLU from 1969 to 1972 before transferring to the University of Toronto for his final season.

And we certainly can't forget one of the Flyers' greatest nemeses, Bill Torrey, general manager of the New York Islanders from 1972 to 1992, who won four Stanley Cups in a row from 1980 to 1983. He was a skating Saint from 1954 to1957.

After basic training, I was assigned to the Office of Special Investigations at the Pentagon, in Washington, D.C., and I wasn't even a general. In fact, I didn't even have a stripe on my sleeve, but I was about to enter training as an intelligence agent in civilian clothes. It was like being in the FBI, but before I solved my first espionage case, my commanding officer convinced me that I had the makings of an officer. Two weeks later, I was on my way to Officer Candidate School in San Antonio, Texas, and six months after that I found myself back in Washington, D.C. as a second lieutenant assigned to the Office of Special Investigation. I was just about to start that assignment when my commanding officer asked me, "What does the Air Force do?" "Fly airplanes," I replied. I had given it some thought, but didn't think I could pass the eye examination. Surprisingly, I did with flying colors. My eyesight was 20/20.

The next thing I knew, I was in flight school in Bartow, Florida, which is halfway between Clearwater and Orlando. By day, we practiced flying T-6 planes. Afterward we took advantage of the great social life nearby and partied with the beautiful young women who were performing in the water skiing extravaganzas a few miles away at the Winter Haven Cypress Gardens. What a life! In fact, we even figured out our own private messaging system. When we took off from a certain runway, we hit the throttle a few extra times to signal that all the guys would be heading for Winter Haven that night or weekend.

All good things must come to an end, and most of the guys in my class in primary flight school were younger and went into jet training in the T-33 and, later, the F-86 fighter. I was almost 24 years old and six-feet-four, and my instructor said that for me it would be twin-engine advanced aircraft, which meant going low and slow. I was assigned to Reese Air Force Base, in Lubbock, Texas, and learned to fly the T-28 and B-25. I really enjoyed flying. Thoughts of making a career in the Air Force and later becoming a commercial pilot danced through my mind.

Instead, my life was about to change forever. I found myself facing one of those forks in the road that I mentioned earlier because one day in November 1953, when advanced training was almost over, they called all of us into the base theatre. Everyone was thinking Korea, and we expected to be given assignments overseas. Instead, they said, "Look guys, the war is winding down and we have a surplus of pilots. You can either sign an indefinite service statement [which meant that they had an option on your services forever] or retire from active duty and join the Air Force Reserve."

Well, here was the step in my life that probably had the most influence on what's happened in the past 83 years—the moment that changed my life forever. But the big problem with this decision was that I had to make up my mind ASAP! So the first thing I did was call my brother, who had spent four years in the Army during World War II. He said, "Hey, you get a chance to get out, you get out."

By then it was too late to get into dental school, so I decided to call the station in Syracuse where I had gotten my real start in broadcasting.

Formerly WAGE, it was now known as WHEN Radio and TV because it later had been purchased by one of the two TV stations in town. Talk about good timing. "Your old job just opened up," the station manager told me. "The guy who took your place, an ROTC grad from Syracuse, just got called a few days ago to go into active duty. The job is yours!"

That was the beginning of the end of my military career, which officially ended a year later when I mysteriously lost sight in my left eye and was discharged from the Air Force Reserve. I hopped into my car and headed home—stopping only for gas, a hamburger here and there, and a few hours of sleep. I really didn't know where my career was headed but I did know one thing: I was not going to be a dentist!

But who knows? If I hadn't made that phone call to my old radio station in Syracuse, I might be pulling teeth today. Or, if I had decided to stay in the Air Force, I would have ended up getting a medical discharge. And by that time, the opportunity to go back to my old radio station may have passed me by and my next move might well have been dental school.

I had a feeling at the time that one way or the other, my life, my future, and my career were about to be determined by a series of decisions that I really could not control. My destiny was out of my hands. Fortunately, that trip back to upstate New York was the beginning of a long, incredibly rewarding, and absolutely wonderful career.

CHAPTER 3

Back to Syracuse with Jim Brown, Boxing, and TV

Back in my hometown, I couldn't be happier. Not only was I getting my feet wet by doing a little bit of everything, but WHEN was jumping into this exciting new television age and I was right there with them, diving head first into an exhilarating new world that was about to open up for me.

And when I say doing everything, I mean just that. On radio, there was a live "man in the street" interview program at noon where I'd stand under the marquee outside the Lowe's State Theatre, right next to the station. There I'd stop people passing by and ask them my question of the day. Sometimes people would give me a hard time, or I'd have to grab them by the arm, because nobody wanted to stop and talk. But it was a great experience.

There was also an afternoon record show and a Saturday morning TV slot called *The Coca-Cola Dance Party*. It was a take-off of shows that Dick Clark, a young Syracuse graduate, was starting to do in Philadelphia, and one hosted by a buddy of Elvis Presley in Memphis, a guy named Wink Martindale, who later went on to fame and fortune in Hollywood. For 30 minutes, I'd bring big names into the studio—people like Sammy Davis Jr., Johnny Ray, and Tony Bennett. Lining them up for both my radio and TV shows was pretty easy. I'd make regular visits to a trendy nightclub outside Syracuse that featured all the big names in show business and catch their acts.

Although I haven't told too many people, I did record hops for $25 a pop (no pun intended) whenever the station management asked me. Back in those days, the extra money came in handy. In addition to that, I also kept it quiet that I was refereeing high school basketball games because my reputation as a tell-it-like-it-is person with referees would have been ruined and would have taken away my best weapon as an outspoken observer.

By then, of course, I had decided that I was going to be a sports announcer. My feeling was that I can best learn the business by trying to do everything in broadcasting, but I didn't want to be a master of ceremonies or a disk jockey. I had no desire to spend my life in the music and entertainment world. But I was willing to try anything. As a result, I ended up doing a lot of things one time only probably because I was the only guy available to do them. For example, I called boxing matches and a 100-mile automobile race. I covered all the big-time local sports events, including those at Syracuse University and the Nationals' run to the 1955 NBA title. I even recreated minor league baseball games over the air—a totally lost art these days. You name it, I tried it.

I can't even tell you who fought in the two preliminary boxing matches that I handled at the War Memorial arena. We knew that a local fighter, Carmen Basilio, was on the way up in the boxing world, and I remember thinking to myself, *Hey, this is a pretty good opportunity to get some experience. Maybe I can make a name for myself.* Hah! Even though I worked at it, went to the gym, and tried to steal as much as I could from the people that really knew what they were doing, it was a disaster. I could hardly speak during the first fight because my mouth was so dry. After I tried another one, I came to the conclusion that maybe I'm going to be a sportscaster, but I'm *not* going to be a boxing announcer.

The 100-mile race featuring Indy 500 cars at the New York State Fairgrounds came right after I got out of the service. I had no idea what I was doing and probably would never have been asked back if I decided I wanted to do more. I had no time for preparation. I was told, *You're doing the race*—like the day before. But I did it: *There they go! Off in a cloud of fumes.* Don't ask me who won.

Besides doing five minutes of sports on the 11 o'clock TV news (Can you imagine that—*five* whole minutes of a 15-minute broadcast?), I got a chance to cover my first love, b*aseball!* I'd grab a 16-millimeter camera (with no sound, mind you) and head to MacArthur Stadium, where the

Syracuse Chiefs of the triple-A International League played. There I'd shoot a couple of hundred feet of film and send it back to the station, about 15 minutes away, where an editor would select 30 or 40 seconds to show live on the 11 o'clock news. Videotape hadn't been invented yet, of course, so this created quite a sensation.

Soon the station gave me the chance to recreate the Chiefs' games on radio. What a thrill! We didn't do away games live. So I'd be sitting in the studio near a Western Union ticker tape machine while the game was going on. The operator would feed me shorthand information like *S1*, and I'd say, "Strike one!" If it was *B3*, I'd read, "Ball three!" A single to center field was SCF, and GBSSO would mean a batter grounded out to short. When sound effects were appropriate—like the bat hitting the ball or a roar from the crowd—I'd work them into the broadcast by hitting a couple of sticks, or with sound effects from a tape. It was great training for being able to ad lib and to think quickly and hone your skills as a broadcaster who happened to be doing a baseball game. And boy did it take imagination and creativity. I could make pitches *a little bit high, low and outside,* or say, *My goodness, did he brush him back with that inside fast ball!* Or I could describe how the center fielder or third baseman made *a great defensive play!* Often the ticker tape machine would break down and I'd have to invent reasons for the break in the action—*We're in a rain delay, folks,* or *A kid ran out on the field and the police are having a tough time catching up to him,* or *The catcher just took a hard foul ball and the umpire is giving him time to catch his breath.* The fans never knew and I had a ball.

I also have to admit that I was an unwitting accomplice in a number of, shall we say, *questionable betting transactions.* It seems that baseball fans used to hang at the bar of the Wood Hotel, located down the street from the station. Some of them worked for Western Union, and they could hear the little clicker despite the crowd noise at the bar. Since they knew well in advance whether a batter got a hit or struck out, they won many a drink by "predicting" what was going to happen.

Best of all, though, I was able to get to know a number of future Philadelphia Phillies, like Jim Owens, Jack Sanford, and Jack Meyer. What a pitching staff, and what a bunch of characters! It was fun recreating their home games in 1954, even though they lost to the Louisville Colonels of the American Association in six games in the Little World Series.

Many nights after I finished the 11 o'clock news, I would go and hang out at a restaurant owned by Norm Rothschild, a local boxing promoter who knew just about everyone in town, especially people connected with boxing. He's the guy who hooked me up with those earlier fights that I attempted to call. I wasn't married yet, so I had some free time on my hands. I was also fascinated by the same people that always sat in the back booth. Some of them looked familiar—like Al Weill, who managed Rocky Marciano, the heavyweight champion of the world at the time. There weren't too many fighters there, but you would see their managers chatting it up with promoters like Rothschild.

Hanging around on the fringes—mostly standing around or sitting in another booth—were people that I liked to call "guys with pointy shoes and snap-brimmed hats." I would often ask Norm, "Who are those guys?" And he would say, "No one in particular." But eventually I learned that these characters, known as "The Boys from Jersey," had a hand in many of the live fights that were televised on Monday, Wednesday, Friday, and Saturday nights. Boxing was really big thing in the early days of television.

Right around this time, Rothschild was handling Carmen Basilio, a local hero from nearby Canastota, New York, who was training hard and preparing to fight for the welterweight championship. Basilio, who was more of a brawler than a boxer, had lost an earlier title fight to Cuba's Kid Gavilan in a tough, 15-round decision in 1953. Basilio later got another shot and went on to beat the defending champ, Tony DeMarco, the Golden Boy from Boston, twice—both times with TKOs in the 12th round. Both of the bruising, toe-to-toe fights became boxing classics.

A little while after he won the title for the first time in 1955 in the War Memorial, which was located not far from Rothschild's restaurant, I asked Norm how he got this fight. I was suspicious because I knew there were so many fighters and so many promoters, and it was pretty obvious that things were happening with mobsters like the Boys from Jersey. I finally got him to tell me, "Well, I handed one of them an envelope one night and I got the fight."

"How many things did you have in the envelope?" I asked.

"A hundred $100 bills," he replied.

One of the highlights of working in my hometown was getting a chance to cover Syracuse University sports, which meant big-time college basketball and football. This involved doing some basketball play-by-play in which I enthusiastically used some of the broadcasting techniques that I picked up from one of my boyhood idols, Marty Glickman, who called games in Madison Square Garden. I also did a weekly show with football coach Ben Schwartzwalder. And best of all, I had the opportunity to get to know someone who in my opinion was the greatest athlete of all-time—Jim Brown.

Jim Brown excelled enough to make it to the Pro Football Hall of Fame after nine brilliant seasons with the Cleveland Browns, when he led the NFL in rushing eight times. But football wasn't even his best sport. It was actually lacrosse. To this day, he is considered the greatest athlete ever to play that game. Even though at 235 pounds he was considerably bigger than other lacrosse players, Jim could outrun anyone on the field. And as with football, he was unstoppable. Because lacrosse matches and track and field events were scheduled at the same time, there were days when Jim would go to the football stadium, compete in a track meet, and then rush down to the lacrosse field and play in the game there. Oh, and he also played varsity basketball. Had Brown wanted to go to the Olympics, there's little doubt that he could have competed in several categories. He was a magnificent, one-of-a-kind athlete, and possibly the strongest man alive, with a body like Adonis.

Jim Brown had come to Syracuse University just before I arrived back in town. He hailed from Manhasset on Long Island, where he had earned the reputation of being the best high school athlete not only in the town's history, but perhaps in all of New York State. More than 40 colleges offered him a free ride. Jim chose the Orange for two reasons: he didn't want to go too far away from home, and the Syracuse alumni raised money to pay his first year's tuition. The problem was that there were people at the university who didn't want another black football player. They had had some issues not long before with a black quarterback named Avatus Stone, who caused a furor by dating a white cheerleader. That didn't make it easy for Brown, who wasn't allowed to stay in the football dorms or eat with the team when he first arrived. Not only that, but they tried to make Jim a defensive player in his freshman year, and he never got much of a chance to show the coaches what he could do.

At the start of his sophomore year, Brown actually found himself in the *fifth* string as a running back. It wasn't until the sixth game of the season that he finally got a chance to play—sporadically. But Jim showed signs of brilliance in a game against Cornell by breaking free for 54 yards on one carry and finishing the day with 151 rushing yards. Even then some of his coaches weren't convinced. After starting the following season against Pitt with a mediocre performance, Brown found himself on the second team in the following game.

Jim was ready to leave Syracuse right then, but his lacrosse coach, Roy Simmons, convinced him to stay. In fact, one of the assistant coaches told me years later that he had made at least a half-dozen trips to the New York Central Station during Brown's freshman year to dissuade him from going home to Long Island. After his game against the Panthers, though, he blew the doors off collegiate football and became the greatest running back in the history of Syracuse. By the time Jim got through his senior year, he was absolutely unstoppable. He took the Orange to a bowl game at the end of the season after setting all kinds of records. In the regular season finale against Colgate, he scored 61 points—including six touchdowns. And, by the way, he also kicked all the extra points. Unfortunately, no black player had ever won the Heisman Trophy, and Brown was no exception. He finished fifth in the voting as Notre Dame quarterback Paul Hornung won the award, even though the Irish had won only two games.

Despite the problems he encountered, Jim helped recruit Ernie Davis, the "Elmira Express," who went on to lead the Orange to the national championship in 1959. At the end of the season, *he* became the first black player to win the Heisman Trophy.

It took 50 years for Brown to come to the realization that he should make amends and leave something behind at Syracuse beside his records. He has since financed two scholarships at the University—one for lacrosse and one for football. Of course, his mark on the playing field will never be equaled.

Right before Brown's senior year at Syracuse, I did have one opportunity to chat with him personally. I was invited by a mutual friend to join them for lunch at the Wood Hotel. We engaged mostly in small talk about football. Other than interviewing him after games, that was the only time I ever sat down and had a conversation with Jim.

I was completely dumfounded years later to learn how the coaches and administrators had treated Brown at the University. Except for knowing about his unhappiness as a freshman, I had no clue what his life was like or how he got to Syracuse. I never read or heard anything about it until a half-century later when his biography, *Jim Brown: The Fierce Life of an American Hero,* was published in 2006. Many observers consider Jim Thorpe the greatest athlete of all time, and reasonably so. But I'll still put my money on Jim Brown!

When I think about it all these years later, it's a miracle that we got anything right on TV back in those days. Nobody really knew much of anything about the business yet, so there was no one to tell us what *not* to do. So we tried just about everything and did anything we wanted. As a result, lots of things happened—much of it not good. In that 15 minutes of news, weather, and sports, we had cameras banging into each other, sets falling down, things not working, and sometimes utter chaos. We had only one take to do a commercial. Remember, this was *live* television. There were no teleprompters or opportunities to shoot it over again. Sometimes the prop—maybe a can of oil or a box of cereal—would be missing from underneath the desk and I wouldn't realize it until it was time to do the commercial. We learned to find ways to work around the problems. One was the use of a "trouble slide," placed in front of the camera when things weren't going right with the picture or sound. I learned in a hurry—like continuing to move my mouth if the sound in the station wasn't working. Viewers at home would usually think that the problem was with their TV sets.

By 1957, I was making about $8,500 a year from my various activities, which included a base salary of $66 a week. By this time, I was married and had a couple of kids, and I didn't really want to leave my hometown. But one day the general manager of WHEN called me in and said, "You know, Al, you're making almost as much money as I am, which means you're ready to go."

My boss was right. I was ready to move on. Especially since I knew that I wasn't going to realize my dream, at least not yet, of doing baseball play-by-play. This was because Bill Veeck, a young sports entrepreneur, had just purchased the Chiefs and moved them to Miami where they would remain in the International League, later becoming the Marlins. (I did meet Mr. Veeck years later when I worked for a while in Chicago. By then he had become the owner of the Chicago White Sox, and he was very gracious to me whenever I visited the old Comiskey Park.)

A few days later, Buffalo beckoned. The good news was that I was going to a larger market. The bad news was that the move turned out to be a huge disappointment professionally, although it did provide me with a giant stepping-stone.

I was hired by WEBR, which was owned by the *Courier Express*, a morning newspaper that would eventually go out of business in 1982. The station lured me to Buffalo by offering me a large increase in pay to do a morning radio show. The real attraction, though, was the fact that the station had applied to the Federal Communications Commission for a television license. It was just a matter of time, they said, and management assured me that I would be the guy to handle all of their TV sports.

It never happened.

The federal government decided that it was not in the public interest for newspapers to own television stations. A number of them did, like the *Buffalo Evening News* and the old Philadelphia *Evening and Sunday Bulletin,* which owned WCAU Radio and TV in its circulation area. Stations like that were grandfathered, but WEBR was left out in the cold. Instead, the Reverend Clint Churchill, who owned a 50,000-watt radio station next door to his tabernacle on Main Street, got the license for Channel 7, WKBW-TV. The station was soon sold to Capital Cities Communications, a group out of Albany that later purchased the American Broadcasting Company, resulting in an enormous profit for Rev. Churchill. CapCities thus eventually owned Channel 6, an ABC affiliate, in Philadelphia. That's how people like Jim Gardner and Dave Roberts later went from Channel 7 to *Action News* in the Quaker City.

For a long time, both the WEBR station management and I tried and tried to get all kinds of stuff, including the Buffalo Bills broadcasts when they came into the new American Football League in 1960. I even applied—unsuccessfully—for the Bisons' triple-A baseball play-by-play vacancy when Bill Mazur left for a bigger job in New York City. Again my dream of finding a path to that big-league baseball job was put on hold. Nothing seemed to click until I got a hold of football and basketball broadcasts at the University of Buffalo. Buddy Ryan was an assistant coach there, which proved to be somewhat ironic. Who do you think was an assistant coach with the Bears the first year I got to Chicago? You guessed it—Buddy Ryan. And when I came back to Philadelphia, who came to coach the Eagles? Good old Buddy!

I did witness one significant football moment during my time in Buffalo. It was something that would have a huge influence on both the college and professional game. It began in July 1964, when the Bills used their 12th-round selection to draft Pete Gogolak, a Hungarian soccer player from Budapest. He had become a highly successful placekicker at nearby Cornell University. I'll never forget watching him at his first workout session with the Bills. Instead of approaching the ball straight on with his toe making the first contact, similar to American specialists like Lou "The Toe" Groza of the Cleveland Browns, Gogolak approached the ball from the left at an angle and kicked it with the instep of his right foot. You could actually hear the sonic boom of the contact, and his distance was consistently much longer than that of his American counterparts.

It was the beginning of a new day for both the Bills and the fledging American Football League. Buffalo won two straight AFC titles. Gogolak's soccer-style placekicking accounted for 102 points in 1964—25 percent of the Bills' offensive total—and 115 points the following year. Moreover, after that season, the New York Giants of the rival National Football League ignored the owner's "gentleman's agreement" against signing another league's players and lured Pete to Yankee Stadium, where he became the Giants' all-time leading scorer. In addition to triggering an expensive battle for players, Gogolak's signing hastened the eventual merger of the two leagues. And today, virtually all placekickers in American college and professional football use the technique pioneered by Pete Gogolak.

Finally after seven years in Buffalo, I got my *BIG* break. I was going to WFIL Radio and TV in Philadelphia, one of ABC's flagship stations in the nation's fourth largest metropolitan area—behind only New York, Los Angeles, and Chicago. Although it was sayonara, Buffalo at the time, I didn't realize that I would eventually be back—at least partially.

(((CHAPTER 4)))

Basketball, Bullfights, and Al's Big Chance in Philadelphia

One day in the fall of 1964, I received a telephone call from a guy named Jack Steck. He was a talent scout for WFIL, the ABC affiliate in Philadelphia, where his wife, Florence, worked as the program director at the radio station. He asked if I would be interested in talking about a job. Would I? Before you could say "the Phillies collapsed," I was sitting in an office a few feet from where Dick Clark had made a national name for himself with a show that became *American Bandstand* when he moved it to Los Angeles earlier that year.

I immediately felt right at home interviewing at the station, which was located underneath old, rickety elevated train tracks at 46th and Market Streets. Why? Because situated right across the street was the Philadelphia Arena, once the home of my former team, the Syracuse Nationals, who had moved to the City of Brotherly Love just the year before and were now known as the Philadelphia 76ers.

Steck came right to the point. "We'd like you to eventually do the weekend sports on TV," he explained. "Right now, during the week, you'll do a radio show and whatever else that comes up."

And that's exactly what happened when I moved to the Philadelphia area and started working at WFIL's brand-new, state-of-the-art building on City Avenue and Monument Road, across the street from WCAU, Channel 10, the CBS station. Whatever they needed, they threw me in. I did a morning quiz show with Paul Norton called *Dialing for Dollars*, and later an afternoon record show. Eventually, I ended up doing high school football games on Friday nights and taping them for Saturday morning television viewers.

Big 5 college basketball—featuring La Salle, the University of Pennsylvania, Saint Joseph's, Temple, and Villanova—was really catching fire in Philadelphia at the time, and WFIL had the radio and television rights. Which meant that Les Keiter, the station's sports director, did the play-by-play. If the city series games were on TV, I got to do the radio. That was the beginning of my lifelong love affair with the Big 5 and, as it turned out, the highlight of my days with WFIL.

All I really wanted to do was sports, and things weren't happening quickly enough on that front. After waiting and playing the good soldier for a few months, I talked to Les and reiterated that I was very interested in doing the weekend sports on television. At the time, I really wasn't that acquainted with Stan Hochman, the *Philadelphia Daily News* sports columnist, or Chuck Bednarik, the retired Philadelphia Eagles Hall of Famer, who were handling those responsibilities.

But rumors were flying around that big format changes were about to be made, and sure enough, Gene McCurdy, the general manager, pulled me aside one day and said, "Al, I know you've been asking me a lot of things, like when am I going to start doing some TV sports? Well, I don't think I'd count on that weekend sports spot right now." Which was code for *You ain't doing it!*

My theory on this—it was never expressly stated—was that Keiter was really happy having two guys who were not professional broadcasters replacing him on weekends. It was pretty easy to figure out why. Les had worked in New York, where the successful eat their young and competition for the choice jobs can be brutal. Therefore, you don't give anybody a shot at something that you've got, and that you're very comfortable retaining. I fully understood, even though I had a contract that said I would do weekend sports and "other things." I eventually did all of the other things, but I never got to do weekend sports.

Not long after that, WFIL's radio and TV stations changed formats, both with hugely successful results. Radio went rock and roll with the boss jocks and stopped carrying live sports action. *Action News* came into the TV marketplace after years and years of the same stale newscasting on all of the other stations. Larry Kane, who came from Miami after making a national name for himself covering the Beatles among other things, was named the news anchor and became one of the most popular personalities in the city.

Early in the summer of 1965, station management asked me to audition for a new rock and roll radio show in the morning. I told them I really wasn't that interested. I said, "You've got the wrong guy. Actually, I really would like to do something else—like sports, damnit!"

A few days later, I was having lunch with two of my best friends from the TV side at the station: George Finkel, a director, and Larry Cooper, a producer. They said to me, "Al, would you be interested in going with Channel 17?" And I said, "Channel what? What is Channel 17?"

"It's UHF television," they replied. And they explained to me that anything above Channel 13 on the dial is a UHF (or ultra high frequency) station, as opposed to the VHF (very high frequency) label attached to the older, traditional stations.

They told me that three new channels would be going on the air—17, 29, and 48—which would double the number of TV stations in Philadelphia. They wanted to make Channel 17 into a sports station. I discovered one small problem when I went home that night. I realized that I couldn't pick up the new channels on my television set. Like everyone else, I had to buy a separate UHF tuner with a circular antenna.

Soon I found myself at another one of those forks in the road when I sat down with Len Stevens, the general manager of the new station, along with Finkel and Cooper. They were the people making all the decisions. After they laid everything out to me, I said, "How much do you want to pay?" It was half of what I was making at Channel 6. I gulped a little but didn't really give it a second thought. "Absolutely!" I said.

After my meeting with Len Stevens, whom I came to regard as one of the most talented executives in the industry, I talked to the bosses at WFIL. "You really don't need me here," I explained. "I'd like to get out of my contract." They said that they understood, and I went to Channel 17 with my eyes wide open. I had been with WFIL for less than a year.

WPHL-TV, as it was known, had taken over a vacant building on Mermaid Lane in Wyndmoor, Montgomery County, just outside the northwest boundary of the city. It previously had been the two-story shelter for the transmitter and tower of Philadelphia's Channel 3. There was actually a hole in one of the walls, so someone put a sign below it that said, THIS IS A HOLE IN THE WALL! How the station got off the ground is an amazing story, as detailed by Stevens when we reminisced over lunch years later.

"An attorney named Aaron Katz had the license for Channel 17, and he didn't know what to do with it," Stevens recalled. "Mutual friends put it together. We became partners…and raised the seed money—$10,000 apiece from 20 people—to buy the license from an entity which had become defunct because the key figure in that operation, the Reverend Percy Crawford [an evangelist who has mentored Billy Graham as a young man] had passed away and the estate wanted to get rid of the Channel 17 license.

"We leased the tower from the previous owners of the building. It was only because the tower was there and it was on the highest ground in the city of Philadelphia—at the top of Chestnut Hill—that we were able to do this, because we wouldn't have been able to afford the cost of building a tower at that point on the Antenna Farm in Roxborough. So all we had to do was to buy the equipment, revamp that station, and put it back on the air with a professional studio and staff. I wanted to televise three things—sports, children's programming, and a nice mix of movies. Initially we tried to get the Phillies, but Bob Carpenter, the owner, didn't want to take a chance on us and I didn't blame him. So we went after stuff we felt we could get."

When I first got to Channel 17, Bill "Wee Willie" Webber was the only other talent. Webber did all the kid's stuff, like introducing the Japanese cartoons *Astro Boy* and *The Eighth Man*. I did everything else, including the taped announcements between shows and an afternoon movie introduction. I even sold some advertising. And, of course, I covered the ball games. The funny thing, though, was not only did we not have a news department; technically, we didn't even have a sports department. We just had programming, but we were the first TV station to go almost all sports. We showed everything that moved and anything that bounced, got thrown in the air, hit with a club, or kicked with a foot. I like to say that we were ESPN before there was an ESPN, and we didn't even know it. Had the satellite been invented back then, we might have become the original ESPN.

We did every sport except ice hockey, although as Stevens recalls, we did try. Channel 48 was going on the air in Philadelphia at the same time and its owner, Kaiser Broadcasting, was able to make a deal with the Flyers. We covered college and professional basketball and football, including the Big 5, the 76ers—I did their road games beginning in 1965—Temple University football, the Pottstown Firebirds, and professional soccer.

"As a whole, though, sports were not profitable," Stevens remembers. "It was kind of a loss leader, developing an audience and reputation for us. The thing that pulled us down in terms of making a bottom-line profit on sports was the fact that part of our contract called for us to bring all of the 76ers' out-of-town games to Philadelphia. Well, when you consider the three-hour time difference for West Coast games—those suckers began at 11 o'clock at night! So not only did we have to pay for phone lines—this is before satellites, even before fiber—we were paying for first class audio phone lines from San Francisco and Los Angeles. The worst part of it was, besides the expenses of carrying the games, we knew damn well that starting at 11 o'clock, we were going to have a tough time selling them. The Sixers at that time weren't the kind of team they are today, and you weren't going to establish an audience at 2 o'clock in the morning, unless they were a contender.

"It was very tough for us because in those days the three existing networks [ABC, CBS, and NBC] paid the stations big bucks to carry their programs. So here's Channels 3, 6, and 10 sitting there, not having to do squat except maybe for an early and late newscast. And they collect money from the networks for carrying the network's shows. We, in turn, had a different burden that they didn't even have. Our burden was to go out and buy and create the programming, do whatever we could to get programs, and then go out to sell and try to break even and, God forbid, make a profit."

In 1966, I first got to know the man I have always considered the best coach to work in Philadelphia during my career on the air. And if that sounds like a great compliment, it certainly is because Philadelphia has definitely had more than its share of excellent coaches. That year, Wayne Hardin, who had done wonders with the football program at the United States Naval Academy in Annapolis, won the Continental Football League title with the Philadelphia Bulldogs.

Four years later, Temple's athletic director, Ernie Casale, convinced Hardin to take over the Owls' floundering football program—which was nothing short of a miracle. The move created shock waves throughout the college football world. Why would Wayne Hardin ever want to come to Temple?

In addition to keeping Navy high in the national rankings, Hardin had developed a pair of Heisman Trophy winners. You may have heard of them. One was a quarterback named Roger Staubach, and the other was a halfback, Joe Bellino. Wayne Hardin's midshipmen also beat Army five straight times in the six years he was there, and I don't have to tell you how important *that* was.

Hardin played for the legendary Amos Alonzo Stagg at the College of the Pacific in California. "He was one of a kind, the Father of Football," Wayne told me. "He started out in life to be a minister and went to Yale. By the time his career was over, he had developed every formation that you can think of—the spread formation, the single wing, the double wing, the 'T.' He had it all. He invented the huddle, and was the first to put numbers on jerseys. He put the forward pass in the game and got it in the rules that it's okay to throw."

"I'm not putting the Owls down," I told him. Temple was not what you would call a power in Eastern football. After Army and Navy, there weren't many really strong teams in Eastern football besides Syracuse and Penn State. *"But why did you take this job?"*

"When I coached the Bulldogs, I used Temple's facilities, and Ernie Casale and I got to be very, very good friends," Hardin explained. "He was just a super guy. I took the Temple job primarily because of Ernie. Number two, I had four kids that were going to be in college at the same time, and their expenses were covered with free tuition and so forth.

"I took the Bulldogs job as general manager and coach with the intent of getting an American Football League franchise right here in Philadelphia. We had backers and hired a good staff and had some good players like Bob Broadhead at quarterback. We won the championship, but the AFL and NFL merged that season. And when they merged, that put the hiatus on any franchise for us."

"You recruited a host of great players," I said. *"People like Randy Grossman, Joe Klecko, Zack Dixon, Jim Cooper, Nick Mike-Mayer, Anthony Anderson, Steve Watson, and Don Bitterlich. All of them played in the National Football League, and Steve Joachim won the Maxwell Award. How did you get them to come to Temple?"*

"When I came to Temple in 1970, I walked across Broad Street to McGonigle Hall, met the president, said hello to everyone. Then I asked, who is the best football player in the area? And they said, 'Steve Joachim, but he's already taken.' Then I went out and talked to his high school coach, who told me that he was already committed to Penn State. 'I didn't ask where he's going,' I replied. 'I'd like to talk to him. While you're on your way to get him, tell him that every quarterback I've ever coached has led the nation and led their league and has had great success. I believe in throwing the football and that's his bag.' Then I looked at the game films and came away interested in only one person on that film. It wasn't Steve Joachim. It was Randy Grossman. I mean he caught every-thing—behind his back, over his head. If he put his hands on it, it was done. Then Steve came down. We had a long talk. I congratulated him and wished him good luck at Penn State. I said, 'If it doesn't work out, give me a call.' He went up there for a year and it didn't work out, so he called me. He came in to Temple, and he and Randy got hooked up again, and it got to be pretty interesting. When I played at Pacific, all of my teammates came from within 90 miles of the campus. I wanted to develop the same thing at Temple. I wanted my team to be a *local* group."

Hardin came oh-so-close to turning the Owls into a major college football power. In 1973, Temple went 9-1 and began a 14-game winning streak that stretched into the following season, when the Owls finished 8-2 and Hardin was named District II Coach of the Year. Wayne's best year came in 1979, when he guided the Owls to a school-record 10-2 mark (the only losses came to nationally ranked Pitt, 10-9, and Penn State, 22-7, after leading 7-6 at halftime) before upsetting the University of California in the Garden State Bowl. They finished 17th in both major national polls.

Temple undoubtedly would have finished higher in the national rankings had it not been for three other heartbreaking losses to Penn State during Hardin's tenure. In 1975, they lost 26-25 at Franklin Field when the Nittany Lions scored late on long kickoff and punt returns, the final touchdown coming on the last play of the game. The following year it was 31-30 when the Owls missed a two-point conversion with no time left on the clock. Then in 1978, Penn State won, 10-7, when Matt Bahr pulled the game out with a late field goal.

"When we went for the two-pointer down at the Vet in that 31-30 game, I wrestled with myself because I said, 'This could be a stepping-stone. We can tie them with a conversion,'" Hardin explained. "There was no overtime in those days and I fought with myself and I said to my-self, 'Oh, come on, coach, what's wrong with you?' My kids were so dis-appointed."

"Now I have to go to the big question right here," I said. *"You estab-lished yourself as a pretty darn good football coach at the collegiate level and even as coach at the East-West game in 1981. But at the end of the 1982 season, you leave college football and everyone is speculating, me in-cluded, as to what the next step will be, what school you will go to. You did not take another job. You retired at the age of 59 and played golf. What in*

the world ran through your mind to say, Well, this is it. I've had enough with success?"

"Al, it's a very tough situation because I remember hearing about Dick Vermeil sleeping on a couch down at the Eagles and I thought, Boy, I've never been that way. But I was getting that way and so I said, 'It's time.' I think when I was in high school and the first part of college, I realized that life is very short, and most of my parents' friends were dying in their 40s. And I remember thinking: *The first 28 years of your life, you get an education, you get married, you get a job, and you have kids. The next 28 years of your life, you work your butt off to make sure you survive. And you take your last 28 and enjoy them.*"

It's hard to believe but in 1967, we were the *only* Philadelphia TV station originating any basketball. We did a total of 90 games—49 collegiate and 41 professional. I also handled an exhibition tennis match between Martina Navratilova and that young sensation from King of Prussia, Tracy Austin, at Bryn Mawr College. I did professional golf the first time the LPGA played its local tournament at Hidden Springs Golf Course near Willow Grove.

We also did soccer, which I knew nothing about. I couldn't remember the last time I had even seen a soccer contest. I learned the game literally on the fly by attending weekend seminars conducted by Pete Leanness, Temple's soccer coach. I also learned a lot from Walt Chyzowych, a legendary star from the school then known as Philadelphia College of Textiles and Science, who was one of the biggest names in the sport, locally and nationally.

Bob Ehlinger, the owner of the new franchise in town, the Philadelphia Spartans, and Hal Freeman, another big soccer buff who was the general manager of the Spectrum at the time, came to us and said that the United States Soccer League was being formed and they wanted Channel 17 to carry their games.

The Spartans' very first game, I recall, was a sellout at Temple Stadium. But my personal high point was calling their contest against the New York Cosmos, featuring Pele, the greatest player in the world. It was the only game I ever broadcast from Yankee Stadium, and I never got a chance to return because the Spartans lasted for only that one season.

I'll never forget that game for another reason. It was the day I quit smoking. I was driving back home over the George Washington Bridge with George Finkel and my throat was killing me. I'm not the dumbest guy on the planet, but not the smartest guy either, and a little thought came into my mind: You're in the wrong business to have throat problems. And I said to George, "This is my last cigarette." I rolled down the window, threw a pack of Tareytons over the GW Bridge, and never smoked again. That was almost 45 years ago.

I started to smoke when I was in the Air Force in basic training. The last five minutes of every hour was time to light up, and everybody was doing it. The cigarettes didn't cost that much; I think they were a dime a pack at the PX. I wasn't a heavy smoker, thank God. I only smoked in pressure situations, such as when I was doing ball games. And during a game, I'd only take about three puffs on a cigarette and that was it. I could spend a whole weekend at home without smoking a cigarette and not even realize it.

A lot of people still had no idea about Channel 17: who we were, where we were, or what we were doing. Most viewers didn't have a UHF converter, and they didn't know what kind of programming we had because they never saw it. Financially, the station struggled and there were days when you couldn't cash your paycheck because the money hadn't been deposited in the bank. But WPHL's management did a masterful job of filling up a whole day with programming—not all sports, of course, but enough that we quickly became known as "The Sports Station" in Philadelphia. One thing helped considerably. When affiliates of one of the major networks—ABC, CBS, or NBC—couldn't clear the time to carry a major event, these shows would become available to independent stations like ours. Often the big networks didn't want to clutter their schedules with sports, especially when such telecasts conflicted with their popular, revenue-producing weekly programming.

That's why little Channel 17, headquartered in its hole in the wall, was able to make television history. In 1967, we became the only independent station ever to carry the NBA Championship Game nationally, and two years later, we were the first station ever to do a football game on Monday night. Yours truly did the play-by-play both times.

The 76ers enjoyed their greatest season in history in 1966-67—they were later voted the best team of the century—and I handled their road games on Channel 17. That team, coached by Alex Hannum and led by Wilt Chamberlain, was an absolute pleasure to watch. But not during the week, said NBC, the network that insisted on carrying only weekend playoff games.

Philadelphia had a 3-2 lead in the championship series against the San Francisco Warriors with Game 6 (the possible deciding game) scheduled for Thursday night, April 24, at the Cow Palace in California. NBC refused to carry it because they wouldn't give up their very profitable network programming, and we hopped right in.

In order to help defray the very expensive line charges, George Finkel and Larry Cooper suggested that we ask all of the NBA teams to help foot the bill and allow the game to be shown in their cities. A number of stations between Philly and San Francisco did pick it up, but because it was shown at 11 p.m. in the East, the response wasn't as good as we hoped. We'll never know how many viewers saw the game, and there's no record of our profits.

Still, the game was a great success, both for the 76ers and Channel 17. Charlie Swift helped me with the broadcast and the 76ers won, 125-122, but times were really different then. Victory parades in Philadelphia were still years away. When we arrived home the next day, about 75 people—mostly family and friends—were at the airport to greet the best team in basketball history. My only regret is that there was no videotape available in those days, so we don't have a copy of the game.

Two years later, the Baltimore Orioles and the New York Mets faced each other in the 1969 World Series with the National Leaguers eventually winning in five games. Game 2 was scheduled for a Sunday afternoon in Baltimore. Since major league baseball had first dibs for use of Memorial Stadium, the NFL game between the Philadelphia Eagles and the Baltimore Colts, scheduled for the same time that day, was moved to Monday night, October 13. The networks weren't interested in carrying the game. Can you believe that happening today? And, once again, Channel 17 came galloping to the rescue.

The late Tom Brookshier did the game with me. Brookie was one of my favorite people. I loved him on CBS on Sundays with Pat Summerall, and I loved working with him that night. I like to think that I prepared like Dick Vermeil for that game. I got to Baltimore the previous Saturday and compiled enough notes to fill three binders. I had more ad libs for one game than I could have used for an entire season. Arriving at the stadium three hours before game time, I got all set up, going over my notes and looking around for my boy Brookie. He finally showed up about 45 minutes before kickoff, tossed the lineup card on the desk and said, "Hey, you all ready to go?"

Well, I was raring to go, with all the notes and all the ad libs right at my fingertips. But as you probably guessed, I got to use hardly any of them. The one thing that I failed to mention was that my color analyst had a great sense of humor. And I was laughing more than I was doing play-by-play that night. I still think that it was a great broadcast because I got to do it with one of the all-time greats.

The Eagles lost, 24-20, but that didn't make any difference. The big news was that we had the biggest audience ever for a UHF station in the United States. It proved that we could draw viewers if we had something worthwhile to broadcast. Granted, it wasn't carried coast-to-coast, but it was the first "Monday Night Football" game ever televised. And that's what counted.

By now almost everyone in the Philadelphia area had UHF converters, and our reputation as a legitimate sports channel was solidified—except in the eyes of major league baseball and certain Phillies officials.

We finally got the rights to do some Phillies games in 1970, the year before Veterans Stadium opened, and we did our first broadcast from the Vet after it was dedicated in 1971. Bill Giles joined the team that year and brought Harry Kalas in with him from Houston along with another guy, Gene Kirby, who had the title of director of broadcasting. The Phillies asked if we would help Harry get acclimated to the city because he had just arrived in town and baseball season was a few months away. They asked if it would be okay if he helped me do basketball. I got to know Harry very well. I took him around and showed him everything I could about the coaches, the players, and the area. I liked him a great deal, and I had no problem working with him. Although at that time no one knew how popular he was going to become, I could tell that Harry Kalas was a gem, and every good word ever said about him is true.

I didn't want Harry's job, but I had wanted to do baseball right from my first day in the business. My company was very interested in using me with the Phillies, and I just wanted something to do, as long as I could be associated with the broadcast team. I remember Len Stevens sitting around a table with Phillies officials, saying, "Why can't we have our own sports people? Why do we have to bring in people from Houston?" But Gene Kirby told George Finkel, our producer, that he didn't want a "minor league" TV station like Channel 17 carrying their games. George, by the way, ended up doing Super Bowls, World Series, and NCAA Final Fours for NBC. He did everything you could do in TV, and I'm pleased as punch that he got those jobs. Anyway, even though they told me that I was going to be part of the Phillies broadcast team, I got turned down because they had already hired Harry, and Andy Musser eventually took over for Byrum Saam when he retired.

Don't forget, in the early days of radio, there was only baseball and college football. There was very little, if any, pro football. College and pro basketball had nothing, and hockey had six teams. So what did you want to be when you decided to go into sports broadcasting? You wanted to be a *baseball* announcer. And when I got that chance in Syracuse with the Chiefs, a triple-A team, Bill Veeck pulled the rug out from under me by buying the franchise and moving it to Miami. Then when I moved to Buffalo, I thought I was going to get a chance to do triple-A baseball there. But that didn't work out because the station I went with didn't have the baseball rights.

I think Bill Giles had a lot to say about everything except the x's and o's of baseball itself—promotions, public relations, things like that. But I think he also had something to say about who was going to broadcast the games, although Kirby was the producer of the broadcasts. Maybe the Phillies front office had heard that Don DeJardin, the former general manager of the 76ers, tried to get me fired because I didn't sell tickets. My reputation as a 76ers basketball announcer was that I wasn't a homer. When I was doing their games, I always thought that I'll call them as I see them and not be somebody that I wasn't. I may have leaned over backward to be impartial when I had the Big 5 teams to do, but I didn't realize that I was supposed to sell tickets. Part of that also might have been because I was the first guy in television to do sports commentary. No one had ever attempted it before.

Anyway, the whole thing didn't work out and when Bill Giles came up to me later when I was at Channel 10 and asked me what I thought of Andy Musser doing the games, I thought to myself, *I don't believe Andy's done any baseball. And they told me they wouldn't use me because I was a minor league broadcaster.* Hey, Andy's a great friend of mine. He worked for the Phillies for a long time, and I'm more than happy for him. But I got the impression that they didn't want me no matter what. And even years later, they wouldn't have used me under any circumstances.

When it became apparent that I wasn't going to be involved directly with the Phillies broadcasts, Channel 17 decided that they needed a post-game show and called it *The 10th Inning*. I told them that I'd love to do it. But this was the dark ages of television; we had no electronics and everything was primitive. In order to edit out one play to show, you had to roll through one of our giant two-inch tape reels to get to the point that you could put down a number on the counter where the play happened. It took forever to get one edit. When I first went on the air, I did a play, talked about it, then went to a commercial. I came back and did another play, and that's the way it went for a while. It was probably the longest postgame show in the history of broadcasting, because it took time to get that stuff wound up. Today you can edit an entire game in 15 minutes.

It was the most difficult job I ever had in my life. I sweated every single moment of it because I knew that I couldn't do a good job. My attitude was not positive, and the sooner I could get rid of that thing, the better I would feel about it. Anyway, I was gone the next year.

Whenever I reminiscence about Channel 17, though, my mind drifts back and focuses fondly on the station's highest-rated show at the beginning, other than occasional basketball games.

Bullfighting!

That's right, bullfighting. And you'll never guess what suddenly caused it to become unpopular. The events originated in Spain and were syndicated by an outfit from New Jersey with voice-overs done in the United States. We ran the shows at 9 p.m. on Saturday nights and drew fabulous audiences for a UHF station. But when the station started transmitting in living color and people saw the blood and gore in all its splendor, the audience dropped considerably. I guess it's okay if you gore the bull—as long as you don't let viewers see the red blood. Bullfighting is probably the only sports event in history that suffered because of color TV.

"That was another sore spot," Len Stevens recalled. "Right after we spent all that money to re-equip Channel 17 and put out a pretty decent five-million-watt signal in black and white, along comes color. Part of our equipment had to be trashed. We lost a lot of money. Aaron Katz and I ran out of money many times. We had to go back to private investors, then we went to a company called AVC. An investment friend of ours put it all together and he made a deal where they would put $19 million into Channel 17, but that money was diluted because we also picked up four other stations in Cincinnati, Pittsburgh, Atlanta, and San Francisco.

"We burned through that $19 million very quickly by the time we had a foothold. You remember Sam Feinberg, our local sales manager. Not many people know this, but there were many Thursdays—the day before payday—that we didn't have the payroll for the following day. And Sam Feinberg would come into the office at four o'clock in the afternoon waving a piece of paper. He would march into the office with the salesmen and girls working there, saying things like, 'I've got a new contract from Schmitz beer. We can make payroll tomorrow.' In other words, Schmitz had just gone for another big chunk of dough to buy— usually the Big 5 or the Sixers, whatever. They would usually buy only sports. Sam Feinberg's clients saved our bacon time and time again because he deliberately waited until Thursdays to sign his contracts. It was touch and go. But we got through."

"It's been almost 50 years since Channel 17 went on the air," I told Stevens. *"I don't think you're aware of what you did. You changed sports in Philadelphia forever. You were there before ESPN. And you've never taken any credit for any of this."*

"It's part of my nature to live an anonymous life," Len replied. "If you want proof of that, just go on the Internet and try to Google me. There's nobody that you know or who you would come in contact with who has had less publicity, deliberately so. I've always been that way. Credit is not something I go for; it's not my nature."

CHAPTER 5

Big 5 Basketball: Indescribable and Unforgettable

The biggest thing we did at Channel 17, of course, was to cover the basketball teams of the Big 5. Without question, that's what got people to buy UHF converters and watch the games. Even today, more than a half-century later, it gives me such a warm feeling when I'm told things like, "You made Big 5 games special when I was a kid." A week seldom goes by when people don't stop me—in a restaurant or on the street— and say, "Hey, I just want to thank you for those years with the Big 5." I mean, that made a bigger impact than anything I ever did, and one reason is the number of Big 5 players and coaches who are still connected to Philadelphia. Many of the fans who come over to say that they loved my broadcasts have their kids with them. They remember that time like it was yesterday.

I had no idea of the impression I made on people when I did Big 5 basketball. I'm proud that the thing fans most associate with me is the Big 5. I only wish I could have been present for all of the past 50 years. I was walking around the Palestra recently and it sank in that I'm tethered to the Big 5 forever because I'm a member of its Hall of Fame.

Ah, the Palestra. What a venue. More basketball games have been played in that arena than anywhere else in the world. And for good reason. There is no other basketball arena like it. Unless you've seen it, you truly haven't witnessed a real basketball game. As many national sportswriters have written, they came to Philadelphia specifically to watch a basketball ball game in the Palestra. They felt that their career wasn't complete until they had seen a ball game there.

The Palestra was one of a kind like Wrigley Field, or the old Madison Square Garden, or Fenway Park. You get the idea. Let's call it unique. That's surely a good way to describe the Palestra. When filled to capacity, like it was most nights, I got the feeling that if I didn't wear earphones, and if I wasn't sitting very close to the guy I was working with, we wouldn't be able to hear each other. I call it "Palestra Loud"—the greatest home court advantage in college basketball.

I had been to Franklin Field for a Penn–Notre Dame football game when I was in the Air Force and I was quite impressed with the atmosphere—the full house and all the pageantry surrounding two college powerhouses, which both the Irish and the Quakers were in those days. But I didn't walk into the building next door. I knew about the Palestra, a little bit anyway, and I knew about the Big 5, then just beginning, but I had no idea what lay within those ancient walls on 33rd Street.

When I arrived in Philly to work at WFIL, I decided to drive down and take a look at the place. There was no one in the building. I walked in and walked down the ramp. As you walk out onto the floor, you begin to get the feeling that this is like no other place. I know it's a basketball floor, but I've never seen anything quite like it, and frankly I wasn't ready for it. There was a loose ball lying around, so I decided I'd throw in a few hoops, but in the meantime I dribbled the ball and couldn't believe the sound I was hearing—the reverberation from every corner of the building. And there was no one there but me and the basketball. The one thing that impressed me was the size of the Palestra. I had no idea how they could fit 9,000 people into that small space. It looked almost like an oversized high school gymnasium, but what a wrong perception that was. I knew the place had been built in 1927—which was a year before I was born.

I broadcast my first games from the Palestra during the 1964-65 season. Les Keiter and I were working with WFIL Radio 560 and TV 6 at the time, and I would occasionally handle the radio play-by-play when Channel 6 carried the game and Les handled the TV end. But the Big 5 doubleheader that I will never forget occurred on Friday, February 26, 1965. There I was at courtside before a frenzied, jam-packed crowd of 9,206 screaming fans, and everything I had ever heard about the Big 5 was fulfilled right before my eyes. The first game was exciting enough. Penn upset Cornell, 79-70, in an Ivy League clash. In the nightcap, nationally ranked St. Joseph's won its 14th straight game, defeating La Salle, 93-85. But it was much closer than that—a typical knock-down, drag 'em out slugfest that people came to expect in a city series game. La Salle trailed by 20 in the second half, but cut the deficit to two points before the Hawks hung on to clinch the Big 5 and Middle Atlantic Conference titles and a coveted bid to the NCAA Tournament. I couldn't begin to describe my emotions afterwards. I was drained, exhausted, and exhilarated, but I couldn't wait to come back for more.

A year later, when I got to Channel 17, we needed a hot product to make a name for ourselves, and I helped talk the Big 5 athletic directors into letting us carry all the home games. That was a miracle in itself because WPHL didn't have any money and had a tough time meeting its own payroll. Luckily, the athletic directors bought in and agreed to minimal rights fees—maybe $10,000 for each school. We did three doubleheaders a week and created an entirely new audience for both our station and the Big 5. It was an experience never to be duplicated. The Big 5 agreed to spruce the Palestra up a bit and installed brighter lights to enhance the color telecasts. The place had been a little dark, and I'm sure that the players' shooting percentages went way up. So did the enthusiasm of the Delaware Valley fans. Many of them had heard of the Big 5— and just maybe had gone to a game or two—but TV gave them a chance to see *all* the games first hand—all the noise, color, excitement, and pageantry of great basketball being played by five Division I schools all from the same area. You couldn't beat it. There was nothing like it anywhere in the country. As soon as we began televising all the doubleheaders, the crowds started to increase. After watching at home, many fans decided that they'd better go and take a look at this place.

This place, the Palestra, was Penn's own home court. Before the Big 5 was initiated in 1955, only the Quakers and Villanova played their games in the Palestra. La Salle, St. Joe's, and Temple played about a block away at Convention Hall. Therefore, doubleheaders often competed against each other on the same night, which meant that fans sometimes had to choose, for example, between watching Tom Gola and La Salle facing Temple and Guy Rodgers at Convention Hall, or Paul Arizin and Villanova playing with Penn and Ernie Beck at the Palestra.

Although the noise level was probably at its highest when two Big 5 teams played against each other in a city series contest, you had to be there to experience the absolute frenzy, intensity, and excitement the

Palestra offered the hometown fans. I've broadcast games in just about every arena in America, and there was nothing louder anywhere—especially when it was full.

Just about all the great players, like Princeton's Bill Bradley and Niagara's Calvin Murphy, and every major basketball power and big-name coach, like Adolph Rupp of Kentucky and Dean Smith of North Carolina, came to the Palestra. A few of them swore that they would never return. Al McGuire, who won the NCAA championship at Marquette in 1977, turned toward the crowd near the end of a loss to Villanova and exclaimed, "I'm never coming back here again." He was true to his word.

The Palestra was a place where you saw—let's put it this way—the best and the brightest of the Big 5's students show off their resourceful, often controversial rollout banners. It was like New Year's Eve and Mardi Gras *rolled* into one. Some of the rollouts were very clever; some were a little extreme, and a number of them elicited hastily convened meetings the following day among local college administrators and students to preserve the peace. I remember one night a banner came fluttering out of the St. Joe's rooting section: "LA SALLE HAS BLUE AND GOLD BALLS." La Salle fans immediately responded with: "IS THAT WHAT THE JESUITS TEACH YOU?" These were a couple of the tamer examples.

And then there was the incredible roar when the teams came out onto the floor. Or even better, when the game began, the first basket by a Big 5 squad brought hundreds of colorful crepe paper streamers flying out of the stands onto the floor. That really was like New Year's Eve. Later on, the NCAA put an end to it, those killjoys. They said that it took too much time to clean up the floor and it interrupted the game. They clearly didn't understand *where* they were!

As a broadcaster, my biggest worry was the St. Joe drummer, who was usually right under our TV booth. When he hit that drum—and it was often—I could feel it from my toes right through the top of my head. Every time he hit that drum, I thought it might be too much for my brain. I had earphones on, but it was impossible to shut out the noise. The intensity was beyond description. I thought the building itself might not be able to take it. I can still feel that drum today.

There were scores of interesting characters bouncing around the Palestra in those days, but none of them were as colorful as the lovable Harry Shifren, the Big 5's unofficial mascot, who was known as "Yo Yo."

An unkempt and disheveled comic figure, Yo Yo bummed cigars from Harry Litwack, quarters from everyone else, and constantly kept fans in stitches by shooting fouls at halftime and mimicking the players. I once got myself in a little trouble with Art Mahan, Villanova's athletic director, when I asked him for a ticket to one of the Wildcats' games in Madison Square Garden and—without telling Art—gave it to Yo Yo. Imagine Art's surprise when he arrived in the VIP section of the Garden to see Yo Yo sitting next to his wife in one of those fancy loge chairs. "Hey, Yo Yo, you're in the wrong seat," Mahan exclaimed. "No, no, I'm in the right place," Yo Yo replied. "Where did you get that ticket?" Mahan demanded. "My friend Al Meltzer gave it to me."

The facilities at the Palestra weren't the greatest, but what could you expect from a building that was almost 50 years old. They were primitive to say the least, but that didn't detract from the mystique of the place. Our vantage point was so high up in the rafters that I could almost touch the ceiling. My interview guests had to climb all the way up on a ladder. It was brutal and a lot of guys turned me down. It was quite a challenge for me if I had to use the bathroom and get back in time for the second half.

It doesn't seem that long ago, but it was a very different time for us broadcasters. I'll never forget interviewing Bob Lanier, of St. Bonaventure, after a game and hearing him say: "We played a *helluva* game." And I remember thinking to myself: *He said helluva game. Oh my God! We crossed the boundary line!* I thought that I was going to lose my job.

Working the Big 5 doubleheaders would get to be a long night, but it was worth it. I started at 6:30 with the pregame show, did both games, the halftime shows, the festivities between the games, the "Star of the Game" shows, and then the recap of all the action. By the time I staggered out of there somewhere around 11 o'clock, I'd be fully exhausted.

Although I worked extremely hard to remain objective in calling the games, I frequently received complaints from fans of each of the Big 5 schools, accusing me of being biased against their teams. The criticism really stung at first, but then I started to save this mail and place the letters in neat piles, one for each school. And I learned a valuable lesson. All of the stacks were about the same.

Not that I didn't deserve criticism at times. Like after the NCAA Tournament Eastern Finals in 1988, when Duke held Mark Macon to perhaps the poorest game of his career and eliminated a Temple team that had been unbeaten for most of the season. After the game, I was doing a standup in the Owls' locker room. I don't remember exactly what I said, but it was something like, "Well, the Owls blew it!" The locker room was really small. Coach John Chaney was sitting behind me, and the whole team was right there within earshot. It reverberated throughout the entire dressing room. Here I was standing with my microphone and the kids were crying. I never felt worse in my entire life. It wasn't like me to say things like that. Why I did it, I'll never know.

One of the most enjoyable highlights of the week during the basketball season occurred every Thursday when all of the athletic directors, coaches, players, and publicity people joined the Philadelphia writers and broadcasters at the Herb Good Luncheon at a hotel near Penn's campus. Even the smaller colleges from Divisions II and III participated. And these people genuinely liked each other. There were more laughs during those two hours when we would joke around, tell lies, and needle each other than I would find on the TV sitcoms of that era. It was all in good fun. When things went well for one school or for a particular "Player of the Week," other coaches would be supportive and full of congratulations.

It wasn't like that in, say, the Atlantic Coast Conference or even the Big East today where there's not a lot of camaraderie. I remember Villanova coach Jack Kraft telling me about an incident in the early 1970s when he took one of his Wildcat teams to the South to play in a tournament. Jack happened to be sitting next to Chuck Daly at a luncheon. Daly was an assistant at Duke at the time and he said to Kraft, "How do you guys do it? How can you be so friendly and talk to each other? I wouldn't even think about sitting next to Dean Smith [of North Carolina] at a luncheon, or talking to anyone else in the ACC. We just don't do that down here."

From day one, I was particularly impressed with how much these guys really enjoyed each other's company and how cooperative the schools were with the fans and with each other. I came from the Little 3 in Buffalo, but Niagara, St. Bonaventure, and Canisius were too separated by distance (with Syracuse going it alone) to be able to pull off such an arrangement. This was my first experience with something like this— big-time college basketball where the coaches worked within 10 miles of each other and were just friends having a wonderful time for a couple of hours to take some pressure off of the events of the week back on campus. And they gave us great material for our shows.

Later, when the Big 5 schools started drifting apart (for a variety of reasons, including money, the birth of ESPN, and the emergence of the Big East) and the weekly luncheons were canceled, I was devastated. I remember telling Temple's PR man Al Shrier that my week was ruined. I didn't know what I was going to do with myself for those few hours on Thursday afternoons. I still miss those luncheons to this day.

Speaking of Temple, one of the finest moments in my life came when Harry Litwack's family asked me to do the eulogy at his funeral in 1999. And I wasn't prepared for it because I didn't know that they were going to ask me until I got there. I didn't have a single note in front of me; I had no idea of what I was going to say. But when I got up to speak, the words just kept coming. A lot of it was Harry, and a lot of it was humorous. I summoned up several stories about Harry—how he had only one losing season in 41 years at Temple, how he won the NIT in 1969, and guided the Owls twice to the NCAA Final Four. And when I finished, I didn't know whether I'd done a good job or not with the eulogy, but the people sure seemed to like what I said. After I went home that night, I sat on the deck of my house and lit up a Garcia y Vega, the same brand of cigar that Harry smoked. I turned on the tape recorder in my mind, I looked up in the sky, and I just remembered, remembered, remembered.

There were so many other great people associated with the Big 5. Some of them are far from well known. One gentleman who comes to mind was Dr. Eugene Gallagher, La Salle's team physician, who collapsed and died at a very young age of a heart attack while sitting on the bench at the Sugar Bowl game in New Orleans in 1974. A few years earlier, I traveled to Bowling Green, Kentucky to televise the Explorers' game with Western Kentucky University. On the flight home, I must not have been looking good because Doc Gallagher took one glance at me and asked, "Are you OK?" I replied that I didn't know. He said, "When we land, you're coming with me. I don't know what you have, but it could be pneumonia and we're going to Chestnut Hill Hospital to find out." It turned out that it wasn't pneumonia and they sent me home to rest for a few days, but from that point on, I always traveled with a doctor. And I'll never forget Doc Gallagher.

In 2006, when the Big 5 celebrated its 50th anniversary, I was asked to name my all-time team. I submitted six players: Ken Durrett (La Salle), Howard Porter (Villanova), Mike Bantom (St. Joseph's), Lionel Simmons (La Salle), and the Steve Bilsky–Dave Wohl backcourt combination

(Penn). Guy Rodgers was before my time here and I never saw him play, so when I think of Big 5 guards, Bilsky and Wohl count as one. I wasn't asked at the time, but I'll say it now: maybe the greatest coaching job in Big 5 history was pulled off by Villanova's Rollie Massimino when he guided the Wildcats to their historic 66-64 upset victory over Georgetown, the prohibitive favorite, for the 1985 NCAA title. No other Big 5 coach can refer to his team as national champions!

After all is said and done, what made me what I am today is Big 5 basketball. That assignment was the luckiest thing that ever happened to me because it gave me an identity that has lasted until today. People don't remember what cities I worked in or what stations I worked for, but they remember me for Big 5 basketball, and fondly! I was very lucky because every school had a great team at one time or another. And the Palestra, big-time basketball, and everything else came together at the same time I began televising the games. That's why I lasted 40 years on the air in Philadelphia.

Albert Samuel Meltzer as a fourth-grader in Miss Shanahan's class at the Croton Elementary School.

When Al was a freshman at St. Lawrence University, he pledged the Phi Sigma Kappa Fraternity.

Al joined the United States Air Force in 1950 and was commissioned in 1952 as a second lieutenant. He then went to flight school, flying the T-6 and then the T-28 and B-25.

On his 80th birthday, Al took a last flight in the T-6.

For seven years, Al was the NFL radio voice of the Buffalo Bills and formed a rare three-man broadcasting team with longtime friend Rick Azur (right) and Ed Rutkowski, a former Notre Dame and Bills backup quarterback.

Big Al, who was no slouch in the height department himself, always enjoyed checking the height of his friend, Wilt Chamberlain, during the Stilt's playing days in the NBA. Officially, it was seven feet and half an inch.

One of Al's career highlights came in the last regular season NBA game at the Spectrum in 1987—the Chicago Bulls were in town—when he served as master of ceremonies for a farewell celebration for Julius Erving, who was retiring after an incredible career.

In 1986, Big Al got a chance to play a round of golf with one of the greatest golfers in history, Arnold Palmer, who had flown into Chester Valley Golf Club to promote the upcoming Senior PGA Tournament, the United Hospitals Championship.

Al also had the chance to interview PGA Hall of Famer Gary Player at the Senior Tournament at Chester Valley.

Big Al stands with legendary Temple University coach Harry Litwack ("The Chief"). Both are members of the Philadelphia Big 5 Hall of Fame.

Al Meltzer poses with one of his best friends, sportswriter Bob Vetrone, during ceremonies dedicating La Salle University's Alumni Hall of Athletes in 1999. Vetrone covered the Big 5 for the old Philadelphia *Bulletin* for many years and later handled PR for the 76ers.

Two of the most popular luminaries in the history of Philadelphia sports, Al Meltzer and Eagles coach Dick Vermeil, watch his Birds go through their preseason paces.

KYW TV's Eyewitness News "Dream Team" (from left): Al Meltzer, Mort Crim, Vince Leonard, Jessica Savitch, and Bill Custer.

Eagles coach Buddy Ryan, one of the most controversial coaches in the history of Philadelphia sports, was a popular fixture with Al on the *Coach's Show*.

Al also hosted a weekly radio show with Eagles coach Rich Kotite on Philadelphia's 1210 Radio. Here they chat with Eagles owner Jeffrey Lurie (right).

CHAPTER 6

Life in the NBA: Not Always Glamorous, But Always an Adventure

During my latter years at Channel 17, I was doing a show called *Hot Seat* with Ralph Bernstein of the Associated Press, and usually a couple of other guys from the media, who would ask very pointed questions. I stole the idea for the show from a Canadian television station and it worked well—but not for long enough.

The Milwaukee Bucks were in town during the 1969-70 season to play the 76ers, and I thought that it would be a great idea to get their rookie sensation, Lew Alcindor, as a guest. Later, of course, he became Kareem Abdul-Jabbar. Though he was only in his first year in the NBA, I knew that Lew was not easy to get on the air and was very difficult to interview, even if you did.

Larry Costello, his coach, and I were good friends dating back to our high school days in Syracuse, when we played against each other in basketball before he became an All-America at Niagara. I called Larry and said, "Would you do me a favor?" And, sure enough, he drove Lew out to Mermaid Lane. We brought him in, put him in a chair on an elevated platform with a single spotlight, and he turned out to be a real good interview.

That night after the game at the Spectrum, I went down to see Costello. Alcindor was at his locker. I had a cameraman with me and as I approached the locker, his back was turned to me and I said, "Lew, would you give me a few minutes?" He slowly turned around and he looked down and said, "Big Al! You know *big* is a relative term. It sticks with you forever!" Here he was, seven-feet whatever, at the beginning of his career, and I thought that was a great statement. I wanted to remember it always, and I have. I've used it ever since.

I had begun doing some Milwaukee Bucks games on the radio the previous season, and would continue to do so until 1970. I was called in to handle the play-by-play on radio whenever their games were televised, and I was also used during the playoffs. Larry Costello's teammate at Niagara, Hubie Brown, was the assistant coach, and when they got Oscar Robertson in 1970-71, they became the fastest expansion team to win the NBA title that season.

As a college player, Costello deserved to be in the Hall of Fame, but he got injured and things never worked out for him. He was the quickest guy with the ball to come down the floor and, of course, he played a major role in the 76ers' NBA title in 1966-67. I saw plenty of quick little guys, but for someone who wasn't five feet ten, he was absolutely wonderful with the ball.

Larry wasn't the funniest guy in the world; in fact, he was kind of serious. But once in a while he would come up with something that would qualify as dry humor. Mainly he was all business, and I imagine that he was tough to play for. When he would sit down and talk, the conversation was solely about basketball. That was his whole life, his only interest. He didn't drink, he didn't smoke, and he went to church every Sunday. He didn't leave anything behind about which you could write in the newspapers. There was no baggage—none whatsoever. But he was a guy who gave you his word and lived up to it.

Another one of my favorite people from the NBA was Alex Hannum, who coached the great 76ers team that went 68-13 during the regular season and won the NBA title in 1966-67. He began his career in the league during the team's formative years when they weren't making any money at all. Every time Alex went into a bar, he'd find one serving a free lunch or free dinner. He knew every such hangout from New York to San Francisco and Los Angeles. He'd frequently take me along, probably because I seemed a little older than some of the guys; in fact I was older than all of his players.

The night before we played for the NBA title against the Warriors—it was about two o'clock in the morning out there in San Francisco and we were staying at the Jack Tar Hotel—Alex said, "Do me a favor, Al. Go to the garage of the hotel and check something out for me." I knew exactly what he wanted. So I took a walk out to the parking garage, came back to the hotel bar, and simply said, "You're in good shape, Alex." He wanted me to see if Wilt Chamberlain's purple Bentley was parked in the garage, and I assured him it was. And he knew that he had nothing to worry about.

We won that game, of course, and we celebrated together down in the bar at the Jack Tar Hotel. I don't remember if Wilt just drank 7-Up or had champagne or an apple juice, but it was a mild celebration. It was calm even in the locker room. Today winning the NBA championship would be cause for an enormous celebration, especially for the benefit of the television cameras.

But once the game was over, we signed off because the station would have had to pay more money to keep the line open. It had already been a triumphant moment for little Channel 17. We formed our own mini-network, and a lot of people all over the country saw the NBA championship decided. As I said before, I would really love to see a replay of the game that helped to put WPHL-TV on the national stage, but that chance is gone forever.

One thing that I will always remember about covering the NBA in my hometown for WHEN was the Onondaga County War Memorial, the arena that hosted the Nats for their final 12 seasons in Syracuse before the franchise moved to Philadelphia in 1963. Syracuse was a unique town in the realm of professional sports—a little city in a big league— much like Green Bay with the Packers. In addition to providing an incredible home court advantage, it was the toughest place for NBA referees to control a game.

On many nights, the refs would dress in their hotel rooms, have a police escort to the game, and an even tighter escort after the games. The fans were not only loud, but at times physical. Referees like Sid Borgia, who was only five feet six, but had a voice that carried all the way back to the cheap seats in the old arenas, seldom lost their cool, but I can remember one exception.

Sitting front row center for all of the games was my good friend, Eli, who hailed from the old neighborhood. Eli had a voice like a foghorn and would constantly remind Borgia of his shortcomings. Finally one night, the little man had enough. He walked over to Eli, asked him to stand up, and punched his lights out. The next day, Maurice Podoloff, the president of the NBA, called Eli, wanting to know what he could do to smooth things over. We had suggested that he sue, but Eli, always the fan, accepted two center-court, lifetime seats instead. Bad move, Eli. The team left town a few years later and became the Philadelphia 76ers. (I asked Eli a couple of years ago if there was any money in his deal. "A check," he answered.)

Here's how tough the Syracuse fans were. My good friend Dolph Shayes, who played with the Nationals for 15 years, remembers one game when they hosted the New York Knicks, their archrival, at the Coliseum. "When the Knicks would shoot free throws, the fans would grab the guide wires that attached the backboards to the stands and rock the basket," he recalled.

The man responsible for professional basketball in Syracuse was Danny Biasone, an Italian immigrant who owned a combination restaurant, bar, and bowling alley in the eastern part of the city. No one really knows how he did it, but he ended up pulling off a minor miracle in 1947, getting a franchise in professional basketball for $5,000 on behalf of a city of a little more than 200,000 people. The Nationals played in the beginning at the state fairgrounds on the edge of town, a venue not really suitable for big-time basketball. In 1951, they moved to the Onondaga County War Memorial, a building that featured the first poured-in-place concrete roof in the nation. (How about that, sports fans? And you thought that I knew nothing about architecture.)

Danny Biasone was the guy who negotiated with Dolph Shayes— stay tuned for that story—and got him away from the New York Knicks for an extra $2,500. He also picked a guy who could really coach—Al Cervi. A street kid who came from Rochester, Cervi had worked in the trucking business. He was one of those "gym rats" who didn't go to college. Al was tough and demanded a lot from his players. But Danny's biggest innovation revolutionized the game of professional basketball. One day after a very low-scoring game, he decided that it was time to jazz up things and put a clock on the court. He kept records for a while and came to the conclusion that the average shot was taken in 24 seconds. So league officials took it for a dry run during the summer before the regular season began and tried it out under game conditions. It worked so well that in 1954, the 24-second shot clock became a permanent part of the NBA game. (The men's college game didn't adopt a shot clock until 1986, when it implemented a 40-second limit. In 1993, it was reduced to 35 seconds.)

Biasone's teams were very successful in Syracuse—the Nats posted winning records in 11 of their 14 seasons and won an NBA title by beating the Fort Wayne Pistons, four games to three, in 1955. But it would only be a matter of time before the smallest town with a major sports team would lose its franchise. That time finally came in the spring of 1963, when Danny sold the club to Ike Richman and Irv Kosloff of Philadelphia for a half-million dollars. The City of Brotherly Love had been without an NBA team since Eddie Gottlieb took the Warriors to San Francisco following the 1961-62 season.

"It was economics, but most people don't know the real story," Shayes explained. "The league had wanted to expand to the West Coast as soon as jet travel came in, but would not do so until teams could play both in Los Angeles and San Francisco—which would make the trip worthwhile financially for the other clubs. When the Lakers decided to leave Minneapolis and go to LA, their owner, Bob Short, approached Danny Biasone because he knew that the NBA no longer wanted Syracuse in the league since we were the smallest franchise in pro basketball. The Fort Wayne Pistons were in the same situation, but their owner, Fred Zollner, was a multi-millionaire who was about to move to Detroit. So Bob Short said, 'Look, Danny, I want to go to the West Coast. We've had it in Minneapolis. I'll tell you what: if you come with me, you can pick any other city of your choice.' Danny Biasone said, 'No, I love Syracuse. My heart's here.'

"Then Bob Short went to Eddie Gottlieb, who was getting on in years, and offered him the same deal. So Eddie Gottlieb made a deal with a group in San Francisco. That, of course, left a void in Philadelphia and also increased expenses tremendously for the NBA. Meanwhile, Biasone saw the handwriting on the wall. Syracuse had been a steady market for a long time with 4,000 season ticket holders. But soon 500 of them started to leave after each season and Syracuse didn't have the cachet to bring in more people. So when those 500 fans left, there wasn't another 500 to take their place. Our attendance was dropping rapidly. Danny was offered a half-million to go to Philadelphia and he took it."

That's how my team ended up as *my* team!

And speaking of my team, I mustn't forget Gotty's good friend, Dave Zinkoff, the legendary announcer for the Philadelphia Warriors, 76ers, and Harlem Globetrotters for many years before he passed away on Christmas Day, 1985. Zink always laced his announcements with a colorful gimmick or a clever saying like "Gola Goal!" for Tom Gola, the former LaSalle All-America. For Julius Erving, who was always introduced last, he would say, "From the University of Mazzachushetts…number six...the captain of the Philadelphia 76ers, Julius...the Doctor... Errrrrrrving! And, of course, he always brought the house down with his nightly plea, "Will the owner of the silver Cadillac...Pennsylvania license plate 123456...please report to the parking lot. Your car is parked with its lights on, motor running, and doors locked." He gave away a salami during every Sixers game as part of a promotion for Hebrew National. Zink also worked for the Philadelphia Phillies at the old Shibe Park long before I arrived in town. His unique voice and inimitable delivery have been copied and imitated more than any other PA announcer in the world. I'm proud to say that I was instrumental in getting one of the streets near Philadelphia's Stadium Complex named after him shortly after his death.

Let me backtrack for a moment to put my NBA memories in Philadelphia in perspective. When I first arrived here in 1964, I immediately found familiar faces. They were a few miles down the Schuylkill Expressway from Channel 6 in Convention Hall. No, they weren't sitting in the stands. They were playing basketball. The Philadelphia 76ers had been the Syracuse Nationals, and my buddy Dolph Shayes was going to be the player-coach. Dolph didn't last very long as a player. He got hurt, but he did coach the team for three years.

Dolph Shayes is a fascinating guy, and I feel fortunate that we have been able to keep in touch over the years. He was only 19 years old when he graduated from NYU with an engineering degree. But he was also six feet seven and, boy, could he play basketball. Everyone assumed that the New York Knicks were going to get him because he grew up in the Bronx, a Jewish All-America with a loyal fan base. But for 2500 bucks, the Knicks lost a guy who would have made them a huge winner for years to come.

"I was always big for my age," Shayes recalled when we reminisced about a year ago. "I remember when I was only nine years old, older kids who were much smaller than me used to wait outside the movie theater and ask to be taken in by adults because in those days you had to be 13. They would see me and say, 'Mister, would you take me in?'"

When Shayes graduated from NYU, there were two professional leagues that would eventually merge into the NBA in 1949. The Basketball Association of America was located in larger cities like New York, Boston, St. Louis, Chicago, and Philadelphia. The National Basketball League was primarily in smaller towns, mostly in the Midwest, with Syracuse being the easternmost team. It included towns like Oshkosh and

Sheboygan, Wisconsin; Royal, Iowa; and Anderson, Indiana. Dolph was the first draft choice of both the Knicks of the BAA and the Nationals of the NBL.

"The BAA had a salary cap of $100,000 for the entire team, and the Knicks said that they could only offer me $5,000, which was the most allowed by the league for rookies," Shayes explained. "Ned Irish, the boss at Madison Square Garden, was the most important person in the BAA, and he was the one who pushed through the salary cap for rookies. He wasn't about to break the rule, although New York did offer me a job with the New York Travel Authority or something like that—the ones that take care of bridges. I asked if I could collect all the quarters at the George Washington Bridge and keep them all. But the National League didn't have a cap, so Danny Biasone, who had started the Nationals two years earlier, gave me $7,500. I decided to take the extra money because in those days the 100 bucks a week was a helluva lot of money.

"I really didn't think pro basketball was going anywhere, although I did watch the Knicks while I was in college. But the team was an immediate hit in Syracuse. We were a very young team with a very aggressive coach. We won a lot of games, played very exciting basketball, and drew very well—8,000 to 10,000 people a game. We were like the Green Bay of the NBA—the David versus Goliath—especially when New York, Boston, and Philadelphia came in—or Minneapolis with George Mikan. The economy was strong because there were a lot of factories in Syracuse and the workers were making pretty good dough. They loved their sports and they really loved our team."

Shayes played for three coaches at Syracuse—Al Cervi, Paul Seymour, and Alex Hannum, who had been his teammate for two seasons with the Nationals. Hannum, of course, later succeeded him as coach in Philadelphia, where he guided the 76ers to the NBA title in 1966-67. Alex also won the NBA championship with the 1957-58 St. Louis Hawks and the American Basketball Association crown with the Rick Barry–led Oakland Oaks in 1968-69, making him and Bill Sharman the only coaches in history to win titles in both the NBA and ABA. Sharman did it with the Utah Stars and Los Angeles Lakers. It's hard to believe, but both Hannum and Sharman were inexplicably omitted from the NBA's 50th Anniversary List of the "Ten Greatest Coaches of All Time" in 1966.

On the other hand, Dolph Shayes did make that NBA 50th Anniversary List as one of the league's top 50 players. He is also included in the

Naismith Memorial Basketball Hall of Fame as one of the top 50 players of the century. Dolph was one of the league's most durable players—15 full seasons and part of a 16th as he appeared in 24 games as player-coach of the 76ers in 1963-64. He did not miss a single game from February 17, 1952 until December 26, 1961 (a streak of 706 games). Generally considered as the first modern basketball forward, Shayes led the NBA in free throw percentage three times (85 percent for his career) and rebounding once. In 1961, he became the first NBA player in history to reach the 30,000 career mark in points, rebounds, and assists. What a legacy!

"And to think that the highest-paid player in the NBA in the 1950s was George Mikan, and he probably made about $30,000 because he was like the superstar of the league," Shayes recalled. "Rochester had some wonderful players, but it was a small town and they didn't pay that well. At Syracuse the salaries were around $15,000. Some players with teams like the Philadelphia Warriors were making $5,000 at that time.

"Paul Arizin was on the Warriors and he was probably making $17,000 or $18,000. Neil Johnston was a raw rookie who came to the team unheralded, and then he became a star almost overnight. So the next year he came to see Eddie Gottlieb, who was owner, general manager, and he probably cleaned up the offices in his spare time. Eddie said, 'You made $5,000 last year, how much do you want?' Neil said, 'I want $18,000.' Eddie Gottlieb went to his pocket, pulled out a bunch of keys and said, 'You want $18,000? Well here—you own the team.' Eddie was a wonderful person, though, and he also had excellent players like Joe Fulks and Tom Gola on his team.

"And, of course, Wilt Chamberlain later became the highest paid player in the history of the NBA. Bill Russell had won a few championships by then and was making about $65,000. The salaries were going up gradually, and Wilt wanted to become the first $100,000 player. He did in the 1964-65 season. When Bill Russell heard that, he went to [Red] Auerbach and said, 'Man, I won championships. Wilt's never won one. He makes $100,000. I have to make $100,001.' So Auerbach gave him that amount and said to Wilt, 'Now you're not the highest paid player because Russell makes $100,001,' or something like that."

Speaking of All-Stars, Shayes told me that it's really difficult for him to name the best player he ever guarded. "Bob Petit, of the St. Louis Hawks, always gave me a lot of trouble," Dolph recalled. "He was just a hard-working guy who never quit. He hit the offensive boards and went to the basket hard. If I played him a good game, I'd hold him to 35 points."

By 1964, good things started to happen in the City of Brotherly Love. Larry Costello also came in from Syracuse. Wilt Chamberlain, who had gone to San Francisco, came back to Philadelphia in a trade for Connie Dierking, Lee Shaffer, Paul Neumann, and $150,000 cash. The Sixers picked up Billy Cunningham, the University of North Carolina All-America, in the draft. He got here in 1965. They had traded for Wali Jones, and they had brought Chet Walker and Hal Greer in from Syracuse—and Luke Jackson, after the 1964 Olympics, as the fourth pick in the entire NBA draft. This was going to be some basketball team.

But Dolph wasn't around to coach it because the owners, Ike Richman and Irv Kosloff, had decided that they wanted to go with Alex Hannum, who had roots in Syracuse as a player and three years as a coach. "My third year, I was 55 and 25. I was Coach of the Year and we had a terrific team, the nucleus of the team that the very next year won the world championship," recalled Shayes, who said that he was fired by Kosloff because his club didn't beat the Boston Celtics in the Eastern Division playoffs. "We had two weeks off and weren't ready for them. That happens in sports all the time."

Dolph characterized his relationship with Wilt Chamberlain as standoffish. "When I was playing, I was a little critical of his foul-shooting, and he didn't like criticism," Shayes explained. "I thought that there was always that thing about us, but he was a wonderful person. Whenever there were things to do for the team, he'd go to events. He was very gracious with the fans. One big problem I had was the fact that he did not want to live in Philadelphia. So he lived on Central Park West in New York City.

"First of all when you play, you practice a lot. Wilt was a night person, so a friend came to me and said, 'Wilt asked me if you can make the practices in the afternoon because he sleeps late and takes the train.' The players didn't like that. Practices were one thing they wanted to get out of the way at 11 o'clock in the morning so they would have the rest of the time to do what they wanted. So we practiced late in the afternoon or early in the evening and, of course, practices with Wilt were farcical in a way because he was so dominant and nobody could handle him. So Wilt would fool around in practices and the players would say, 'Dolph, just sit him down so we can get a good workout.' But Wilt was very well liked by the guys on the team. He had a wonderful personality and they all got along together."

At any rate, everyone knew that the 76ers had the makings of a dynasty. As a matter of fact, when the NBA celebrated its 35th year back in 1985, that 1967 Philadelphia team was selected as the best team in pro basketball during that period. The 76ers ran through the Boston Celtics and then took on the *old* Warriors, who were now the *new* Warriors in San Francisco, and, in six games, won the NBA title. Charlie Swift and I happened to do that game because the NBC network wasn't going to televise even the championship game unless it was played on the weekend. We got a chance to televise it across the country, celebrate with the team, and all was well.

The following year, even though the 76ers had home court advantage, they lost a seventh game to the Boston Celtics in the Eastern Division Finals at the Spectrum, and that was about it for the greatest team in basketball. By the way, Philadelphia had gone up three games to one and seemed to be in complete control, but it was obvious that they were distracted—and for good reason.

Dr. Martin Luther King had been assassinated on April 4, 1968, the night before Game 1 of that series, and, although there was some talk of postponing the game, the teams reluctantly agreed to play. I remember that Wilt and some of his teammates were upset that Alex Hannum hadn't called a meeting to get their opinions, especially since Red Auerbach had done exactly that with the Celtics. Any momentum that the Sixers might have had wasn't there, and the Celtics came back to end the dynasty.

Alex lived to see another day, but Wilt? He went back to the West Coast. Not to San Francisco, but to Los Angeles. A trade was made on July 9, 1968, and the 76ers got Jerry Chambers, Archie Clark, and Darrall Imhoff from the Lakers for Chamberlain. It was a notable transaction for a number of reasons. Imhoff, you may remember, was the center for the New York Knicks who had the dubious distinction of guarding Wilt the night he scored 100 points in Hershey. And it was the first time in history that a reigning NBA Most Valuable Player was traded the following season. This was not a good three-for-one deal for our 76ers.

I was still doing the Sixers games in 1970 when Irv Kosloff hired a guy named Don DeJardin as the team's general manager. I don't remember where he came from; I do know that he only lasted in the job until 1974. But he was after me *Big Time*! He wanted to get somebody else to do the games because, in his mind, I wasn't enough of a "homer." He felt that I shot my mouth off a little bit too much. I was critical when the team was playing poorly—which was happening more frequently.

I wasn't around when the Sixers later established the most dreadful record in franchise history. In 1974, a coach named Roy Rubin came in to guide the team to a won-loss record of 9 and 73. In less than seven years, Philadelphia went from being the *best* team in the NBA to the *worst* team in pro basketball. And that record still stands today.

When Fitz Dixon bought the Sixers in 1976, he made sure to make good use of the talents of Pat Williams, a former catcher in the Phillies minor league system, who had been hired by Jack Ramsay as the team's business manager in 1968. Williams left the 76ers the following year to join his hero, Bill Veeck, and spend four years as general manager of the Chicago Bulls. Williams returned to the 76ers in 1974. He would spend the next 12 years as their GM and would acquire a reputation as the "Bill Veeck of the NBA," in honor of the man who was arguably the greatest promotional genius in major league baseball history when he ran the St. Louis Browns and, later, the Chicago White Sox. Williams quickly lived up to the reputation that preceded him years earlier when he had been voted baseball's Outstanding Minor League Executive when he operated the Phillies' farm team in Spartanburg, South Carolina.

Now Pat was back as Philadelphia's general manager with a reputation that preceded him. Just like Veeck, Williams was determined to put people in the seats at the Spectrum. And he was an idea man. Like getting "Victor the Wrestling Bear" to take on all comers at halftime. But the idea I remember—though perhaps I shouldn't—was "Little Arlene," who won an eating contest. I believe that there were five opponents. In all, she consumed 76 hot dogs, 30 pizzas, a half-dozen Cokes, and she easily beat all of her challengers. How did she do it? Easy. She was surrounded by curtains and she would go behind them between challenges and—I don't know how else to say it—throw up. This was pure Bill Veeck.

But people started to come and see the 1976 Philadelphia 76ers. There was a guy named Julius Erving, from the University of Massachusetts, playing in the competitive American Basketball Association during the years of the wars between the two leagues. He was in a contract dispute and he didn't want to report to his team, the New York Nets. So Pat Williams went and talked to the GM of the Nets, who happened to be the former Villanova star, Bill Melchionni. They finally made a deal—no, it was a *steal*—and the Doctor was purchased by Philadelphia for a measly *three million bucks* because the Nets had just paid $3.2 million for a franchise in the NBA and they couldn't afford to keep their superstar.

The key to the Sixers' success came during a conversation between Williams and Fitz Dixon when Pat asked the owner's permission to make the deal. "Who is Julius Erving?" Dixon asked. "The Babe Ruth of baseball," Williams replied. "Do it!" ordered the owner.

By then, Billy Cunningham had become the coach of the 76ers, and they had players like George McGinnis, Caldwell Jones, and Mo Cheeks. They made a trade to get a great shooting guard named Andrew Toney, who we all later remembered as "The Boston Strangler" because he just destroyed the Celtics. But the big move was Moses Malone, obtained from Houston on September 15, 1981 for Caldwell Jones and a later first-round pick. That trade, of course, paid big dividends in 1983 when the 76ers swept the Lakers in four straight games for the NBA title. And who will ever forget Malone's bold prediction of "fo, fo, fo," meaning that his team would sweep every series. He came close—only a loss to the Milwaukee Bucks in Game 4 of the Eastern Conference Finals spoiled that prognostication.

At any rate, when the team arrived home from LA, there was an understated reception. As I think back to the return home of the '67 NBA champs, there were only a few dozen people there, and most of them were relatives and close friends. How times have changed. Sometimes you play for a ring, but in this town, you play for a parade. The Doctor stayed in Philly until the end of his career, and the 76ers picked up Charles Barkley later on. They also added Allen Iverson, but there have been no rings, no parades, no titles since the magical '83 season.

It's easy to understand why. Harold Katz, who owned the Sixers in the '80s, was involved in a move that almost destroyed the franchise. In 1986, he traded Moses Malone, who led the club to that '83 championship. This was just the beginning. The trade was made with the Washington Bullets for Jeff Ruland, who came here with a bad knee and only played a few games.

There's more. Katz also traded two future first-round draft picks. It didn't end there. The Sixers traded their first-round pick Brad Daugherty to Cleveland for Roy Hinson. Harold thought Daugherty was too soft. You want even more? Daugherty played nine years for Cleveland and averaged 19.5 points per game. Hinson was traded away a year later.

Although I would never trade my experiences in the NBA for any-thing—especially handling the 76ers' road games for Channel 17 from 1965 to 1970—traveling with a pro basketball team was really never that glamorous. Far from it! But I must say that there was one traveling com-panion who made my life an absolute joy—a guy named Bob Vetrone, who handled the color and analysis for me. In the beginning, he was work-ing at the Philadelphia *Bulletin,* where everyone knew him as "Buck the Bartender." Eventually, Bob became the public relations director of the 76ers, and that's where he did most of his work with me on the telecasts.

As they used to say about the late, great evening newspaper, "In Phil-adelphia, nearly everybody reads the *Bulletin.*" Well, the same could be said for Bob Vetrone: *Everybody* knew him. Not only in Philadelphia, but all over the world—especially where basketball was discussed. I would venture to say that Bob Vetrone knew more people on a first-name basis than anyone in the city's history. Mayors, political leaders, sports and entertainment celebrities—you name anyone and I guarantee you that Bob knew more people than they did. Not only that, but I never heard a bad word about him from anybody in all the years I knew him, right up until the day he died in 2005. Bob was really one of a kind with an enor-mous sense of humor. Beef, as I called him, was a wonderful, wonderful guy, and it was always a pleasure to be in his company.

As I implied earlier, when you travel on the road in the NBA, it ain't a lot of fun. But Bob and I got to room together. There are a lot of stories that will never be told, but I will tell you that I miss him dearly—even today. There was always something about him that touched me. Bob knew his basketball and he did a nice job on the air. He wasn't really a "professional broadcaster," but I liked that because we were able to con-verse comfortably, and it wasn't a contest about who was going to get the air time.

Bob knew everyone in the NBA, which made my job much easier when I was on the air. There wasn't a coach or general manager in the league that didn't know him. And wherever we went, Bob would be part of the conversation before the game. He was always respected as an impor-tant part of the league because his reputation preceded him in many ways.

Shortly before Bob died, he called me and said, "I want you to come with me to the Bryn Mawr Rehabilitation Center. Tommy Gola is there." I didn't know that Gola, the former La Salle All-America and NBA All-Star, had suffered a fall, but I said, "Absolutely!" We spent a couple of hours there, not just visiting but talking to him. Tommy had some severe medical problems, and Beef wanted Tommy to know that he would be more than happy to help him with anything he needed. And that's the way Bob always treated people. Later when he was down on his luck, his friends quickly came to his aid. Like the people at La Salle University who hired Bob as sports information director, a position that enabled him to qualify for much-needed health benefits in his final years.

Bob and I often talked about one of the craziest New Year's holidays we ever spent together, beginning on December 31, 1968. Coach Jack Ramsay's 76ers had just beaten the Bucks in Milwaukee before a handful of fans who braved the 10-below-zero weather. It was so cold that Philly sportswriter George Kisida went through the stands in the arena, asking fans, "What are you doing here on New Year's Eve?" George was just a wonderful guy. He was a great reporter who had a unique perspective.

As a weary band of players and media members left the arena to wait for cabs to the airport, we had no idea what was in store for us on this cold, cold night. Al Domenico, the team trainer who also served as tour director, had booked an 11:30 flight to Chicago with a connection to Philadelphia. Teams didn't have the luxury of traveling by charter back in those days, but if all went right, we would celebrate the New Year in the air en route home. But all did not go right.

We waited and waited for cabs, but they never showed up. We wanted to make a phone call (this was before anyone had cell phones), but the arena was locked and Al McGuire's nearby bar, for some unknown reason, was closed on New Year's Eve. By now the wind chill was about minus 30, and Sixers rookie Shaler Halimon ended up with frostbite on his ear. It was a miracle that we didn't all get pneumonia.

Finally, we spotted a cab, persuaded the driver to call a few of his friends, and rushed to the airport for the flight to Chicago. The plane was a twin-engine prop, and it bounced like a basketball as we flew over Lake Michigan. After what seemed like hours, we landed in Chicago. By now it was 1969, but we had very little to cheer about as we raced to the terminal, arriving just in time for the trip to Philadelphia.

At least, we figured, we'll be on the flight home. Except there was a little problem—no pilots or flight attendants. They were coming in from Los Angeles, circling above, attempting to land. Also, there was no food on the plane and the airport restaurants were closed. Some of the players had beverages in their bags, so we used the beer that made Milwaukee famous to toast in the New Year. We took off at three o'clock in the morning and arrived in Philadelphia four hours later. It was not long after that experience that I moved on to bigger and better things after being convinced that traveling on the road with the NBA could turn your hair white.

There was one other memorable road trip. In 1967, the year the Sixers won the NBA championship, they played the Celtics in a seven o'clock game one night at the Boston Garden. I walked in about 5:30 and I heard a bouncing ball. I looked and the only lights lit were above the stands. I looked again and saw Wilt. He was shooting free throws. So I just kind of wandered over and said, "Here, I'll feed you." We later started talking about free throws and he told me that when he was in high school and college, he was a better free-throw shooter than he was with the pros. Nobody was around—it was just the two of us. And he said, "Are you a basketball player?" I replied, "Oh yeah. I was a very good high school player." He said, "Did you shoot free throws?"

"I patterned myself after a guy like Dolph Shayes," I replied. "I loved the way he shot free throws. And I'm probably as good today as when I was playing ball." So Wilt said, "Well, how about a little something on the side here?" I said, "Sure. How much?" He said, "Best out of ten for a million dollars."

I immediately said, "Of course." I thought to myself, *I'm going to win a million dollars!* He stepped up to the line and made seven out of ten free throws. Now, I hadn't shot a free throw in years, believe me. And I didn't have a million dollars in my pocket, although I knew I wouldn't have to pay, anyway. But my ego was at stake here. So I stepped up to the line and I made eight out of ten! I walked up to him and I said, "There it is. Do you want to write me a check or how do you want to do it?" He replied, "I'll send it to you in the mail."

Speaking about unforgettable experiences, the 1977 NBA Finals between the 76ers and the Portland Trail Blazers was a classic. More to the point, though, Game 2 was a mess. Philly had a two-game lead on the Trail Blazers, but toward the end of that second game at the Spectrum, Darryl Dawkins—all six-foot-eleven, 251 pounds of him—got into a fight with six-foot-nine, 215-pounder Maurice Lucas, the toughest guy on the Portland team, and that tussle ignited the Trail Blazers for the rest of the series. Lucas, who was Portland's enforcer, came racing in to confront Philadelphia's "Chocolate Thunder" after Darryl had flipped and body-slammed Portland's Bobby Gross to the floor. As he and Darryl squared off, little Doug Collins—later the 76ers' coach—tried to restrain Gross. Darryl swung, Gross ducked, and the punch squarely hit Doug. Meanwhile, Lucas came charging down the floor and got into it with Dawkins. Both of them were ejected. Afterwards, we found out that Darryl went into the locker room and lifted all of the walls of the stalls out of their foundations. He also ripped out one of the urinals. He practically destroyed the place. The Sixers won that game going away, 107-89, to go up two-zip, but they ended up losing four straight to coach Jack Ramsay's Trail Blazers.

Here's all you need to know about Jack Ramsay, one of the classiest guys in the game. Jack was having his practice before one of the NBA finals that year, and all you could hear was the squeaking of sneakers, the ball bouncing, and Jack. Then the Sixers came out. Gene Shue was the coach. Darryl Dawkins was wearing a painter's hat backwards and Lloyd Free was doing something else of the showboating variety. All of the big men were trying to make 30-foot, three-point plays—and they were all having a great time. It actually wasn't as much practice as it was fun time. I hoped that they would be more serious about the game. It was like kids in camp—that's what Philadelphia's practice was. With Jack Ramsay, though, it was like being in the Marine Corps. Later on it occurred to me that I should have known right then and there that Jack was going to have his team ready. I don't think that anyone could blame Gene Shue as much as the group of characters on that team. People like Dr. J and Bobby Jones were okay, but they also had a lot of strange people. Still, it was definitely a fun team!

Ramsay was all business in basketball, and yet he was a really nice guy. He got along tremendously with the other coaches. Earlier in his career, he had recruited very successfully for St. Joe's, a school that was outsized in its competition with the Big 5. Jack turned out to have an excellent basketball mind, not only as coach of the Hawks and Trail Blazers, but also as general manager of the Sixers the year they won the NBA championship. Jack probably influenced the careers of more basketball coaches than any man who ever coached the game. He was also responsible for a lot of marriages in the Big 5.

Another highlight of my NBA career came in the last regular-season game at the Spectrum in 1987. The Chicago Bulls were in town, and they asked me to serve as master of ceremonies for a farewell celebration for Julius Erving, who was retiring after an incredible career. I still have a picture of myself that night, wearing my tux and black tie. The place was packed. The Bulls were all out on the floor to watch everything, and it was truly a love affair. Dr. J had the best connection with Philadelphia fans of any NBA athlete ever. There were a lot of great guys on that 76ers team who should have won at least one or two more NBA championships. But Doc was special. That night made me feel like I was doing a rock concert. There was a deafening roar the entire evening. And when Patti LaBelle started to sing "Wind Beneath My Wings," I started to cry. It was that emotional. I thought to myself: *This is it. He's going to retire. What's it going to be like now?*

Dr. J was an absolute gentleman, and here's a small example: I was in a restaurant with my wife one day. We were sitting alone, and Doc came in and said, "Are you with anybody?" We said, "No," so he sat down with us and talked for about an hour. He was always available in any situation. When I'd go into the locker room, the first guy I'd head for would be Dr. J. Bobby Jones got dressed early and left, Moses Malone was a little difficult to interview, Mo Cheeks had very little to say, and so in most cases our savior was Julius. He was an innovator who will never get full credit for the game as it's played today because during his time, he could play that game like no one else.

And that about says it all for my memories of the NBA.

CHAPTER 7

Camelot at Channel 3 Eyewitness News

I f I wasn't the busiest TV guy in America at Channel 17, I suppose I came close. I covered the 76ers, Big 5 basketball, college and pro football, and everything that moved on the playing field.

I had also joined the world of pro football on a number of other fronts. The Buffalo Bills had recently changed radio stations, and they asked me to come up and do their play-by-play. In addition, I picked up weekly narrating and voice-over gigs at HBO, Tel Ra Films and NFL Films, resulting in a tremendous amount of national exposure—and lots of additional travel. I guess you could say that I was the ultimate free-lance sports announcer.

Then came another *Fork in the Road*. And that's why, when the phone call came from Philadelphia's KYW TV Channel 3 about taking over the sports job, I jumped at the opportunity. I had already decided not to sign another contract with Channel 17, because of the station's financial situation. Moreover, I could still do the Bills' games and continue with my Milwaukee Bucks basketball assignments. Last but not least, there was much more money involved.

I was in for quite a shock, though, when I reported for work my first day. I walked through the entrance, went toward the elevator and said to someone, "I'm looking for the newsroom." The person pointed over to the left and said, "There it is!" And I walked over and looked through the door. I couldn't believe my eyes. The newsroom was about as big as a standard dining room. I later learned that this area was originally supposed to be the mailroom, but because *The Mike Douglas Show* was taking up all the usable space, this tiny section was all that was left. I had a cubicle that was about twice the size of a phone booth, which was very uncomfortable because of my height. I had a shower curtain instead of a door, because there was no room to swing open a door. You couldn't even have a private conversation with anybody because others could hear you all over the place. It was really tough. When you have bad working conditions, it has an effect on you. And these were really bad working conditions. Fortunately, the people were great to work with and the news director was a wonderful guy. You couldn't ask for better cooperation.

A few months later when I came in to work, there was a tremendous amount of commotion going on near the newsroom. Everything was pitch-black because the electricity was off. I wondered what in the world was going on. I'm not sure if it was a monkey or a chimpanzee, but whatever it was had been on *The Mike Douglas Show* with an animal trainer, I assume. The creature had wandered away, found the newsroom, and absolutely destroyed it. In one sense it was terrible, but in another sense it might be a wonderful blessing. I immediately thought: *We're going to get a big, brand-new newsroom out of this.* And that's what happened. They moved us upstairs, where they had been saving space to rent out, and we got ourselves a first-class newsroom.

Anchorman Vince Leonard and weatherman Bill Custer were already working at Eyewitness News when I arrived. Vince knew Philadelphia like no one else, and Philadelphians knew him. Bill was not just any weatherman. He was from the farm country around State College, Pennsylvania—a Nittany Lion through and through. And he did something that no TV personality had ever attempted, at least in a large city: He grew a real garden in front of the station at 5th and Market Streets.

The station soon brought in Mort Crim, a popular reporter from Louisville, Kentucky, who had been considering a run for Congress, and Jessica Savitch, a talented 24-year-old native of South Jersey, who attended Ithaca College and was working in Houston, Texas.

Crim turned out to be, in my opinion, the best anchor who ever delivered news in this town. And I'm including the revered John Facenda, who mainly had an exquisite speaking voice. But Mort had more than that. He backed it up with great writing. That's right: he wrote his own material. He was not just a rip-and-reader. He actually *knew* the news.

Jessica was not just a very attractive blonde. She was extremely bright, an incredibly hard worker, and so ambitious that she never turned down the chance to do the big story. She also initiated the two- and three-part news series, a staple of TV news today. These series were soon being copied by other stations, and it wasn't long before all of the national networks were knocking on her door.

It was a perfect fit for five people who had no inkling how this was going to turn out or how we would eventually complement each other and become what the *Philadelphia Daily News* called "the greatest news team in the city's history." And for most of the '70s, according to the critics, we formed the best local news team in the nation!

The guy responsible for it all was Jim Topping, who turned out to be the best news director I ever worked for, and that includes a lot of news executives at a number of television stations. He did an incredibly superb job of putting the pieces together and synchronizing the five people on our team. He just knew that the whole would be so much greater than the sum of its parts.

To begin with, Jim added the city's first 5:30 p.m. show. No one else in town was doing anything before 6:00, but it didn't take very long for the other channels to copy us and try to catch up with our popularity. Jim also offered me an opportunity that, as far as I know, a sportscaster had never been given before: the chance to do a five-minute segment of sports commentary on the 5:30 show and a shorter version at 6:00 and 11:00. No one had ever done this kind of commentary on television, and talk radio hadn't really gotten off the ground. I was opinionated, but it was not considered a detriment. I just said what was on my mind, but I didn't try to encourage those who disagreed with me to go swallow razor blades. It wasn't like one of today's ego-driven sports and political rants; it was more like a well-reasoned newspaper column. I wasn't always *that* opinionated, but like a good referee, I called them as I saw them. And from that day on, the mail came pouring in, because when you talk about *controversy,* when it comes to sports broadcasting in this town, I invented the word.

I'm not certain who first applied the name *Camelot* to the Channel 3 news team. It could have been a newspaper columnist or maybe a magazine writer. But I do understand why the term was used. After spending 50 years in the television news business, it has been my experience that few, if any, on-air news teams ever brought together the same ingredients that this combination of unique people did. It wasn't that we were more talented than other teams; certainly there are others with as much drive, ambition, and will to succeed. There were other news teams that were just as active in their local communities as my colleagues.

I know it's a cliché, but if there's a single word to describe the uniqueness of this particular Eyewitness News Team, it has to be the much-overused word *chemistry*. You hear that a lot in sports. It's very hard to define but quite easy to recognize. In a word, our team had it. It wasn't just on-air chemistry; it was the kind that generated genuine friendships. We actually *liked* each other and formed bonds between families that transcended work. We got together at each other's homes, socialized, and enjoyed each other's company. I believe that it was the deep regard and respect that we all shared for each other that sparked such magic when we appeared together on TV. There simply was none of the petty jealousy and behind-the-scenes bickering that sometimes characterizes the relationship of television personalities. Each of us delighted in the others' success. We truly worked as a team. We covered for each other, watched each other's back, and had some great times together.

The one get-together that I remember the most was the 100th running of the Kentucky Derby. Mort Crim and Vince Leonard were co owners of an airplane with Herb Clarke, the weatherman at Channel 10. And, of course, I had flown in the Air Force. One day, Mort said, "Why don't we hop on our plane and we'll all go down and see the Derby. At this late date, we'll never get a room, but I've got a contact."

His contact was none other than Harland Sanders, the honorary "Kentucky Colonel" and the distinguished, white-bearded founder of Kentucky Fried Chicken. We fully expected him to pull a couple of hotel rooms out of his back pocket, but we never dreamed that he would do what he did and say, "You boys aren't going to stay at any hotel. You're all going to stay at my house! No, I don't want to hear about it. Plenty of rooms!" And there were.

So we flew down to Louisville's international airport, Bowman Field. The Colonel met us with his white limousine, resplendent in his white suit with the little black string tie that he felt compelled to wear. He took us to his house in Shelbeyville, which was a classic antebellum residence. You wouldn't call it a mansion by any means, but it was something to see. He treated us very well. The day after the Derby, when we wanted to sleep in a little bit, guess who came banging on the door at 6:30 in the morning. Who else but the Colonel. And he came bearing wheat germ pancakes, biscuits, and red eye gravy.

The Derby, which was celebrating its centennial, is held at Churchill Downs, right in the heart of Louisville, and there aren't many people who can get a parking space right next to the track except that guy in the white suit with the white limousine. After the Colonel took us to his private box, he asked, "Are you boys hungry? I'll be right back." We saw him walking across the infield—he made sure that *everyone* saw him—and the next thing we knew, old Harland came back to our box, carrying two big tubs of Kentucky Fried Chicken, one under each arm. We may be the only people in the world who have ever had Colonel Sanders bring us KFC in buckets at the Kentucky Derby and then get up and make breakfast for us the next morning.

There were more memorable trips. Unfortunately, though, management got very upset because three members of its five-member Eyewitness News Team were in an airplane together. We weren't too worried about it, but they were. I don't remember more than two of us flying together after that.

It didn't take us long to realize that Channel 3 was about as good as it got. But with its popularity came problems—including a great demand for talent, especially Jessica's and Mort's.

When Jessica Savitch started getting telephone calls almost every day for about three years from all three national networks, it became a very large problem because she was still under contract to Channel 3, and they weren't about to let her go. After a while, something like that can get into your head, especially when things aren't going well. So she often locked the door to her office, and sometimes I could hear her crying behind it. At one point, a guy was shadowing her every night after work, so the station arranged for a cop to wait in the office to escort her home.

Finally, Jesse took a job at NBC in New York. Now when you're a local anchor and you go to New York, and they put you on the network news on the weekends, this can be a problem. It wouldn't have been a problem for me or for Mort or for Bill or for Vince, because we had considerable experience in different TV markets. But you've got to know New York, because it's an entirely different animal. You've got to know the network, you've got to know the business, you've got to know the way people think. It's like a player coming up from triple-A ball and suddenly playing in the major leagues. It got very testy.

Jesse was treated very badly by her colleagues, who were jealous as hell of her for having her own weekend anchor show—people who had been at NBC for years and had been bypassed for this coveted position.

When you look at women who are in television right now—sports as well as news—they are mostly blonde, but she was the first blonde woman on the air. Because Jesse was so young, she had problems that I'm sure she would not have had if she had remained in Philadelphia a little longer. She didn't have any friends at NBC. It got to the point where she was facing some serious issues, and she started using drugs.

NBC has to take some share of the blame, because they should have handled Jesse's situation with more compassion. They should have let her gradually work her way into a national network situation. They should have provided a more positive atmosphere where viewers could see how good she really was, and that she wasn't just hired because she was a good-looking blonde who could read the news.

Mort Crim was more than an associate to Jesse, even after he left Channel 3 for the Midwest. She often went to him for advice. When things really got tough for her, she would go to Chicago or Detroit and spend time with him and his wife and kids. He acted in many ways like a father, because she was so very young and desperately needed guidance.

Life soon became very tragic for Jessica Savitch. She was divorced. She lost a husband to suicide, and on October 23, 1983, she herself died in an automobile accident that almost defies description. She was at a restaurant in picturesque New Hope, in Bucks County. It was very late, there weren't many lights, and she had parked her station wagon without noticing that she was next to a ditch that had about three feet of water in it. She took a wrong turn and the car flipped over. The windows could not be opened. She and her companion, and even her dog, perished in the darkness.

After Jesse left Eyewitness News to go to New York, Mort Crim decided it was time to move. He had several offers and elected to go with CBS in Chicago. Mort's story is a crazy one. When he went to Chicago, he replaced Bill Kurtis, who left that job to anchor the new morning show on CBS in New York. But it took only six months for the network honchos to realize that the new CBS show wasn't going to make it. Kurtis returned to Chicago and wanted his old job back, but there was no way that two people could sit in one seat, so Mort decided to look around. He landed at WDIV-TV, the NBC affiliate in Detroit, and stayed there for 22 years as anchor and senior editor. He had his own production company, his own airplane that he could fly around the nation, and there just wasn't a better newsman in the entire Motor City. Mort has since retired—well, almost retired. He still writes books and now lives in Jacksonville, Florida.

Meanwhile, I was getting restless. When the people at KABC-TV in Los Angeles expressed interest in me, I jumped at the opportunity to fly there for talks with them. But there was one minor problem with that scenario: my contract with Channel 3 didn't expire for another year or so. I did get to spend a few days in sunny California. KABC made me a nice offer, which was contingent on what Channel 3's owner, Westinghouse Broadcasting Company, would do about my contract. Boy, did I find out in a hurry. A few weeks later, I was getting off a plane in Buffalo and a guy came up to me, smiling and shaking my hand. I figured, hey, it's a fan! But not so fast. The guy was giving me a piece of paper with that handshake—serving me with a summons, a notification that I was being sued by the Group W people for breach of contract—not in Philadelphia, but in New York City. How about that, sports fans?

At first I kicked an idea around with my lawyer, Glenn Goldstein, who also served as my agent. Perhaps I could sue Westinghouse Broadcasting for the release of my contract, which would allow me to take the job on the West Coast. But Glenn reminded me that Group W could delay legal proceedings indefinitely, which meant that I wouldn't get any money and I wouldn't have a job. Also, there was no absolute guarantee that I would win the case. We finally decided that going through with a lawsuit wouldn't be the best idea for two reasons—they could keep me out of work for a while, and they could let the situation drag on to the extent that the legal fees would far surpass any kind of money I would make.

Meanwhile, something very strange happened which I still can't explain. I received a call one evening from a person high up in the chain of command at the ABC network. ABC, of course, operated Channel 6, our major competitor in Philadelphia and my former employer. The station's general manager, Larry Pollack, didn't want his folks associating with anyone from other stations in the city. Now here's a high-ranking network executive telling me that they had heard about my problem. If I was interested in the LA job, they would be more than willing to pick up the legal expenses in New York against Group W. How do you like that? I thought. I always knew that the ABC people wanted me out of town, but I never realized how badly they wanted me out of town. Well, it didn't happen—at least not then. But it did happen later after my contract legally expired.

Relatively speaking, only a few years of my half-century in television were spent at Channel 3. But I never found the situation elsewhere to be anything like it. While there was certainly camaraderie and even some friendships within all the teams on which I've worked, nothing ever came close to the feelings we Camelot folks had for each other.

Well, I guess there is one exception. It happened when station management hired a weekend sports announcer from Seattle, where rumor had it that he had been run out of town. His name was Rod Luck, and the first show he ever did in Philadelphia tells you everything you have to know about the crazy situation we were dealing with. It seems that the Saturday 6 p.m. news was running late, and the producer cued Luck to wrap up his segment immediately. After the show was over, Luck stormed into the newsroom, slammed the producer into the wall, and bellowed, "DON'T EVER DO THAT TO ME AGAIN!"

Rod Luck's thing was getting deeply involved in his stories. One day, I received a frantic call from the coach of the local indoor soccer team. He wanted me to do something because Luck was banging his players into the sideboards as he kicked the ball around with them. The coach felt that someone was going to get hurt. The same thing happened with players at football practice. Luck even jumped into the pool one time when he was covering a swimming workout. There were many other incidents, and I mentioned them to management to no avail. Not only that, but I started to get upset after I heard that he was carrying a loaded weapon. I never again walked to my car in the parking lot after the late news unless other members of the news team were with me.

Finally, "Lotsa Luck" did himself in. One night, he was found in a room at the old Sheraton Hotel on JFK Boulevard. He was in bad shape. It looked like someone had beaten him up, but he told authorities that he had actually done it to himself. Thankfully, the general manager of KYW-TV had had enough and he fired him.

But that wasn't the end of Rod. When I returned to Philadelphia from Chicago to work at Channel 10, guess who was back at Channel 3? But not for long. By then, Luck was heavily into physical sports like boxing and wrestling. The fights in Atlantic City were big-time, and he regularly featured the performers on his show. Station management finally said sayonara for the second time when it was learned that a limousine was ferrying him back and forth to Atlantic City, where he was being taken care of, as they say.

Rod Luck wasn't the only character on Eyewitness News. Channel 3 was a Westinghouse station and so was KDKA-TV in Pittsburgh. The western Pennsylvania station had a sports announcer named Bill Currie, who was a leading personality there and much in demand as a luncheon and dinner speaker. He was known as "The Mouth of the South," a nickname he had acquired years earlier when he did play-by-play for sports teams at the University of North Carolina. Westinghouse decided that it would be a great idea for ratings to move Bill to Channel 3. By then, I was long gone and working at Channel 10. I couldn't believe what I was watching when I tuned in to catch his Philadelphia TV debut amid much fanfare. Currie was dressed like Happy the Clown. He was wearing a plaid sport coat with a big flower in his lapel and a bad hairpiece.

When the "Dream Team" left KYW-TV in 1977, Eyewitness News was number one in ratings. Channel 3's ratings went right through the floor after that disastrous debut, and it took a few years for KYW to be competitive again. As you can imagine, Bill Currie didn't last long. Still, you wonder how management could hire characters like Rod Luck and Bill Currie. I think they did so because they treated sports like fun and games and were always looking for someone who was "different." But Philadelphia is a tough TV town. Viewers want their news and coverage straight and fair. Gimmicks just don't work.

But the depth of the special friendship I had with my real friends at Channel 3 is evidenced by its endurance. It's been a long time since I worked at Eyewitness News and yet, during all of those years, the team kept in touch by phone, by mail and, as often as possible, by personal visits. We vacationed together in places like Las Vegas, and we had a great reunion in Colorado near Bill Custer's home before he passed away in 2006. Unfortunately, Jesse Savitch is also no longer with us, but Vince, Mort, and I—along with our wives—continue to stay closely in touch. And as each year passes, telephone calls and visits become more valuable and more special.

My time at KYW was the pinnacle of my broadcasting career. It truly was my Camelot. All of us, except for Jessica, might have stayed on forever if the Westinghouse management hadn't decided it wanted to de-emphasize the talent—despite having the best news team in Philly and maybe in the country—to concentrate on electronic news gathering.

But that's a story for another chapter.

CHAPTER 8

Life with O.J. and the Buffalo Bills

I n 1971, right after I switched from Channel 17 to Channel 3, the Buffalo Bills decided to change radio stations for their football broadcasts and asked if I'd be interested in being their new play-by-play man. They were familiar with my work because I had previously done University of Buffalo games. But now I was working in Philadelphia, so this would involve commuting back and forth for 20 games, including the exhibition season.

It's sometimes funny how things work out. WEBR, the station that was now hiring me to call the pro football games, had originally brought me on board back in 1957, when they promised me that I would be their sports guy once the FCC approved their application for a new TV station. That never happened because of "public interest" gibberish.

Since then, however, WKBW obtained the TV station, and they also operated a powerful, clear-channel radio station. Not only that, they were the big rock station in Buffalo, and arguably the most popular outlet in western New York. Naturally, the Bills wanted WKBW to be their flagship station, because they reached a huge audience with those 50,000 watts. So what goes around does indeed come around.

This turn of events also meant that I got into work with Channel 7's sports director, Rick Azur, a good friend from my earlier days in Buffalo, who now had the TV job that never materialized for me. Rick and I formed a three-man radio team with Ed Rutkowski, a former Notre Dame and Bills backup quarterback, who was doing political work for

Jack Kemp, another former Bills quarterback who would soon run for vice president and make a bigger name for himself nationally.

You don't hear of many *three-man* radio teams, but that's what the Bills wanted. Rick did the color and coordinated everything that was going on with the broadcast. Eddie's job was to tell me what went on with the players in the field. My job was to tell him what was actually happening *on* the field. Right from day one, when we went up to Niagara University for preseason training camp—in those days they had six exhibition games—we connected beautifully and had very little trouble. We practiced diligently and got along famously. My early fear was that we would be jumping all over each other. But it got to the point where everybody knew where to come in, and how to come in, and it ran smoothly for seven long years. Later, I recommended Rick Azur for a job at Channel 3 Eyewitness News in Philadelphia, but they hired Rod Luck instead. (Enough said!)

My arrival coincided with some pivotal turning points in the fortunes of the Bills. O.J. Simpson, the Heisman Trophy–winning, All-America running back from USC, had already been on the scene for two years, but was being tragically miscast as a "decoy" by coach Johnny Rauch. Think about that for a moment. Here was the best running back in all of college football, the number-one draft choice in the land, being used as a *decoy*. But he never complained, even though, I'm sure, he would rather have been playing in a larger, more glamorous city like Los Angeles. The Bills had "earned" that number-one draft pick by finishing the 1968 season with a 1-13 record. (The Philadelphia Eagles and Pittsburgh Steelers each won two games that year, much to the consternation of their fans.)

By the 1972 season, Rauch was gone. He was replaced by Lou Saban, who had originally been head coach of the Bills in the early '60s. In 1964 and 1965, the Bills went 12-2 and 10-3-1 en route to consecutive AFL championships. Saban was the only man ever to accomplish that feat, and was extremely popular in upstate New York. He was Coach of the Year twice, but he left to take over the University of Miami and the Denver Broncos before returning to the Bills (by now in the NFL) from 1972 through 1976.

When Lou came in, his first move was to get the best offensive linemen he could find—people like future Hall of Famers Reggie McKenzie and Joe DeLamielleure, who played in 185 consecutive games as O.J.'s lead blockers. I mean, what a tremendous line! They were known as the "Electric Company," a moniker coined by Bud Thalman, the Bills' PR director at the time, "Because they turn on the Juice who supplies all the electricity." Needless to say, Saban was credited with developing O.J. to his full potential, and quarterback Joe Ferguson had a wonderful job—just give the ball to the best running back in the National Football League. What always amazed me was the fact that O.J. was so good and that every team knew exactly what he was going to do on every play: *O.J. left, O.J. right, and occasionally O.J. catching a pass.* Still, nobody could stop him.

Unfortunately, we were in the same division with the Pittsburgh Steelers at the time, the AFC East, and there were no wild cards in those days. Consequently, we got to play only one postseason game with O.J.—a 32-14 loss in a Divisional Playoff in Pittsburgh in 1974. That was a particularly disappointing season, because Saban got the team off to a sizzling start—winning seven of our first eight games—before things started turning the wrong way.

Two significant moments stand out in my mind from that '72 season when Lou Saban took over. O.J. surpassed the 1,000-yard milestone for the first time, rushing for a total of 1,251 yards. And the Bills finally played their last game in decrepit War Memorial Stadium, a forgettable 21-21 tie with the Detroit Lions that gave them an even more forgettable 4-9-1 record. The following year, Buffalo dedicated its sparkling new Rich Stadium in grand style by pulling out a pulsating 9-7 win over the New York Jets before the first of many sellouts—77,425 fans.

The highlight of my seven years with the Bills came in the last game of that '73 season in New York, on December 16, when O.J. became the first back in NFL history to rush for more than 2,000 yards. (Remember, they played only 14 games in those days.) Simpson had rushed for 219 yards the previous week against New England to move close to his historic milestone, but as kickoff time approached at Shea Stadium, the weather couldn't have been worse. It was absolutely terrible. The field was covered with so much swirling snow that the yard markers were impossible to read. Fortunately, the Bills had the game under control from an early point. They won, 34-14, and O.J. quickly took care of the existing NFL rushing record of 1,863 yards, set by Jim Brown in 1963. Then, picking up four and five yards at a clip with relative ease, O.J. finished the game with 200 yards, giving him the record of 2,003 for the season.

Afterwards, O.J. was surrounded in the locker room by a crush of media people and well-wishers. Standing on the fringe of the crowd, I looked out over the room and saw this guy waving to me. It was Mario Andretti, the auto racing legend. I walked over and said, "Mario, what can I do for you?"

"I have my two kids here," he replied. "Would it be possible for you to introduce me to O.J. and get his autograph?"

"Sure," I said, "no problem at all." It didn't hit me until a week later when I realized that the great Mario Andretti had asked me to do him a favor. We had never met before, but he had seen me on television. And he knew who I was.

There was another memorable vignette from that day. Because the outcome was never in doubt and the weather was atrocious, most of the New York Jets starters headed for the sidelines early. But not quarterback Joe Namath. Years later, we attended a banquet together and I asked him, "Joe, why in the world did you stay in that game against the Buffalo Bills?"

"Because I was the leader of the team," he replied. "I was the quarterback, and I owed it to the franchise."

Now fast forward to Friday, June 17, 1994, less than 23 years after that magical day in Shea Stadium. I'll never forget my first reaction when I saw O.J. being chased down the LA Freeway in that Bronco. I was editing a piece of film at Channel 10 at the time, and everybody started gathering around the TV monitors. I couldn't believe what I was seeing. O.J.? My friend from Buffalo? Later, I watched some of the trial, and I can't explain the change I saw. But after I found out that he had money and fake IDs and passports—and after listening to some of the evidence at the trial—if they'd ask me, I'd say, Yeah, I think he did it. It really hurt. It honestly hurt because here was a guy who had wasted his life.

The O.J. that I knew and the O.J. that other people know now are two entirely different people. I covered him for seven years, and he was undoubtedly the most cooperative athlete I've ever known. As far as I'm concerned, there wasn't a more cooperative superstar in any other sport or at any other time. He'd walk through a hotel lobby or an airport—in those days, most NFL teams didn't fly by charter—and would stop and talk to everybody and sign autographs. He was the most charming person you could ever meet. He never turned anyone down. I remember one time watching him hold up his teammates while he answered every last question from a high school kid, because that's the way he was. There were many times when the team bus would be ready to leave the ballpark after a game, but it had to wait because O.J. would still be giving interviews in the locker room. Maybe his pads would be off, but he'd be sitting there with his pants and shoes and the rest of his uniform still on. The other guys on the team didn't mind at all. They all loved him, especially the offensive linemen who received Rolex watches as gifts after his record-breaking season.

Because I didn't live in Buffalo, I would arrive on Saturday and leave on Sunday. On road trips, the team would fly back to Buffalo, and I'd catch a plane back to Philly. So I didn't have much personal contact with O.J., but he knew who I was and what I was doing. I really admired him. I remember telling someone years ago that the O.J. I knew was a magnificent person, a super guy, and a super athlete. He was warm and gregarious. He genuinely liked people. He was the same old O.J. in Buffalo as when he was in junior college in San Francisco. Even after he retired, he was a spokesman on hundreds of TV commercials. And was he ever popular with the ladies!

During training camp at Niagara University, the Buffalo players lived in cottages that ordinarily housed senior students during the academic year. So did Bud Thalman, who had been at Annapolis with Roger Staubach and Joe Bellino before taking over as PR director of the Bills. Next to his room was his office, which contained the only telephone in the building. I just happened to be sitting in there one afternoon when the phone rang. Bud picked it up and said, "Yeah, I'll get a hold of him." So the next thing I knew, O.J. came rushing into the office, had this quick conversation, and left. I said to Bud, "What was that all about?" He said, "That was Priscilla Presley!" There were no cell phones in those days. And no secrets.

In Buffalo, our radio booth was right next to the TV booth, so I always got a good look at who was hosting ABC's *Monday Night Football*. The first MNF game at Rich Stadium was classic Howard Cosell. He was there with Frank Gifford and Dandy Don Meredith. There were 80,000 fans at Rich Stadium, all fueled up on a cold winter's night, and none of them were Howard Cosell fans. Just before the player introductions, Howard did what only Howard could do. He walked out on the balcony in front of the press box and raised his hands upward like the Pope greeting the faithful at the Vatican. The response was, let's just say, underwhelming—the loudest booing and most expletive-laden response in the history of the National Football League. And Howard played it to the hilt.

Cosell knew what he was doing. He knew what it would take to become the real Howard Cosell—*Controversy!* Now it's a staple for all sports talk radio. He became the best-known man on sports TV, and when you add the ABC network and *Monday Night Football*, you could like him or hate him, but either way, you were going to watch the game. He became, in a sense, bigger than the events he hosted. It became obvious to me that night that Howard, at least in his own mind, had become bigger than the game.

The late Gene Kelly, who did play-by-play during the Philadelphia Phillies' run to the National League pennant in 1950, told me that Cosell was a classmate of his in grammar school in Brooklyn, and what viewers saw during his broadcasting career was what Kelly saw back then. As Gene put it, "Howard let everyone know that he was the best and the brightest."

Cosell eventually went to law school and became the legal advisor to Little League Baseball. Along with that came a part-time, unpaid radio show. Then after practicing law for eight years, Howard quit his $30,000-a-year job to take his first full-time radio gig with ABC in New York for $250 a week. Along the way, he hooked up with a young heavyweight fighter named Cassius Clay, who just loved to shoot off his mouth. But one thing about the future Muhammad Ali was that he could talk the talk and walk the walk. He could back up what he said. He was good for Howard, and Howard was good for him.

For all of his fame and fortune, however, the real Howard Cosell wasn't what you saw. He was a very insecure person with an ego that was completely out of control. I think that this story tells it better than anything else. When Howard retired, he wrote a book. Why I'll never know, but he trashed just about everyone he had ever known or worked with in the broadcasting business. And when he passed away, he died a man without friends—lonely, disliked, and eventually largely forgotten. But while he was working, Howard Cosell was the biggest name in the industry.

And speaking of celebrities in the world of boxing, Les Keiter was the sports director of Channel 6, who reported a lot of big-time boxing on radio and television. He told me that his first encounter with Howard Cosell was just before the first heavyweight championship bout between the unbeaten champ, Floyd Patterson, and Ingemar Johansson of Sweden, in 1958 at Yankee Stadium. Keiter was assigned to do the blow-by-blow action, and Cosell, the color and analysis for the ABC radio network. Before the opening bell, Keiter reached over and tried to shake Cosell's hand to wish him luck—a customary gesture for broadcasters before a major event. Howard turned his back and said, "Relax, kid, you'll get used to working in the big time."

CHAPTER 9

Covering the Broad Street Bullies, But Missing the Parade

I n 1965, shortly after I arrived at Channel 6 from Buffalo, the National Hockey League announced that it was doubling in size and would expand from six to 12 clubs. The decision on the final franchise came down to a pair of cities separated by 98 miles—Philadelphia and Baltimore—with the Maryland city having the edge because it already had a relatively new arena for home games. Philadelphia could offer only two antiquated hockey venues. The Arena, with a seating capacity of a little more than 5,200, was built in 1920. Convention Hall opened 11 years later, but could hold fewer than 12,000 fans. Neither facility would satisfy the NHL.

Into the picture came Jerry Wolman, the charismatic, 34-year-old owner of the Eagles, who was worth upwards of $36 million, with most of it earned in the construction of apartment complexes and commercial buildings. When he guaranteed to have a new facility completed within 16 months—and Philadelphia mayor James H.J. Tate offered a five-acre tract across the street from the soon-to-be-constructed Veterans Stadium—the deal was made. The city held possession of the land, Wolman agreed to a 50-year lease, and Philadelphia had a new NHL franchise. The City of Brotherly Love was now a major league city in every way.

Wolman's $12 million dream opened in 1967, and for the next few years we joined the usual capacity crowds of 17,000-plus fans watching the new Philadelphia Flyers, skating their way to becoming a contender.

They didn't make too much of an impression in those early days, but in 1971 a new coach was hired. His name was Fred Shero, the father of a fellow alumnus of St. Lawrence University, who was working his way through the New York Rangers' system. Gradually, the team we quickly learned to know and care about became the infamous "Broad Street Bullies," who battled, brawled, and scrapped their way into the National Hockey League record books less than seven years after becoming an expansion franchise. In addition to ruling the Canadian game, they brought a new meaning to the old joke: *I went to a fight and a hockey game broke out.* But how we loved them!

I was calling the 76ers' games at the time, and I remember watching from the press box as Fred put his young team through practice sessions at the Spectrum. He would also watch the 76ers practice from that same press box on occasion. Some of the similarities between professional hockey and NBA basketball are quite intriguing. Each sport has five men operating at the same time, but hockey adds a sixth player—the all-important goaltender.

I always thought that I knew a little bit about hockey. But I learned a tremendous amount just watching Shero running his drills in a highly unorthodox style. Undoubtedly, the most interesting and colorful coach that the city has seen before or since, Freddie spent considerable time in Russia learning his drill system. Years before, his parents had fled from that country to Canada to avoid religious persecution—the same reason that my parents came to the United States. You could say that "Freddie the Frog," as he was known, was also an intellectual. On the road, he also spent considerable time in the library reading and studying. He was an excellent motivator and used unique methods to communicate with his players. For example, instead of admonishing a player in front of teammates, he would leave a handwritten note in his locker. His messages, scrawled in chalk on a blackboard, were classics. Who can ever forget the immortal words that he posted before Game 6 of the Stanley Cup Finals in 1975 against Boston: "WIN TODAY AND WE WALK TOGETHER FOREVER!"

And so they did! Twice!

Start with captain Bobby Clarke, who was drafted as a 19-year-old diabetic, and goaltender supreme Bernie Parent and you have in my opinion the two all-time best athletes in the city of Philadelphia. Then add another great Hall of Famer, Bill Barber, to the ranks of Barry

Ashbee, Tom Bladon, Bill Clement, Bruce Cowick, Terry Crisp, Gary Dornhoefer, Andre "Moose" Dupont, Bill "The Cowboy" Flett, Bob "The Hound" Kelly, Orest Kindrachuk, Ross Lonsberry, Al MacAdam, Rick MacLeish, Simon Nolet, Don "Big Bird" Saleski, Dave "The Hammer" Schultz, Bob Taylor, Ed Van Impe, and the Watson brothers, Jimmy and Joe. And guess what? You have the most inspirational team in the city's history!

Each one of these players contributed immensely to the Flyers' success. But nothing was more meaningful than Rick MacLeish's winning goal in probably the biggest game in their history: their 1-0 win over the Boston Bruins that brought the Stanley Cup to Philadelphia for the first time. And no player epitomized the Broad Street Bullies more than Dave Schultz, that mild-mannered, soft-spoken gentleman who became an absolute terror, the baddest dude in the NHL, once he got on the ice. There were better players in the league, better players on the Flyers team, maybe even better players in the minor leagues, but as far as I'm concerned, the biggest name in hockey in the mid-'70s was The Hammer. I spent time with him in Utica, New York, when he was coaching a minor league team there. They traveled by bus, and the inside of that bus looked like an old-fashioned Pullman railroad car. The trips between games would be anywhere from 300 to 500 miles. He just loved coaching, and his players loved him. The Hammer? Nah. That must be another guy!

It's also worth mentioning that many of these kids who grew up in small Canadian towns like Flin Flon, Moose Jaw, Smithers, Thunder Bay, and Trois Rivieres, have elected to spend the rest of their lives and raise their families right here in the good old Delaware Valley. For a long time, many of them continued to skate together in the Philadelphia area in Flyers alumni exhibition games. Not only that, but four of them—Clement, Kelly, Kindrachuk, and Schultz—elected to be sworn in as U.S. citizens in 2010. Clement took his oath in a moving ceremony before a sellout crowd at the Wells Fargo Center prior to a game with the New York Rangers.

As a broadcaster, I find hockey a very difficult sport to describe. I have never played it. But I have always admired the sportscasters who not only can keep up with the flying puck and the explosive action on the ice, but also can pronounce the names of the ever-increasing number of NHL players who hail from the Czech Republic, Finland, Russia, Sweden, and other foreign countries, without missing a beat. I commend every one of them, especially the most remarkable hockey announcer of them all—Gene Hart, the longtime voice of the Flyers.

What an interesting guy he was! A former schoolteacher, Gene once ran the old Aquarama, Philadelphia's "Theatre of the Sea," that was located across the street from what later became Veterans Stadium. He was a dedicated patron of the opera, and could speak Russian well enough to pass as a native. He demonstrated his fluency in that language when the Russians played the Flyers back in the 1970s. Gene was a true intellectual with a voice as smooth as a skater in the Ice Capades. His delivery was more urbane than anyone I have ever heard in sports. I would say that Doc Emrick was probably the best hockey technician I've ever heard, but Gene was not a technician. He had a unique, gentlemanly way of narrating a rough game with a beautiful voice and great diction. It was like a college professor stepping in to do a night of hockey action down at the Spectrum. Gene knew the game and he knew the players, and he was as personable as anyone could be.

Who will ever forget Gene Hart's famous Game 6 call in 1974: "Ladies and gentlemen, the Flyers are going to win the Stanley Cup! The Flyers win the Stanley Cup! The Flyers have won the Stanley Cup!" Or his signature phrase: "Good night and good hockey!" Unfortunately, Gene passed away well before his time at the age of 68 in 1999, and I miss him to this day. I not only miss his broadcasts; I miss his friendship and his occasional phone calls when he would invite me over to his house for a chat. That's how I got to know him.

Gene Hart was blessed with an exceptional family. Old-timers will remember his wife, the former Sarah Detwiler, who thrilled countless vacationers at the South Jersey shore by riding the diving horse off Steel Pier. Gene's daughter, Lauren, a beautiful vocalist, was the anthemist *par excellence* for the Flyers, a role she undertook while he was still broadcasting the games. Believe me, there was nothing like it in the annals of professional sports when she teamed up with the legendary Kate Smith via computer-generated graphics to sing Irving Berlin's "God Bless America" before important NHL games. Lauren's rendition of the American and Canadian National Anthems was spellbinding enough, but her duet with Kate Smith was guaranteed to bring goose bumps, if not tears, to anyone who cares about our nation.

I am old enough to remember Kate Smith when she sang and sold war bonds on the radio during World War II. Flyers fans, of course, remember her as the team's good luck charm, who sang "God Bless America" as no one else could, either in person or on a recording. Her first live appearance at the Spectrum came on opening night of the Flyers' initial Stanley Cup season on October 11, 1973, and I'll never forget the thunderous applause that greeted her. In later years, Kate brought the team a lot of good fortune—everything but another Stanley Cup.

When the Flyers won their first Stanley Cup in 1974, there had been no history of championship parades in Philadelphia. Hell, when I was with the 76ers and they won the NBA title for 1966-67, we got off the plane and were greeted by a vast crowd of 75 relatives and friends. But that first Flyers victory parade, witnessed by a couple of million fans, set the stage for later Phillies and 76ers celebrations. Hopefully, we will see the Flyers and Eagles receiving similar accolades when they bring home those elusive Stanley Cup and Super Bowl championships.

The Flyers' first victory parade started out with plans just to drive down Broad Street toward Independence Mall, where Kate Smith and other celebrities would be gathered. But it was scheduled for a Monday, and I already had an obligation. The Maxwell Club had their annual golf tournament at North Hills Country Club, and I was booked to play with Temple's athletic director Ernie Casale and football coach Wayne Hardin. We played, had a lot of fun, and went into the clubhouse. The TV was turned on while we were eating. I looked up and saw a live telecast on Channel 3, where I was working. The more I looked, the more I wondered, *What's going on?* Well, I couldn't get a heck of a lot of information because it wasn't a true broadcast. All they did was put a camera on the top of the station, which was located right across the street at Independence Mall, and shot whatever they could see. The voice-over turned out to be our anchor, Mort Crim, who knew absolutely nothing about hockey, but could still describe what was going on better than anyone else.

I had no idea that this was going to happen. I remembered that it was mayhem in the Flyers' locker room after the game was over. I can't tell you exactly what I did in there, but I was busy doing my interviews, and I really didn't get to talk to anyone about what might be happening in the next few days concerning a celebration. At any rate, I completely missed the information. Whether they gave something out on a piece of paper or just made an impromptu announcement, I'll never know. Parades didn't really turn me on anyway, because we had never had any before for a sports team in this town.

I'm told that one incident did come out of the parade. There was a group of people who gathered in front of Channel 3 and wanted a piece of me because I had predicted Boston in six! Even though there were guys from the city papers who had picked the Bruins, I received, for one full year, the kind of letters that looked and smelled like the linings on the bottoms of parrot cages. They were addressed to "Dumb Al." I wasn't the only target, but I was the only one the fans could get to and attack. Maybe it was a good thing that I wasn't there to watch the parade.

That parade set the tone for celebrating victories by sports teams in Philadelphia. It used to be all about the Mummers, but by now it's come to include the Phillies and the Sixers, and hopefully someday the Eagles. They talk about winning a ring in sports. In Philadelphia, they talk about having a parade. And parades they do well.

Now for a confession. After the Stanley Cup championship game in Buffalo the following year, I finished my standup for the 11 o'clock news and went into the Flyers' locker room. It was late and there wasn't anyone there. The Stanley Cup was standing all by itself on a folding chair. Everyone had gone, but the cup was still sitting there. I couldn't believe it! I looked around and figured I'd check it out. Then I took a peak inside the cup, and there was still some champagne in the bottom. I couldn't skate worth a damn, though I could do figures like 1 and 11. But here was a chance for a little hockey immortality of my own. I looked around—there still wasn't anybody there—and I stole a sip out of the Stanley Cup. I don't know what kind of champagne it was, but to me it tasted like vintage Dom Perignon!

Bernie Parent, the great goaltender, had just helped the Flyers win the Stanley Cup, and he was invited to headline the Pro-Am at the IVB Golf Classic at Whitemarsh Valley Country Club. I was picked to play in his fivesome. Now the 10th hole where we teed off is right next to the road at Whitemarsh. Everything to the right was out of bounds, because it was adjacent to a highway. The entire course was to the left. I don't know how many people were there watching, but I know most of them were waiting for Bernie. That was just as well, because I had a tremendous case of stage fright.

To be invited to play with Bernie was entirely unexpected. It was different when I played rounds with Arnold Palmer and Nancy Lopez a few years later. I was fully prepared for all of the hoopla, especially since I would be paired with Nancy at my own club. But I wasn't ready for this. I had forgotten that "Only God saves more than Bernie Parent." It was a madhouse! Everyone wanted to see Bernie. By the way, Bernie wasn't much of a golfer, but no one expected him to be. He was dressed like he wasn't a golfer; he was wearing a style of pants that golfers don't wear. But he was having a great time, because everyone wanted to talk to him, shake his hand, and get an autograph or a picture with him. Bernie was having the time of his life. He didn't care what he was doing with the golf ball.

I, however, was very serious about golf at the time. I got up to the tee, I looked down there, and I couldn't take the club away. I froze. My mind froze, my body froze, and I just could not take that club away. Everything was absolutely surreal. It's like being on stage and forgetting your lines. It was a unique experience for me, to say the least. Finally, I dragged the club back and I hit the ball. And when I tell you that I hit the ball a mile, you can believe me. There was only one problem: Because of the way the 10th hole was positioned, I hit a screaming hook that covered four fairways. I immediately picked up the club and started to walk as fast as I could so I could avoid having anyone talk to me, stare at me, or give me a bad time. After I calmed down, I had a great time. I have no idea when that happened; it could have been at the turn. But finally, I got to the point where I could relax a little bit. Before that, I admit that I was somewhat intimidated.

Now let's skip ahead a few years. I will never forget the 1979-80 season when the Flyers set a North American professional record that still stands to this day by going unbeaten in 35 straight games (25 wins, 10 ties). Then they swept Wayne Gretzky's Edmonton Oilers in the opening round, and they quickly eliminated both Fred Shero's New York Rangers and the Minnesota North Stars in five games before losing the Stanley Cup Finals in six games to the New York Islanders.

I covered the final game up in Long Island, and it is probably the bitterest loss I ever witnessed. Bob Nystrom scored the deciding goal of New York's 5-4 win in overtime, but everyone remembers the Islanders being way offside on the goal that gave them a 2-1 lead in the second period. Linesman Leon Stickle never called the infraction, although he admitted afterward that he had blown the call. "I guess I blew it," Stickles was quoted as saying after watching the replay. "Or maybe I was too close to the play. I just missed it." Now in all fairness, we will never know if the Flyers would have won the cup that year, because they still would have faced a Game 7 back at the Spectrum.

Before the 1984-85 season, the Flyers brought in Mike Keenan to succeed Pat Quinn as coach. I was anxious to meet him, especially since we had the same alma mater. When we finally got together, I remember telling Mike, "If you play your cards right, you can own this town." I explained how the Flyers had set Philadelphia on fire back in 1974 and 1975 when they won those Stanley Cups, and I described how the fans wanted to canonize coach Fred Shero and players like Bobby Clarke and Bernie Parent. We agreed that Philly was not a hockey town before then—it was a football and baseball town—but when they won that first Cup, it was dynamite! And if it ever happened again with Mike as coach, the city couldn't do enough for him. If he won that thing, he could stay here forever! Later he did win it, but unfortunately with someone else— the New York Rangers. I didn't realize how tough a coach Mike Keenan was. It's a shame that he never won it all in Philadelphia.

Maybe Peter Laviolette will be the Flyers' good luck charm. He came close to performing a miracle in 2009-10 when he took over a team that was, to put in mildly, in disarray, guided them into the playoffs by winning a shootout on the very last day of the season, and then coaxed them all the way to the Stanley Cup Finals, where the Chicago Black Hawks finally prevailed.

$$(((\; \text{CHAPTER 10} \;)))$$

Other Towns Come Calling, But There's No Place Like Home

B y 1977, the old gang of mine at Channel 3 Eyewitness News was gradually breaking up. Vince Leonard and Bill Custer stayed together for a while, and then Vince said his goodbyes and took off for Camelback Mountain in Arizona. The next thing I knew, he was asked to anchor the afternoon news, then the early evening news, at KPNX-TV in Phoenix. He did so from 1980 to 1989, and eventually moved to his present home, Las Vegas.

Bill Custer also found another job near the big mountains that he loved dearly—the Rockies. He became the weatherman in Denver, and he also wrote a weekly column for a local newspaper. And he built himself a house in the foothills of the Rockies. Bill was finally home in the West, which surprised the heck out of me because I thought he'd never leave the East. He was very successful and eventually retired before passing away in 2006.

Eyewitness News lost another talented personality in 1977, although station management never realized what they were throwing away. Glenn Brenner, a local kid from Abraham Lincoln High School in Northeast Philadelphia, was handling weekend sports after spending seven years in the Phillies' minor league system. He had also been recruited for basketball out of high school by La Salle's Joe Heyer, but he decided to give baseball a shot. Brenner was a funny guy, but not everyone at the station appreciated his sense of humor. One day on the air he said, "The Eagles played today like a stale glass of Schmidt's Beer." The following Monday morning the Schmidt's people came knocking on the door of Channel 3 and complained. I have no way of backing this up, but I understand that the wife of general manager Alan J. Bell, who didn't like Brenner to begin with, was instrumental in getting him taken off the air. Glenn hung around for a while and then hooked up with WUSA-TV (Channel 9) in Washington, where his popularity then just exploded. He was arguably the most loved sportscaster in the history of our nation's capital when he died of a brain tumor on January 15, 1992. He was only 44.

After Mort Crim went to Chicago with CBS, I reached another *Fork in the Road* and decided it was time for me to move on. I accepted an offer in the same city with WMAQ-TV, a station owned and operated by NBC.

Before leaving for the Windy City, my going-away party was a personal classic. It was held at Cavanaugh's on Market Street, across the street from the old Philadelphia *Bulletin* building. Tons of people showed up. Billy Cunningham, Penn's Chuck Daly, and all of the other Big 5 coaches, Bob Vetrone, many writers and sportscasters (including my co-author), and other college officials were there. It wasn't anything formal. They gave me a few gifts, some of which I will never show to anybody. But basically it was very nice. Billy and Chuck spent most of the time during the party huddled together and talking privately. Only later did I learn why. Cunningham, who was coaching the 76ers, asked Daly to come along and join him as his assistant. This led eventually to a very successful career in the NBA for Chuck. He coached the Detroit Pistons to the NBA World Championship and became one of the most respected basketball minds in the country. For my money, he was also the best TV basketball analyst, whenever he was called on to provide color. I'm sure that Billy had the idea of bringing Chuck into the NBA in the back of his mind for a long time, but I like to think that he suddenly just came up with the idea at my shindig and made the offer spontaneously. Unfortunately, Chuck Daly passed away recently, and I lost another friend much too soon.

Then it was time to settle down in my new surroundings, located on the top floor of the Merchandise Mart. The original home of NBC in Chicago when they became a radio station, WMAQ was filled with all kinds of history. It was an enormous operation—about 25 times larger per square foot than Channel 6—because it housed a thriving film setup in addition to its radio and television studios. I was really in the big-time now, and I thought I had it made! I had a nice car, and I lived in the Lake

Point Tower, a beautiful glass complex just off the Navy Pier. From my apartment about 35 floors up, I had a tremendous view of Lake Michigan and downtown Chicago.

But moving to Chicago, as it turned out, was the biggest mistake I ever made in my life. I was unhappy from day one. In all fairness, it wasn't because of Chicago, a wonderful city that was very good to me and welcomed me with open arms. The station paid me well as its sports director. It was a heck of a job, but there was a problem. There were mornings when I'd wake up in a cold sweat, remembering the wonderful times at Channel 3. I had pulled the plug and here I was—very unhappy because my roots were too deep in Philadelphia—but I found it difficult to make friends in the Windy City.

Moreover, I still had a commitment to NFL Films, from when I did the weekly show with Charlie Bednarik for HBO's *Inside the NFL*. I had been doing occasional work for NFL Films for a while—voice-overs, previews of upcoming games, or reviews of the week—but right before I left Channel 3, HBO came to town. They had an idea for a new weekly show and, lo and behold, who did they call on to host it? Chuck and me! I remember that Marty Glickman sat in on our first planning meeting. He was doing some basketball work for HBO. I reminded Marty that I watched him as a little kid when he was a star halfback at Syracuse.

HBO didn't do the show from the sumptuous NFL complex that they have today in Mt. Laurel, New Jersey, but from their primitive studio in a basement on 13th Street in downtown Philadelphia. We used an old-fashioned film camera which made so much noise that they had to place a pad over it. There was no air conditioning and the hot lights were brutal, but it was fun. It was a wonderful experience, but compared to today, it was like pioneer times as far as television was concerned. We had a scoreboard crudely made of wood, and we slid the names of the teams into the openings in the wood. The basic premise of the show had us predicting the winners of the upcoming NFL games—"Who do you like this week, Charlie?" Obviously, I deferred to him a lot because he knew much more about football than I did, but I made sure that I asked him the right questions.

I enjoyed Bednarik very much. We had worked together at a couple of Pottstown Firebirds football games when I was at Channel 17. Charlie also was a weekend sports announcer at Channel 6 with Stan Hochman when I first arrived in Philadelphia. Charlie is a remarkable person, but he's also the kind of guy that I wouldn't want to cross. When Charlie gets upset, he really gets upset. He resents the money being paid to professional athletes today, and he is quite outspoken about it. Although he's had some issues with the club over the years, Charlie still does work for the Eagles. There's also a simpatico relationship there because the fans, most of whom have never seen him play, love him immensely. We saw a vivid example of that recently when the Eagles honored the 1960 NFL champions at Lincoln Financial Field on the 50th anniversary of their title. Charlie got the biggest ovation.

Midway through the NFL season, I had left Channel 3 to go to Chicago—which meant that I had to fly into Philadelphia every Monday morning, then fly back to Chicago to do my late night sports show. In the old days of flying, as everyone will remember, if there was bad weather in Chicago, the plane had to circle over someplace in the Midwest for an hour or so before it could land. These days, they don't take off unless they know they can land. There were a number of evenings when it was snowing, and I was sitting alone in that airplane, wondering what in the hell I was doing there. When I finally arrived at O'Hare, the station would arrange to have me picked up and taken to the studio, where I could try with whatever time I had to put the 5:30 show together. Sometimes we almost didn't make it. Because of my commuting difficulties, I knew that my work with HBO would be over by the end of that season. It would have ended anyway because they moved the show to New York, where it is still running after more than 30 years (now on *Showtime*) as the longest-continuing sports show on cable TV.

There was another reason for my wanting out of Chicago—the most important reason: I terribly missed my children, who were living by themselves back in Philadelphia. I flew back every weekend, not only to do the show, but to see my kids, check things out, and make sure that everything was okay. I had been married a couple of years after I got out of the Air Force, and we had three girls. My oldest was Gwenn, then Karen, and finally Helene. My first wife and I separated and got divorced after we settled in Philadelphia. The kids stayed with me and were in their late teens at the time. Every single week, I'd be reminded that my kids were back in Philadelphia, and I just couldn't do it anymore. Not only that, Chicagoans wanted everyone to root for the home teams, and I couldn't do that either. But knowing that my kids were living by themselves was the deal breaker.

As far as my job was concerned, I did some Big 10 basketball play-by-play and got a chance to see a spectacular freshman at Michigan State. His name was Earvin Johnson. His nickname was Magic. I wonder what ever happened to him. When I saw him, even as a six-foot-eight freshman playing in the backcourt, I knew that he was going to be something special. But for the most part, I was married to news, weather, and sports back at the studio, which was entirely unsatisfactory. I wasn't involved with what I loved—play-by-play—and I wasn't getting any closer to my dream job: broadcasting major league baseball.

Late in 1977, I had only been in Chicago for a short time and the phone rang in my apartment one night. It was Phil Jasner of the *Philadelphia Daily News,* saying, "Did you know that Charlie Swift just took his life?" I was shocked. Charlie and I had worked together on the 76ers and Big 5 basketball. Phil suggested that maybe I'd be interested in calling Jim Murray, the general manager of the Philadelphia Eagles, because Charlie had also done Birds analysis.

I had just finished my seventh season doing Buffalo Bills games, but in the back of my mind I thought, *Maybe I will give Jim Murray a call. He's going to need another announcer.* Jim and I talked for a while and he said, "You know, we could possibly work something out, but this would be for radio only. That's all we've got. I can't promise you anything else." I thought it over, but I quickly figured that just doing Eagles radio would not be a good gamble for me. There was no television involved, so I passed it by. I'd have to start up all over again in Philadelphia. That's when they brought in Merrill Reese, and Merrill has been doing the play-by-play regularly since 1978.

One night, while I was covering a Bulls game at the Chicago Stadium, Eddie Rush, the veteran NBA referee, came over to the press table before tap-off and said, "Al, how you doing? We miss you back in Philly." It punched me right in the stomach, and there were tears in my eyes when I drove home that night. A thought overtook me: *Maybe I need to do something about this.* A few days later, I talked to the WMAQ station manager, who had worked previously at WCAU in Philadelphia, and let him know exactly how I felt. I didn't hold anything back. I told him that I liked Chicago, but I was 50 years old and I wanted to go back to Philadelphia because of my family. He said, "Maybe we can arrange something to get you into New York where you could maybe split the week, commute back and forth, and still live part time in Philadelphia." That was a heck of an offer. They were as nice as they could be. But I said, "No, I've got to go back to Philadelphia." My mind was made up.

Then I decided to make a few phone calls. I checked in with some friends at Channel 10 in Philadelphia. I found out that they had just let go of Vince Papale, the former fan favorite of the Philadelphia Eagles, and were about to hire another person to work with Jim Kelly in their sports department. Eventually, I talked to Dan Gold, who was the new general manager at Channel 10, and to Eric Ober, the station's news director, who would eventually become president of CBS News. I told them that I heard that the station might have a job opening and, if so, I'd be interested.

While I was thinking about Channel 10, Mort Crim called me and said that WDIV-TV, his NBC station in Detroit which was owned by the *Washington Post/Newsweek* Group, wanted to talk to me. It really wasn't the right thing for me to do because my heart was set on returning to Philadelphia, but I thought that at least I should give it a shot.

Soon I was sitting in a room at an upscale hotel in downtown Detroit's Renaissance Center, talking to the guy who ran the *Post/Newsweek* Group's broadcast operation. He explained that they knew all the reasons why I wanted to go back to Philadelphia, but they thought that I would be interested in their generous offer. "I think we can work something out," he said. Then he laid out the details: "As the sports director, you'll have your own producer and two shows Monday through Friday. You will also be involved with University of Michigan football and basketball." And best of all, he told me that I would be the extra man on weekends with the Detroit Tigers' home games. I was finally getting a chance to fulfill my lifelong dream of being a major league baseball announcer. Then he said, "We'll sign you to a contract which obligates you for only one year, but will obligate us for the entire life of the contract," which was the first three years. Then to top it off, he handed me a piece of paper—a blank check—and said, "Just put the number down that you think the job is worth, and that's what you'll get." I was numb. I didn't know what to do, but I said that I couldn't make the decision right away. "That's okay," he replied. "Let's get in touch with each other in a couple of days."

So I went home, and the first thing I did was talk to Beverly, who was then my fiancée. She had been married and divorced and was working as a nurse after earning her bachelor's degree at night from Villanova

University. I was already long divorced when we started dating, and we eventually married in 1980. We had a child, Jordana, who was born in 1982. We call her "Jordy." I wanted her to go to the Communications School of Syracuse University, but she ended up going to Colgate. I thought I'd maybe get one of my kids into the business. Oh well, you can't win them all!

Beverly came out to Detroit with me a short time after my interview, and they gave us the grand tour. Then she said to me, "Al, why are you leaving Chicago?" I thought about it for a second and replied, "Well, you know, you're right!" I immediately called the *Post-Newsweek* people, thanked them for the offer, and said, "I'm going back to Philly." I didn't have the job at 'CAU yet, but I thought that I had a commitment at the time—at least in my mind. In the meantime, I had formally cut my ties with WMAQ. My oldest daughter, Gwenn, came out to Chicago and helped me pack up the car. Then we drove straight through back to Philadelphia. At last I was home—about to be challenged by another *Fork in the Road!*

CHAPTER 11

Big Al Pulls Off the Only Local TV Hat Trick (Plus One)

S hortly after I returned to Philadelphia, I stopped by a restaurant on City Avenue near Channel 10 and made a deal with Dan Gold and Eric Ober. Jim Kelly and I would each do a weeknight show, split the weekends, and handle the Eagles' preseason games. Jim was very involved with CBS—particularly with golf—and eventually ended up doing the Senior Golf Tour for the network. Jim was a good guy, but he had his eye on CBS, and I had my eye on Philadelphia.

Jim Kelly was very competitive. I can't say that we were the best of friends, but he knew how to do his job. We split the Eagles games in a highly unusual manner. I would do the first half, and he would take over the play-by-play for the final two quarters. I can't remember seeing games handled that way before or since. But it worked.

This was going to be it for me. It was 1978, I had just turned 50, and I was content to stay at WCAU-TV and live in the Philadelphia area forever. Ralph Penza and Joan Dinnerstein were doing the anchoring at the time, and CBS was *the* television network to work for in many ways. The quality was still there, and things were running smoothly. The station was very successful, and it had a great reputation. A lot of guys—including Frank Chirkinian, "the father of televised golf," who produced the U.S. Masters telecasts for almost 50 years; Tony Verna, one of the best directors in the business, who invented instant replay; Tommy Brookshier, and Jack Whitaker—had gone to the CBS network in New York when Jack Schneider, the station manager at 'CAU, became president of CBS and brought along some of his boys.

The only thing that didn't sound real good to me was when station management said: "By the way, we can only pay you about half of what you were making in Chicago." But for some reason, the financial terms no longer seemed that important, and I said, 'You've got a deal." That deal lasted for 20 years!

I did the sports at 6:00 and 11:00. It was a studio job—not the baseball job I always wanted, but that wasn't going to happen. So I took the offer, made a decent living, and all went well for a very long time. I got a chance to cover everything that happened in this town, and it was great fun because lots of stuff happened—both good and bad, as it usually does in Philadelphia sports.

In June 1981, I helped my friend Herb Lotman get the first McDonald's LPGA Classic off the ground at our country club, White Manor, in Malvern. Lotman owned Keystone Foods, which provided hamburgers and chicken for the McDonald's chain. I was involved in making the initial presentation when the club expressed interest in hosting the tournament on an annual basis. I conducted the drawing for the traditional Pro-Am on the Monday of tournament week. I didn't arrange it that way, but as luck would have it, I ended up in a foursome playing with Nancy Lopez, a future Hall of Famer. It was a really warm day, but about an hour before tee time, I decided to hit balls, because if I was going to be on the first tee, there were going to be a lot of people around—not to see me, but to see Nancy. Still, I didn't want to look bad. (Where have we heard *that* before?)

Unfortunately, I forgot to wear a hat. After slamming balls all over the place for about 45 minutes, I started to perspire. I drank loads of water, but it didn't do me any good. I got to the point where I couldn't stop perspiring, and I wasn't feeling that great. I started off hitting the ball pretty well, but when we got to the 14th tee, I sat down when everybody else hit, but I couldn't get up. The officials immediately called for help, took me away in a golf cart, and packed me in ice. The physician on duty, Elliott Goodman, happened to be my golf partner during the week. He told me that I had heat stroke, because I was drinking water at every hole, and I couldn't stop perspiring. I didn't realize that I was really close to having a serious problem. They got me home safely, and they told me that Nancy had called the club to find out how I was doing. The next day, she called the club again to see if I was okay. I thought to myself, *That's such a nice thing to do, and by a celebrity no less.* I mean she was really concerned! I stayed home recuperating for a couple of days after that. But the fact that she called twice to make sure that I was okay is something I'll never forget. You meet some athletes who are a pain in the butt, but you also meet some who are the genuine article, and in her profession, women's golf, Nancy is just like Jack Nicklaus and Arnold Palmer— a class act through and through!

I first met Billy Werndl in 1966 when we were both working at Channel 6. He had just graduated from high school and was assigned to the mailroom, but I could tell right away that this guy knew sports like no one else. One day, I came up to him and said, "Kid, someday we will be working together again." We've laughed about that many times over the years, because we did end up working together for 15 years at Channel 10. I called him "Billy Ball" because he was so feisty—much like Billy Martin, the great manager of the New York Yankees. I gave him that name with the utmost respect because he was the best producer I've ever had.

Billy had more contacts than almost anybody in the city. He went to every practice and got to know every athlete, coach, and official of every professional and college team on a first-name basis. I mean, he was an encyclopedia. Take the NFL player draft, for example. No one in the nation analyzed it better. Everybody in sports will tell you that he was extremely enthusiastic about his job. Billy thought that every story was important. So much so that I often found myself bailing him out of trouble with the bosses after he would campaign very aggressively for a film crew, because we didn't have one assigned to us. I don't know how many times I'd get phone calls from Billy saying, "Look, they promised me a crew and I'm here with the Flyers [or the Eagles or the Phillies] waiting to do an interview." That was a constant battle for 15 years. I must admit there were days when I almost lost it, because news and weather always had priority—with sports hanging by its fingertips eight rungs down the ladder.

No matter what sport it was, Billy Werndl was priceless. At Eagles home games, for example, I had to stay outside the locker room after the final gun because we were telecasting live. Billy would go into the locker room and bring players out for me to interview. That was not an easy thing to do—especially after losses—but he always came through. I felt a tremendous loss when Werndl took off for San Diego, where he hosted a popular "Philly Billy" radio sports talk show for more than a dozen years.

One day in the fall of 1981, we got a tip that the quarterback on Graterford Prison's football team could throw a football 70 yards in the air. So we took a film crew out to the prison in Skippack Township, Montgomery County, drove through the gates, and got patted down—the whole nine yards. As we walked through the hallway, the prisoners were all smoking and hanging out, and many of them shouted, "Hello, Big Al!" So I was feeling pretty good: *Hey, they recognize me. My ratings must be pretty good in the Big House!*

We went out onto the field and saw the team practicing, just like a bunch of high school or college kids—except these players were not your normal schoolboys and there wasn't a lot of grass. For one thing, they played exclusively a "home" schedule. But it looked like decent, semi-pro football. We walked around and talked to the players, and then I asked the coach, "By the way, before we get started, do you happen to know what your quarterback is in for?' He glared at me and replied, "No, and I don't want to know!" *Okaayy.*

We watched this quarterback tossing the ball for a while and finally got to the point where I said, "Let's go for it. Let's find out how far he can throw the ball." So he flung the ball a couple of times but fell way short of 70 yards. So we figured: Well, there's no sense taking a seven-step drop; just start at the back of the end zone and run up and when you hit the goal line, let it fly! He'll get a nice head start and wherever it lands, it lands. I don't know how many yards short he threw the next few times, but I think midfield was as far as he could reach. So 70 yards became 50 yards, and our story didn't have quite the bite that we thought it had. But then we realized that our piece certainly had something else. It had the unique feel of what's going on inside of a real prison with real prisoners. You could see it on the viewfinder of the camera, and you could feel it as they shouted, *Big Al!* Then they proceeded to tell us, loudly, what's bad about Graterford in no uncertain terms, many of them not suitable for family viewers. I got to the point where I thought to myself, *I better get out of here!*

As it turned out, we got a very good story because after we looked at all the video, we got a lot of interesting audio that we didn't know we were getting. Not only that, but Billy told me that a guy came up to him and said that there was going to be a problem at the prison in a couple of weeks. Shortly afterward, that's exactly what happened—they had a prison uprising. It began on Wednesday, October 28, 1981, when an escape attempt went awry and a group of prisoners took 38 hostages, including three guards and three civilian employees. Fortunately, the siege ended peacefully five days later on Monday, November 2.

In 1986, Arnold Palmer flew into Chester Valley Golf Club to promote the upcoming Senior PGA Tournament, the United Hospitals Championship. How it happened I'm not too sure—I think there was a drawing of some kind—but guess who got a chance to play with one of the greatest golfers in history. I was stunned. Arnold arrived by helicopter after flying his private plane into Philadelphia International Airport. We meet on the first tee, and just as we got ready to hit, it started to rain. And I was thinking to myself, *Don't rain! Please don't rain! I am playing golf with Arnold Palmer.* At the time, I was close to a 14 handicap, because I was playing a lot of golf and I didn't want to embarrass myself.

As soon as we got on the first tee, Arnold treated me like an old friend: "Hi, how are you? What are you doing?" And all that kind of stuff. During the entire time we were playing, he was talking to me and I was asking him all kinds of questions. Meanwhile, I was playing pretty well, but the rain got so bad that it was decided that nine holes would be enough. A friend of mine said that I had a 44 on the front side. Playing with Arnold Palmer, I thought I could have had a 144. All I remember was that we talked the whole time. It was just like being with a friend and hitting the ball for nine holes while talking about anything—not just golf. Obviously, Arnold did talk about golf, because I asked him lots of questions. And along the way, he would offer little tips about the game. And I kept saying to myself, *I'm playing golf with Arnold Palmer!*

But we had to quit after nine holes. We went inside the dining hall and there was Arnold, surrounded by his entourage, the people connected with him. It couldn't have been 15 minutes later when I looked around and the entourage had grown into a vast crowd. Word got around that Arnie was there, sitting down and shooting the bull with everybody. People in the back would ask him a question, and he would answer. He even told us things that weren't even asked of him. I think the Q&A lasted damn near two hours. I was only able to ask him about one thing: "Arnie, I understand that you have 2,000 putters in Latrobe." And he replied, "More!"

Then Arnie told a story on himself. He said that he earned $5,000 for the first tournament he ever won in 1955. It was at the beginning of his career when there wasn't a great deal of money. "The trouble is," he explained, "I went downstairs after dinner and I came back to the room and told Winnie that I had lost the $5,000 gambling. And she said,

'Arnie, that's the first and last time that will happen if you want me to stay and be your wife.'" And I wondered, *Is he telling everybody that story?* But that's the way he was—as wide-open as can be. It wasn't quite the Jack Nicklaus era yet—the glory days of golf were still a few years away—but Arnie was the friendliest, most accessible famous person that I ever ran into in my life. He was exactly what he was said to be. There was nothing phony about Arnold Palmer. It was a day I'll never forget, and we took a picture together on the first tee. If you came to my home and looked around for pictures, that would be the one that you would see right away—*Arnold Palmer and Al Meltzer.*

In 1987, I covered the national collegiate football championship game when number-two Penn State beat the top-ranked University of Miami, 14-10, in the Fiesta Bowl in Phoenix. That's the year when coach Jimmy Johnson's Hurricanes pranced around in fatigues and went out of their way to let everyone know that they were bad guys. Michael Irvin was their top wide receiver and Jerome Brown, who later died tragically as a member of the Philadelphia Eagles, was their best defender. Miami's players also said during the week that nobody liked their team and that everyone liked Penn State coach Joe Paterno. A number of them remarked to me more than once, when I attempted to do an interview, that they knew I was really there to cover my friend, Joe Pa.

As it turned out, I was standing next to Paterno when the game ended. I had worked my way down to the field with my cameraman. I knew Joe pretty well because he used to come into Philadelphia regularly to play Temple, and we would reminisce about the old Penn State–Syracuse rivalries when he was just a young guy. This upset over Miami was perhaps the biggest win in the school's history, so I grabbed my microphone and I talked to Joe while running beside him across the field. All the time, I was thinking to myself: *Hey, I've got a big story here; I've got Joe Paterno!*

Afterward, when we got back to the remote truck, we realized that there was something we didn't have. We didn't have the interview. My cameraman—and I'm not going to mention his last name—was a Penn State alum who forgot to turn the camera on. But Tommy, I still love you.

On August 6, 1989, my producer, Jeff Asch, and I covered the American Bowl in London as the Eagles beat the Cleveland Browns, 17-13. No one could have imagined 10 years earlier that there would be an NFL game in London. But sure enough, here we were in ancient Wembley

Stadium. Actually, we came dangerously close to not covering the game, because our equipment got impounded by international authorities beforehand. It seems that we didn't have the correct paperwork, and our cameras, microphones, and sound equipment were sitting back in the United States. Fortunately, everything arrived just before kickoff, but we had some uneasy moments.

Meanwhile, while the Browns and Eagles were practicing together and banging each other around practically every day at Crystal City, we were having a wonderful time touring London with our own car and driver. It was like a vacation. We were joined by an old friend, Ernie Accorsi, who worked in Philadelphia early in his career. He was then Cleveland's general manager and would later become the successful GM of the New York Giants.

Before the game, the Eagles and Browns bounced each other around so much that tempers flared on more than one occasion. There was the customary pushing and shoving—which you would expect from football players, especially the ones who were attempting to make the teams—but Browns coach Bud Carson, like many of his NFL counterparts, didn't appreciate the extracurricular activities. It wasn't his intention to get rough at any time in the preseason, because his players could get hurt. "I think I've had enough of this crap," he said, joining a whole list of coaches who have used those words when talking about Buddy Ryan.

Wembley Stadium is the Yankee Stadium of Great Britain. I was extremely interested to see how 85,000 fans were going to react, because the British are not accustomed to seeing our kind of football, even though they call their version of the sport by that name. And they reacted just like fans at a British football game. They enjoyed it immensely. But I think they were cheering at the wrong moments most of the time.

By the way, I have to say that Jeff Asch was as good a producer as you will find anywhere. And the reason is that Jeff knew television. He was a great idea man who gave me many fascinating suggestions about features and things of that nature. He knew what was good on TV, and what wasn't. Most producers do not get that involved. He knew how to put it together, and he knew how to maintain contacts in the sports world. And besides being a tremendous help, Jeff was a helluva nice guy who became very close to a number of prominent coaches and athletes.

One of them was Sixers star Charles Barkley. On Friday nights, Charles would frequently hang out with Jeff and some of the other local sports announcers at TGI Friday's on City Avenue. So Jeff got to know him very well. On more than one occasion when we were tipped off that Barkley might be in some kind of trouble, Asch would stake out his condominium, which was located around the corner from the station, and get him on camera when he came out the door. We also sent Jeff to cover the trial in Milwaukee after Barkley was accused of throwing a man through a plate glass window. The jury found him not guilty, and we had an exclusive.

There were other unforgettable moments during my time at Channel 10. On March 28, 1992, in the East Regional Finals of the NCAA Tournament at the Spectrum, I had a perfect view of what is widely considered the greatest shot in college basketball history. With 2.1 seconds left in overtime and Kentucky leading by a point, Christian Laettner, of Duke, took a full-court pass from Grant Hill, dribbled once, turned, and hit a jump shot at the buzzer to give the Blue Devils a 104-103 win.

I was in the press box and, of course, it was full. At the end of regulation, I decided to look for a seat closer to the action. I saw an empty one right in the front row, so I worked my way down to the floor, sat down, and looked over to see who I was sitting next to. It was Senator Ted Kennedy with his new wife, Vicki. Now what in the world was Teddy Kennedy doing at a Duke–Kentucky basketball game? The answer is that the University of Massachusetts had been eliminated by Kentucky, 87-77, in the previous Sweet 16 game, and he, of course, was one of the distinguished senators from that state. Did we talk? No!

When I was a 10- or 11-year-old kid just beginning to listen to sports on the radio, I first learned about the Rose Bowl, which was the biggest football game of the year. There weren't 32 Bowl Games then, just one game when the two best teams in the nation—usually from the Pacific Coast and the Big 10—played in the Rose Bowl on New Year's Day. There would be three feet of snow outside my window at home, and the announcer would be talking about people in shirtsleeves, the sunny day, and the beautiful green grass. This was long before TV, and I marveled how his description made Southern California and the Rose Bowl with its 100,000 fans sound so much more glamorous than Syracuse, New York and Archbold Stadium's crowd of 35,000. I thought to myself: *Gosh, that must be wonderful!*

I finally got the chance to travel to Pasadena more than 50 years later when undefeated Penn State was invited to play in the 1995 Rose Bowl against PAC-10 Conference Champion Oregon after going unbeaten in the regular season, their second as a member of the Big 10. That was the year that the Nittany Lions got shafted out of the national title when the Associated Press, the coaches, and others declared Nebraska, another unbeaten team, the national champs.

The teams did not practice at the Rose Bowl. The Penn State team was quartered in Costa Mesa, a beautiful community in Orange County, and practiced nearby at the University of California–Irvine. The usual media crowd would come to interview Joe Paterno. He'd give them the standard answers and that was it except for one day when I was starting to walk off the field and Joe hollered across the way, "Al, come on over!" I realized that he was singling me out from all of the other media folks, and I was quite thrilled. We sat by ourselves for about half an hour, and do you know what he wanted to talk about? *How are things going with football in Philadelphia?* He was very interested in hearing how the pros were doing, how the local coaches were doing, and how the schools were doing. I didn't have a camera or a tape recorder with me. But it was quite an experience, because I was talking to the greatest football coach in history. As old as I was, I was truly impressed.

Later when I was with Comcast SportsNet, I went up to Happy Valley to do a special documentary on Paterno with Mark Jordan, my cameraman. Joe took us through the whole nine yards of Penn State football history and a million other interesting things that had happened to him. My question for him was, "Joe, when are you going to retire?" He was 70 years old at the time. I was 68, and I was retiring in two years. And Joe said, "Probably when I'm 75." I know that he's past 84, and he's the winningest coach in college football history with more than 400 victories. May he live forever.

After the Lions defeated Oregon rather handily, 38-20, I was in the press box in the Rose Bowl stadium, trying to see out the windows overlooking the field. The only problem was that they were no larger than most kitchen windows. I was sitting in a row of chairs about three rows back, and I couldn't see the field. In fact, I couldn't see anything. I thought to myself: *This is the Rose Bowl?* I'm used to press boxes that cover the entire half of the stadium. The game hadn't started yet, so I walked out and took the elevator down to the field. As I walked through the same tunnel that the players had just used, I heard this roar and for the first time in my life I saw the Rose Bowl and some 100,000 people in shirtsleeves and the beautiful green grass. What an experience! And I thought at that moment about the times when I was a little kid wondering what it must be like. You never know where you're going to end up in life, but as a kid you remember these things.

Looking back at my stay at Channel 10, I must agree with Charles Dickens: *"It was the best of times; it was the worst of times."* In my last years there, I ended up being on a show that started at 4 o'clock in the afternoon and went off the air at 6:30, when the local news gave way to the national network news. During that two-and-a-half-hour period, I only had maybe three or four minutes of airtime. The station honchos just didn't like sports. They thought weather was the only thing people cared about, even though our station had made a lasting impact in the world of sports. Under my direction, I had persuaded the powers at WCAU-TV to be the first local station to actively pursue avenues for televising such live local events as the Pennsylvania Derby horse racing classic from Keystone Park, scholastic football and basketball championship games, and the much-anticipated La Salle–Louisville basketball game in 1983-84. But station management changed frequently, and sports still didn't matter to the suits in the front office.

The worst day came when Drew Barry, the new news director, said to me, "Philadelphia isn't a sports city." The bosses' feelings had been graphically evident for a long time. When I did player interviews after the Phillies won the World Series, every reporter was sent to sports bars in the region for live shots of fan reactions. Because of this, the news show ran overtime with the "man in the street" coverage, and I never made it on the air. Another time, I was at one of Dick Vermeil's news conferences after an Eagles game. Before it started, I was standing there, holding the microphone with a wire on it and as I turned around, I saw that there was nothing at the other end of the wire. My cameraman wasn't there. He later told me that the station had called him to go to Camden and shoot a fire.

The camera guys were always great. One time, a couple of them told me that they were having lunch in an out-of-the-way restaurant. They heard some familiar voices in the next booth. It turned out to be the station's general manager Steve Cohen and, would you believe, Howard Eskin. I went to Cohen and asked him what this was all about. He said that they were just discussing old times at Philadelphia's Northeast High School. Sure they were! Shortly before I retired, there was Howard Eskin handling the half-hour sports show after the Sunday night news.

My two biggest disappointments in 50 years were not going to the Winter Olympics in 1992 in Albertville, France and in 1994 in Lillehammer, Norway. Ron Burke, who was then doing weekend sports, was sent to cover the games. He did very well, but from that experience I got the message from the news director: it was going to be me against them. They didn't like my complaining all the time when they screwed me over.

Almost as disappointing was missing the greatest upset in college basketball history—Villanova's riveting, 66-64 win over Georgetown for the NCAA basketball crown in 1985. I can't blame that one on the station, however. It was just a poor decision on my part.

When the NCAA postseason tournament schedule came out that year, it was obvious that we were going to need three people to cover the games, because Villanova, Temple, and Penn had all been selected for the tournament. I chose Temple because they were the highest rated local team in the tournament, and Villanova had been blown out by Pitt in its final regular season game. So as I followed the Owls, Joe Pellegrino covered the Wildcats. I don't have to tell you what happened after that. Suffice it to say that Coach Rollie Massimino's Wildcats went all the way to the championship game, in Lexington, Kentucky, long after the Owls had been eliminated by those same Hoyas, 63-46, in the Eastern Regionals. So I saw Villanova's greatest basketball moment on TV. But I wasn't there.

Incidentally, that game was the last college contest played without a shot clock. The NCAA adopted the 19-foot, nine-inch line nationally in 1986, and extended it to 20 feet, nine inches in 2008-09.

Two years before I retired, the National Broadcasting Company flipped stations with the old Westinghouse Broadcasting Company (Group W), which bought CBS (Channel 3). Channel 3 then became a CBS affiliate, and we at Channel 10 became part of NBC. Our bosses brought in a new general manager, a guy from Chicago named Pat Wallace. His first day on the job, I said something on the air—an offhand remark, which frankly I am noted for. I think I said something cute, I'm not even sure. Afterward, I walked into my office and the new general manager, whom I had never met before, was standing there. "Why did you say that?" he asked. "What?" I replied. Then I thought to myself, *It's going to be a long ride here for the next two years!* The next thing I knew, I was talking with my friend Herb Clarke, who also had white hair, and we figured, *Well, they're going to be making a lot of changes and, what the hell, we're retiring soon, anyway.* As it turned out, they cut my workload in half—instead of two shows, I only had one. They made it pretty well known that they didn't want me anymore, even though I still had about a year left on my contract. They thought that since I was only doing one show, I shouldn't make as much money. My contract stated that I would be paid a certain number of dollars, and they were trying to mess around with that. So I called my agent, Glenn Goldstein, and I said, "You know, I think somebody here is going to let me go because I'm 70 years old and I've got white hair." He called me the next morning and said, "All is well. I called the general manager of your station and I mentioned a couple of things to him like age discrimination, and I got a call from a lawyer at NBC in New York, and they said, 'No, of course not. We'd love to have Al!'"

So not only did they love to have Al, they were going to let me retire on the 28th of September, which would have been 44 years exactly since I had my first full-time job in broadcasting. And not only that, they were going to give me a bonus. They wanted to give me a going-away party, and I told them what they could do with it. Not only did I get a little bonus, I got separation pay. I got all the goodies that come with leaving and then some. The time I spent at Channel 10 was uncomfortable for me to say the least. But it paid off in the end and helped me cover some of the bills.

Before leaving Channel 10 in 1998, I took advantage of a golden opportunity to take a final shot at one of the "consultants" brought in by NBC to improve its ratings. Television is very big on bringing in these "experts," who get paid big bucks to tell us how to do our jobs.

At one such meeting in a conference room at the top of the old Adams Mark Hotel on City Avenue, a woman started explaining what the consultants were looking for. Of course, they weren't looking for me, because I had white hair and I was going to be gone soon, anyway. She said that she was going to play tapes to give us an idea of what some news directors thought of sports, etc., etc. I think I counted eight news directors interviewed on those tapes, and not one of them was in love with sports. Some of them might have been fans, but they thought that carrying sports as part of a news program was a waste of time and money, even for a couple of minutes. They conveyed the attitude about sportscasters that "you're here but we really don't need you." Then this woman said, "This is the kind of a show that we want in sports." She rolled the first videotape that showed two guys doing a two-man show in San Diego. They were talking to each other like in a sports talk show today. Then she stopped the tape and said, "This is what we're looking for."

One of the principals in that clip from San Diego happened to be a guy named Ted Leitner. Many people won't even remember him because he lasted in Philadelphia for only a year. When I was at Channel 3, he was at Channel 10. He was a guy that for whatever reason—I have no idea why—didn't want to associate with the other sportscasters in town. There weren't many of us, but we had a cozy little fraternity. We were always ridiculed by the newspaper people as being the guys with the bad makeup and hairdos who never knew anything about sports. We were always given the worst space in every press box we worked in, because the newspaper guys ran the press box. Ted didn't connect with people in Philadelphia, because as it turns out—and it was pretty obvious when you watched him—his shtick was negative. He always found something that was wrong or bad or not good enough. If the team won, it was because of some lucky break—that kind of thing. He was always looking for a place to dig where he could find something negative and use it. That's the way he reported sports, and that's why he lasted here for only a year.

Ted Leitner was being used by the consultant to give us an example of what we should be doing in Philadelphia now that NBC owned the station. I can't remember exactly what I said—and I know this person was probably a nice lady—but apparently I decided to let it all hang out, and I told her about the experience that the number-one guy in San Diego had when he was in Philadelphia. I'm not sure if she was crying at the end or not, but I had an effect because I was leaving and it didn't make a damn bit of difference to me.

Leitner's attitude toward his colleagues in Philadelphia reminded me of some other incidents involving Larry Pollack, the former general manager at Channel 6, who didn't want any of his people associating with their counterparts from the other stations. Years ago, I had made plans to run a charity celebrity golf tournament at White Manor Country Club—where I was a member—with the proceeds going to the Variety Club. Pollack called the country club and said that we couldn't have the event because Channel 6 was already sponsoring a Variety Club telethon, and (although he didn't say it) my event would overshadow his. A few nasty telephone conversations ensued in which he said I could have the event if I changed the name to the "Jim Gardner Tournament." Needless to say, I responded with a few epithets that I hadn't heard since my days in the military. But I didn't do the tournament, and I also left the club.

Anyway, Steve Levy came over to work at our station from Channel 6 after sitting out a year because of contractual restrictions. His closest friend over there was Jim O'Brien, the popular weatherman. They did everything together, and even motorcycled one time to Alaska. But after Steve was put on the air at Channel 10, Jim never spoke to his best friend again. That's the way it was. *You were my friend, but the hell with you now because you work across the street.* Jim O'Brien later died in a tragic skydiving accident.

Big Al enjoyed talking sports with Phillies All-Star Pete Rose, who was an expert on just about every sport, especially college football and basketball and dog racing.

Big Al had two chances to hoist the Stanley Cup—here in his office at WCAU- TV 10, and also in the Buffalo Auditorium after the Flyers won the coveted "Holy Grail" for the second straight year in 1974-75.

"Colonel" Harland Sanders, the distinguished, white-bearded founder of Kentucky Fried Chicken, hosted Big Al and his Eyewitness News colleagues Mort Crim and Vince Leonard (right) at the 100th running of the Kentucky Derby in 1974.

Not only did Colonel Sanders host his friends from Channel 3 at his house, he served a breakfast of wheat germ pancakes, biscuits, and red-eye gravy. The Colonel also gave a cooking lesson to Big Al and Vince Leonard.

Life on the road in the NBA was anything but glamorous for Big Al. Catching 40 winks on an airplane was often an art form.

Philadelphia mayor Ed Rendell was on hand to honor Big Al when he retired from WCAU-TV 10 after 20 years in 1998.

Al Meltzer served as master of ceremonies for a gala fundraising pep rally to restore Villanova University football at the Academy of Music on December 4, 1981. Featured at the festivities were comedian Bob Hope (right) and Philadelphia mayor Bill Green.

Pictured with Al and his bride, Beverly (center), after their wedding on August 17, 1980, are Al's daughters, Gwenn (left), Karen (second from left), and Helene (right).

Helping Big Al (center) celebrate his wedding are his brothers and sisters (from left): Raymond, Harriet, Sanford, and Irving.

Al's wife, Beverly, and their daughter, Jordana.

Al poses with Wilt Chamberlain at the Big Dipper's Bel Air estate in California after their historic interview on April 29, 1999, six months before Wilt's death.

Big Al and former Flyers great Mark Howe were both inducted into the Philadelphia Sports Hall of Fame in 2011. Here they are standing with Mark's dad, Gordy, a member of the Hockey Hall of Fame.

Al's proudest achievement was being the first member of the media to be inducted into the Big 5 Hall of Fame. Here he is shown at the display in the main corridor of the Palestra.

CHAPTER 12

Keeping Up with Colorful Birds Like Buddy, Dick, and Leonard

One of my first assignments, when I arrived at Channel 10 in 1978, was hosting a weekly show with the Eagles' brilliant new coach, Dick Vermeil. It didn't take me long to realize what made him different than most of his professional counterparts. It was apparent at his initial press conference: you asked Dick a question, he gave you an answer. No matter what happened, he always gave you an answer. No clichés, no "coach-speak." He was very candid about his feelings. I don't know how you can describe it other than to say he was as honest as the day is long. Dick was a tough coach, and he expected a great deal out of his players. But on the other hand, as we found out later, he was in love with his players. He didn't just like them as football players, he liked them as people.

The first time I ever did a show with Vermeil, I remember telling him during the break: "The camera loves you, Dick. And if you decide not to coach football, I think television would be a great thing for you." I would only see him on Tuesdays. His wife would bring his clothes from their home, because he hadn't seen her since the game on the previous Sunday. He always slept on a cot in his office next to his film projector. So if he woke up at 3 o'clock in the morning with an idea and wanted to look at something, he could do just that. Dick loved to win and he took losses extremely hard, because he worked like hell during the week.

When you sleep in your office and you get up at 3:00 a.m. to run something on a projector that's next to your bed, it's hardly a surprise that Dick was burned out when he left. You can only drive yourself so hard for so long. He was always on the move. That's why I'm glad he went into television, I'm glad he got back into football, and I'm glad he won a Super Bowl. He was enormously successful here as a spokesman and motivational speaker. Everybody knows Dick Vermeil and everybody loves him in this town, with justification. For a West Coast guy who initially didn't want to come to Philadelphia, he became not just a football coach, but a dearly loved resident. And he still lives here. He could have gone anywhere he wanted when he stopped coaching, but he loves the area and, of course, its people.

Dick was tough, but he was fair. All the players had enormous respect for him, but he sometimes had a problem because he held on to some of them too long. When you fall in love with your athletes, it's very difficult to let go. But he got them to a Super Bowl, and he was a very successful coach—there's no doubt about that! Dick Vermeil was one of the greatest guys I've ever met in sports. We were privileged to have him for as long as we did. The only thing was that he won the Super Bowl for the wrong city. But Dick is still an institution in Philadelphia, and he hasn't coached here in years. I would say that he's the most beloved coach in the city's history.

Speaking of beloved people, Jimmy Murray, the general manager of the great Super Bowl XV Eagles, was one of a kind. I first ran into him through my Big 5 connection when he was working as Villanova's sports information director. If you don't like Jim Murray, you don't like people. He's the genuine article. He was in the right job because meeting people was his strength, and frankly, if he wanted to, he could have developed a comedy act. He was that funny—a master of classic one-liners. He also served as Leonard Tose's aide de camp, and not too many people could handle that.

Leonard Tose, by the way, was one of the all-time great owners of any professional franchise. Just ask any coach who ever worked for him. Dick Vermeil always benefited from the fact that Leonard loved him and never bothered him. He just let him coach. The first time I experienced the generosity of the man, I hadn't been in town long. I was at a restaurant in South Philly with my wife, Beverly, and a couple of other people. After dinner, I waited for the check. It never came. Leonard knew I was in there. He didn't come over or say anything and I didn't see him, but he picked up the check. That was the way he was. He would do anything for his football team, and he was the guy who talked Dick Vermeil into leaving sunny California for the woods of Pennsylvania.

Unfortunately, all of the other things said about Tose are true. Although he was unique, Leonard had this big problem. He couldn't hold on to his money. The stories are legion about him losing scads of money at the casinos and about Dick Vermeil paying his rent, among many other things. But anyone who covered an Eagles football game or a Monday media luncheon always had the best meal he could dream of. Tose fed the media surf-and-turf with wine for Monday night football. On Monday mornings, it was Lobster Newberg. His taste in food was awesome.

As I mentioned earlier, if you're into Philadelphia sports, both the good and the bad come with the territory. I'll never forget one of the really bad things—the sale of the Philadelphia Eagles and the astonishing chain of events that preceded it. I was in bed one Sunday morning in December 1984, and Hugh Gannon, who handled much of the weekend sports at Channel 10, called my home and woke me up with startling news. He said that the *Arizona Republic*, a newspaper in Phoenix, was reporting that Leonard Tose was about to sell his team to a local syndicate and move the franchise to that faraway city. Leonard was attempting to pull a "Robert Irsay" and sneak out of town in the middle of the night just like the owner of the Baltimore Colts did earlier in 1984 when he packed all of the Colts' belongings into moving vans and took off for Indianapolis.

It turns out that people in the Eagles front office had been visiting Phoenix, checking out office space and even schools for their children. By selling 25 percent of the team to James Monaghan, an Arizona real estate developer, and moving the team there at the end of the season, Tose would have pocketed enough cash to wipe out his substantial gambling debts. Fortunately, Philadelphia mayor Wilson Goode stepped in, restructured the club's lease for Veterans Stadium, and made some other concessions to force Tose to change his mind.

Believe me, my life wasn't the same for about a month—chasing Leonard, staking out Leonard's house, waiting for Leonard, going wherever Leonard went day and night—because we knew that the sale of the team was inevitable. One night, we were babysitting Leonard while he was meeting with the other NFL owners at the Waldorf Astoria Hotel in New York City, trying to get them to bail him out of his financial woes. When we finally spotted Tose, I tried chasing him through a revolving door while carrying a camera with a microphone and cable attached to it. Talk about getting all tangled up.

The embattled Eagles owner was still buried in debt—some say it was as high as $42 million—when he avoided bankruptcy a year later by selling the franchise for $65 million to Norman Braman, a onetime Eagles water boy who made a huge fortune with a chain of drugstores and luxury automobile dealerships for Rolls Royce, Bentley, and Maserati. What happened to Tose was absolutely tragic. For all of his gambling problems and poor spending habits, Leonard was genuinely a great guy and a wonderful owner. He always picked up the tab, treated everyone as first-cabin, and was arguably the best owner in the National Football League. And to think that he purchased the Eagles from Jerry Wolman for $16 million!

People tell me that perhaps my most biting, yet thoughtful TV commentary probably occurred on Tuesday, December 11, 1984, when Leonard Tose was attempting to move his Philadelphia Eagles franchise to Phoenix:

> "The Eagles are a public trust," I said. "Now they're as much a part of this city as Billy Penn—a public trust that has been mismanaged to a point where it has to be moved like a piece of furniture.
>
> "Leonard Tose is $40 million in debt, certainly not the problem of people in this area. And I know you've been lied to. For the last 50 years plus, you have supported the franchise—the problem is Leonard Tose.
>
> "How he accumulated his debt is not the point. The point is he can, and has, run a great franchise into the ground. And now he wants to bail out…and there isn't a thing that you can do about it. I realize that the mayor is trying to get local money together—the deal in Phoenix is unbelievable—and from a financial standpoint it wouldn't be worth the money. But they want a franchise in Philadelphia and Leonard Tose is drowning in red ink.
>
> "Yes, you have been betrayed. Yes, he can move the team. Yes, there's a chance someday that we'll get another NFL franchise, because this is the fourth largest TV market and it means huge dollars to the networks.
>
> "But I've said it before, and remember it always: Sports is a business. Now, if you haven't learned that by now, then learn it. Don't be naïve enough to think that you owe it anything or it owes you anything.
>
> "And if, in fact, Leonard Tose does move, I hope…it's in the middle of the night."

I don't want to sound pompous, but I always felt that I was part of the conscience of those people who watch and maybe learn from us. I reported the sports news and also its ramifications. The Tose situation was a case in point. What an opportunity to show righteous indignation. Granted that Leonard was the owner of the Eagles and, in effect, had the right to do with the franchise whatever he wanted. But he had no right to pull the team out of Philadelphia capriciously. For almost three decades, the Eagles have been among the NFL's very top clubs in attendance, and at one point during that span they had only *five* winning seasons. Imagine that! Because of such fan loyalty, Tose had no moral right to dislocate, and thus violate such public trust. As we all know, if it hadn't been for the Phoenix newspaperman breaking that story, the City of Brotherly Love could have been without an NFL franchise for a long time—maybe forever.

Norman Braman was a native Philadelphian who lived in Florida for part of the year and the south of France the rest of the time. He was your classic absentee owner who had no interest in the city of his birth—even though he made a bundle of money from the sweetheart Veterans Stadium deal that his predecessor never had the opportunity to enjoy. Philadelphia fans and the media never warmed up to him, because he came galloping in as the new "savior" of the Eagles, but reneged on his promise to move back to the city. His players didn't care for him either.

Braman was more content selling those fancy, expensive cars down in Florida, vacationing at his villa on the French Riviera, and flying in for Eagles games on his private jet. At the height of the arbitration hearings during the NFL players' strike in 1987, it was learned that when Norman had to open his books, instead of losing $7 million as he had claimed, he had actually made $7 million the year before. In 1990, Braman paid himself a $7.5 million salary as the club's owner, according to testimony at an NFL antitrust trial. He was the wrong guy at the wrong time. We thought that Norman had gotten away with murder when he sold the team to Jeffrey Lurie for almost $200 million in 1994, but it didn't turn out quite that way, for which I shed no tears.

There was also no love lost between Braman and the new coach he hired in 1986: the irrepressible Buddy Ryan, who referred to his boss as "the guy in France." Buddy and I happened to go back a long way together with a number of crazy twists and turns—beginning at the University of Buffalo in the '60s, when he served as an assistant coach and I was handling UB's play-by-play on the radio. Who do you think was an assistant coach with the Bears the year I got to Chicago? Good old Buddy. And when I came back to Philadelphia, guess who the Eagles hired as their coach? Same guy! At his first press conference at the Vet, he spotted me, came over, and said, "Big Al, quit following me around!" Then he said, "I'll do the coach's show on Channel 10, but I want you to pay me more money than you paid Dick Vermeil." Then he proceeded to regale the media with such lines as: "If I lose, you can't help me. If I win, I don't need you!" And: "Now there's a winner in town!"

You knew that something different was about to happen in Philadelphia. Buddy, of course, had been lifted on the shoulders of his defensive team when the Chicago Bears won the Super Bowl. Mike Ditka, his boss, never forgave him for that. There was never any love between those two, because Buddy had been picked to be defensive coordinator by the owner, not by the coach. When Ditka got the job as coach, he got Buddy Ryan as a gift...or a curse. George Halas brought him in because he had done great work with the Jets under Weeb Ewbank with that patented "46 defense." And that continued with the Eagles, at least on the defensive side of the ball, where no one else ever did it better for the Birds. And I say that with all due respect for their coordinator Jim Johnson, who passed away in 2009. Offensively, it was another story. Buddy left that phase of the game entirely up to others. How many times did you hear that he told Randall Cunningham, one of the Birds' best quarterbacks ever, "All you have to do is make a couple of plays and my defense will take care of the rest and we'll win them all."

Buddy had his show with me on Channel 10 once a week, and he'd come in on Monday night with his wife, Joanie, who was very charming. On occasion, Beverly would join me and we'd meet the Ryans at the long-gone Marriott Hotel across the street from the station on City Line Avenue and talk over a pleasant dinner. We talked about a lot of things, including the theatre. When Buddy was coaching the Jets, he and Joanie loved to go to the theatre. He was a big-city guy and knew his way around New York. But he was conversant in a lot of topics other than football. Those dinner conversations were always very enjoyable. Unfortunately, Joanie is not well today and is struggling with Alzheimer's disease.

As it turns out, Ryan was deep into the horse trade and had a farm down in Kentucky, which I visited after he retired. He even named one of his horses "Fired for Winning" because of you-know-who. His twin boys from his first marriage are both working today as successful coaches in the NFL. Rex is the head coach of the New York Jets, and Rob is defensive coordinator of the Dallas Cowboys. Buddy also had quite a military background. He was the youngest six-stripe soldier in the U.S. Army during the Korean War, and was a master sergeant by 18 or 19. He didn't talk much about what he did in the war, but you don't get to be a master sergeant in the Army at that age unless you do some heroic things.

Whenever I socialized with Buddy Ryan, I always thought I was talking to two different people. At dinner, I knew a friendlier, warmer part of him. But when he went on the air, the *other* Buddy showed up—the Buddy who just loved to twist the knife. For example, Buddy let everyone know that he hated Mike Ditka. He also didn't like Dallas coach Tom Landry. This went back to the NFL strike in 1987, when he accused the Cowboys coach of running up the score against his replacement players, which led to a lopsided 41-22. Some of the Cowboys' starters, like future Hall of Famers Randy White and Tony Dorsett, crossed the picket line to play against the Birds that day. Ryan, of course, wanted nothing to do with these "scab" players who were forced on him, but he honored his contract and coached them through three embarrassing losses. He also humiliated them whenever he could and referred to them as "dumb jerks," wishing all along that he could have his regular players, who were picketing in front of the Vet. Later that season, after the strike was over, Buddy got even with Landry and the Cowboys with a 37-20 Eagles victory. Instead of having Randall Cunningham take a knee in the closing seconds, he ordered his quarterback to throw for a one-yard touchdown. That certainly got everybody all up in arms.

The first game right after the strike had started was against Buddy's old team, the Bears, and boy, did I get bounced around! I walked through the gate at Veterans Stadium, where the trucks and buses enter. I was walking toward the entrance to the press box, but before I got behind the gate, a group of the guys who were picketing—none of them football players—tossed me around like a rubber ball because I was covering the game. It was an unusual, disturbing incident and the kind of thing I don't want to go through ever again. These people, whom I'm sure are ordinarily very peaceful, law-abiding citizens, were not their normal selves in this situation. They were mad as hell, and they went after the first person they could get their hands on and blame.

Buddy Ryan, of course, had no love for Norman Braman, and he resented the fact that the Eagles' owner didn't spend much time in

Philadelphia and lived in a chalet in southern France during much of the year. He didn't like Braman personally, although he took his money and coached his team. I think that Buddy would have been much friendlier with Leonard Tose, because Tose was a free-spender who knew the horse business, and he would have liked Leonard's style.

I do know that Reggie White, who was one of the best defensive linemen in the history of the National Football League, also had no time for Mr. Braman when he played for the Eagles. Reggie felt that the owner was not committed to building a championship team in Philadelphia, and he frequently mentioned the names of the talented veterans among his teammates who were permitted to leave the team as free agents. Finally, in 1993, Reggie joined his fellow defectors and signed a $17 million contract with Green Bay. He eventually won a Super Bowl with the Packers. Reggie had come to Philadelphia from the World Football League and was known as "The Reverend." He was as nice a guy as you would want to meet. He was very gentle—except, of course, on the football field. And Reggie was so good that he was dangerous. Tragically, the Rev. White passed away suddenly in 2004, two years before he was enshrined in the Pro Football Hall of Fame. A great tackle and an even better guy!

Another player who earned my respect was Ron Jaworski, the quarterback who took the Eagles to the Super Bowl in 1980 and played in the NFL for 17 years. I liked Ron a great deal. I thought he had a lot of guts. Most of the time, he didn't play with great football teams during his decade in Philadelphia. They did go to the Super Bowl that one year, but otherwise the Eagles were not a powerhouse. The Eastern Division had Washington, Dallas, and the New York Giants. Somebody wasn't going to make it in every year, and most of the time it was the Eagles. So Ron really suffered through a lot of defeats. He did the best he could, never complained, and took incredible hits, baby. I mean, if you looked at the video, you'd say *he's never getting up!* I can't remember the game—it might have been with the Chicago Bears—but Ron got nailed from the blind side and when he hit the ground, there was a gasp in the press box. We thought he was really hurt. He was always positive in the locker room, and the Jaws you see today is the same Jaws you saw as a football player. He appreciated the fact that he could play in the NFL and he had a job that he did well. Ron stayed in the Philadelphia/South Jersey area and became a big part of the community. He owns a lot of property around here, including golf courses, and is a popular part of the scenery. Not bad for a guy who sat on the bench for the LA Rams and came to

Philadelphia from Youngstown State in Ohio. Ron grew up just outside of Buffalo, a small-town kid who did not look like an NFL quarterback until he put on the uniform and threw the ball. He was a self-made quarterback, and I think the fans appreciated that. They also appreciate how hard Ron worked to become a highly respected analyst for ESPN on *Monday Night Football.*

Thinking of Buddy Ryan always reminds me of the NFC Divisional Playoff Game against the Chicago Bears on New Year's Eve, 1988—the infamous Fog Bowl. The Eagles had flown into the Windy City a day early, and Ryan stood up in the bus taking the team from the airport to the hotel and barked to the driver, "Take a drive around Soldier Field and honk your horn, because I want everybody to know that Buddy's back!" I think we took a couple of trips around the stadium. But that was Buddy in all his glory. The Chicago media couldn't get enough of him, although I'm sure that Mike Ditka got too much of him.

The Fog Bowl is a little story in itself. I came prepared with a heavy overcoat, thermal underwear, boots, and a scarf. I was wearing everything for cold weather. I got out of the hotel room the day of the game and I thought it was 60 degrees, at least it felt that way. (Actually, they told me later that the temperature at kickoff was 34 degrees, which was still unseasonably mild for Chicago at that time of year.) The Eagles were in the Bears' red zone nine times and did not score any touchdowns, primarily because Keith Jackson, the best tight end in the league, dropped a pass when he was wide open. The Birds had two other apparent TDs wiped out by penalties.

Early in the second quarter, I looked over from my seat in the press box, and just like you see steam slowly come over the edge of a cup of tea or coffee and then drop down, that's exactly what it looked like on the playing field. It was foggy because it was very warm and Lake Michigan was very cold. As the fog quickly enveloped the entire stadium, I went downstairs and got right behind the Eagles bench. All I could see, besides moving shadows, were the tops of the goalposts on either end of the playing field. I could not understand why the game wasn't stopped. I mean, you absolutely couldn't see! The broadcasters all said they couldn't make out anything, but the referee disagreed, so they continued play. If they had just waited 20 or 25 minutes before halftime and then resumed the game, there wouldn't have been a problem, because the fog didn't last all day. It eventually dissipated and the second half was played on a clear field.

Had the fog not rolled in, there's no doubt in my mind that the Eagles would have beaten Chicago instead of losing 20-12. The Eagles had them dead to rights in the first half, but they just couldn't capitalize. The Bears caught a break because quarterback Randall Cunningham couldn't complete long passes in the fog and threw three interceptions. He still threw for 407 yards, a new Philadelphia playoff record. Randall was the finest pure athlete who ever played here. He could run like the wind, throw the ball, kick the ball, and do everything a great quarterback should do. And Buddy always repeated his famous statement: "Randall, just go out and get me a couple of touchdowns and I'll take care of the rest." It is also fair to say that the Eagles could have advanced far in the playoffs that year had they won this game, because they did finish first in the NFC East by winning six of their final seven regular season games. That was the best record in the NFL during that stretch. Who knows? Maybe that game cost the Eagles the Super Bowl.

As I walked out of the Eagles locker room after the game, who did I see out there waiting but a bunch of Chicago players. And Buddy and his old players stood there hugging each other. Their middle linebacker, Mike Singletary, had tears in his eyes. So did Buddy. It was an emotional moment. It was like friends who hadn't seen each other in years. Buddy's players loved him, and that scene will stay with me forever.

When Buddy was on the air at Channel 10—we didn't have a live audience in the studio the first year—we just talked about the games. He was very candid about what was going on. If somebody wasn't playing well, that player's name would come out in the conversation. He'd also throw in a few lines here or there just for laughs. Then later when we got a live audience, he would take questions. Buddy had no idea what people were going to ask him. Nothing was set up in advance; they would just ask Buddy what he thought about something. And Buddy would tell them exactly what he thought. "Buddy, why don't you go to midfield after the games are over?" Or, "Sometimes even before the games are over, you leave the field and you don't shake hands with the other coach. Why?" He would reply, "I used to do it underneath the stands." But that was a lot of malarkey.

Ryan was not a phony in that respect. The façade he put on was for the public, because it was good for business and he made more money. As I figured it out, the other Buddy was a football giant, meaning that he was the best defensive coach in the National Football League bar none!

Unfortunately, once the Eagles got into the postseason, they couldn't win a playoff game. That was the one thing that eventually drove Buddy Ryan out of town. Braman then gave the job to Rich Kotite, because it hardly cost him any money. Rich was a good guy—I really liked him—but I don't think he was ready to become a head coach. Things kind of deteriorated after that, and we went into the Dark Ages of pro football here in town for a while.

In addition to my program with the Eagles' head coach on Channel 10, we arranged for Ron Burke to host a show with Randall Cunningham. Then we really hit pay dirt when we brought in one of Buddy Ryan's top defensive players, Mike Golic, the former Notre Dame star, and gave him his TV start while he was still playing in the NFL. Mike had been drafted by the Houston Oilers before the 1986 season, and came to the Eagles the following year. He turned out to be consistently the best interview at the Eagles training camp at West Chester, and was actually good enough to do stand-up comedy right on the field. Not only that, but Mike always went along with anything my producers asked when they were adding little pieces or trying out funny segments for the show. They had him doing crazy things because they wanted to take advantage of his great personality. Mark Jordan, my cameraman, and Mitch Goldstein, who produced the show, then came up with the idea for a title, "Golic's Got It." Mike's piece began as a three-to-five-minute segment of *The Randall Cunningham Show*, but it got to be so good that we decided to expand it to ten minutes. Finally, we gave him his own football variety show, and he eventually won an Emmy.

Golic did things on his show that were just out of this world. They were always taped on Tuesdays, the players' day off. Once before the Eagles played the Washington Redskins, he went to a pig farm and wrestled a bunch of hogs, because the hogs symbolized the Redskins fans with their big snoots and behavior. In Cleveland, they have the "Dog Pound," so Mike went to a dog pound and started playing around with the dogs. At the end of the piece, he took out a can of Alpo dog food and ate the whole can. I mean, where else can you find somebody crazy enough to do something like that? Mike went up to a coal mine before the Eagles' game with the San Francisco 49ers. He was a little apprehensive about going down the shaft—they tell me that he wasn't sure he wanted to be that deep in the heart of Pennsylvania—but he hung in there and actually gave some karate lessons while in the coal mine. Before the Eagles played the Oakland Raiders, Mike found a Little League football team called the "Raiders," and he took on the whole team. It was one player against 11 or 22. Gimmicks like these attracted many viewers. So did the episode before a game with the Denver Broncos when, unfortunately, Mike had to cut short his stay in the corral after trying to get close to the horses at the Cowtown Rodeo in South Jersey. He learned quickly that there's a big difference between a plow horse and a bronco.

ESPN called Mike when they heard that he might be retiring after playing one season in Miami in 1993. He then ended his eight-year NFL career. ESPN used him in various ways as a reporter and interviewer, and they finally got him involved doing football color and play-by-play. A couple of years ago, they hooked him up with another guy named Mike (Greenberg, that is), and they now have a popular morning show on ESPN called *Mike and Mike,* which is simulcast across the nation on TV and radio. He now gets great exposure and loves what he does. Mike Golic has two sons playing on Notre Dame's football team, a daughter who is an Olympic-quality swimmer, and a brother, Bob, another Notre Dame grad, who also played in the NFL for 13 years with New England, Cleveland, and the Los Angeles Raiders. Quite an athletic family, those Golics.

Mike became a great hit with us at Channel 10 primarily because he wasn't putting anything on. He was a really good guy who also liked to laugh a lot. Mike embodied the idea that "what you see is what you get." It's no wonder that he is now an immensely popular national personality on ESPN.

CHAPTER 13

Big Al Has Mitch Williams All to Himself as the Phillies Rise and Fall

After surprisingly making it to the 1993 World Series, the Phillies' Game 6 against the Blue Jays in Toronto turned out to be one of the low points in their history. The Phils were coming off a 2-0 Curt Shilling masterpiece shutout that cut Toronto's lead to three games to two. They went into the ninth inning at the Sky Dome leading 6-5 when manager Jim Fregosi decided to throw Mitch Williams in to close things out and send the Series back to Philadelphia for the decisive Game 7.

It never happened. With one out and Rickey Henderson and Paul Molitor on base, Joe Carter smacked a 2-2 pitch for a three-run homer, and the Blue Jays had their second straight World Series title. It's hard to believe, but this was the first time in major league baseball history when a come-from-behind walk-off home run won a World Series.

I was covering the Series for Channel 10. I left my seat in the press box during the seventh inning and worked my way down to the field level of the stadium. I wanted to check on my exact broadcast location, which was next to the back door of the Phillies' locker room. I watched the ninth inning on a little monitor that I was using. I saw Carter hit the ball and knew the game was over. But I was standing outside the rear door of the clubhouse and not at the front where most of the media would be gathering. The back door was open and the Phillies were just beginning to file in, so I said to my cameraman, "Let's go in." It suddenly occurred to me that I was now inside the locker room all by myself, because everybody in the media was outside, still waiting to get in the front door.

And there, sitting all by himself in a corner, was Mitch Williams. For a brief moment I thought to myself, *Is it fair to go over to him right now and interview him?* I didn't know him that well, but I went over and said, "Do you mind if I talk to you?" In a situation like that, I guess he could have punched me in the nose, but Mitch always had too much class for anything like that. He said, "No, go ahead." I asked the usual questions like, "What happened?" and how he felt, and he answered everything politely and completely. He gave me great answers, for which I was grateful.

By then the reporters had started to come in, but just prior to that, some of the players, including Dave Hollins and Danny Jackson, had come over and given me a bad time, cursing and yelling things like, "Leave him alone!"—and much worse. Not only that, but one of the local sportswriters stepped on my microphone line, and I couldn't do any more interviews for a while. The writer just happened to have his foot planted on my line, and I couldn't budge him off it. What was I going to do, push him? He was doing his job, but I couldn't do mine. Did he do it on purpose? I'll never know. But I did get my exclusive interview with Mitch Williams.

Mitch has since come back to Philadelphia's Comcast SportsNet as an analyst on the Phillies' pre- and postgame shows. He also has a baseball show on national satellite radio and is doing great work for the Major League Baseball TV Network. And I'll tell you right now, Mitch was born to be a broadcaster. I've really been impressed. Of all the former major leaguers who have done that job, he is among the best. Not only that, but he has developed into one of the most popular sports figures in Philadelphia. He turned a negative into a positive by being so cooperative and accessible during a time when many other athletes would hide in the shower or disappear completely from the public spotlight.

Even though it didn't involve a World Series game, many baseball fans consider "Black Friday" in 1977 as the real low point in Phillies history. I agree. That was Game 3 of the National League Championship Series when the Phils had a seemingly comfortable 5-3 lead with two outs and nobody on base in the ninth inning. The home crowd was on its feet, cheering as loudly as I've ever heard them. I won't bore you with the grizzly details, but they included three bad defensive plays, a blown call by the umpire, and a terrible decision by manager Danny Ozark. You get the picture. The Dodgers won, 6-5, and took the next game, 4-1, in atrocious weather following a two-hour rain delay. They went on to the World Series instead of our guys.

Anyway, on Black Friday, all the local sportscasters, including yours truly, set up their equipment to do live wrap-up shots after the game on the second deck near all the statues just outside Veterans Stadium. We had come out and stood on top of our remote trucks with lights, a microphone, and a monitor. It was a little easier to do it that way rather than fight the crowd. After the Dodgers scored, I decided I'd better get out of the stadium quickly, because the fans were going to be leaving, and they were going to be in a foul mood. We had a couple of Rent-a-Cops surrounding the truck just to make sure there was no problem. But as I climbed up on top of the truck, I saw fans pouring out of the exits, people who were in a really bad mood. I was okay until the light was turned on. Of course, in order to be seen on camera, I had no choice. So the fans spotted me. They started to climb up on the remote truck and then began to shake it. We were close enough to the edge of the deck that if they had pushed the truck over, we would have tumbled down a full level to the ground below. I grabbed everything I could grab. I saved my microphone. I probably didn't save the lamp, and I don't think I saved the monitor. I really can't remember how I got on and off the air, because I couldn't see anything. All I know is that it was my turn, and I talked into the microphone and whatever video they were showing back at the station, which I couldn't see. We got some help from the police once I went off the air, and everything was okay after that. For about a five-minute period when they were climbing up on the remote truck, I thought to myself, *This could be a huge problem*, because if I fell from the truck, I would fall on concrete. That was the worst experience I ever had doing a postgame show.

The next night, during the famous rain-delay game that never should have been played, they decided to put me in the Phillies dugout. Dick Enberg was the network announcer and he said during the rain-break, "Now down there in the Phillies dugout to interview Tug McGraw is Philadelphia sportscaster Al *Metzler*."

My moment in the sun and Dick Enberg couldn't even get my last name straight!

If Black Friday was the low point for the Phillies, the 1980 season certainly made up for it as the Whiz Kids won the first World Series in their 97-year history by beating the Kansas City Royals in six games. Actually, in many ways, the '80 Series was anticlimactic after what had happened in perhaps the most exciting National League Championship Series ever played. It was certainly the Phillies' greatest comeback, especially after they dropped two straight games to the Houston Astros and had their backs to the wall. They stayed alive by winning Game 4 in 10 innings to even the Series at two apiece, but I'll never forget Game 5 on Sunday night, October 12, in the Astrodome.

Garry Maddox drove in the winning run to get the Phillies into the World Series, but I never saw any of it. Can you believe that? It was one of the biggest moments in Philadelphia sports history, but I couldn't see or hear what was going on. All I know is that they were losing 5-2 and Nolan Ryan was pitching. When I saw Ryan pitching with a three-run lead after seven innings, I figured it was time to leave my temporary seat, which was high up in the stands, get down below as quickly as possible, and get ready to do the postgame show.

By the time I worked my way down, things had happened. The Phillies took the lead with five runs in the top of the eighth inning, and the Astros tied it with two in their half of the inning. That's when I was totally blocked out because I was stuck behind a bunch of groundskeepers and a glass door behind home plate for the last few innings. That piece of glass provided the only sightline for the ground crew that took up all of the viewing spaces as they were entitled to do. But we couldn't see a thing. When the door finally opened after the Phillies had won it in the tenth, I ran out onto the field with my microphone and my cameraman and the first guy I ran into was Dick Ruthven, the winning pitcher who had retired the last six batters.

Ruthven was walking off the mound, so I threw my mike in front of his face and got him to say a few things. I also remember Phillies PR man Larry Shenk was standing there, but he hadn't been with me very long because all during the latter stages of the game, he was walking around the Astrodome. Just walking and walking. I got the impression that he *wanted* to hear what was going on, but also *didn't want* to hear. When he heard the crowd cheering, it upset him, and when he didn't hear them, he knew that something good was happening. But he never saw the Phillies winning part of the game, either.

Pete Rose, I believe, was as responsible for winning that pennant as anyone. I got to know him a little bit, particularly in Spring Training.

Pete loved sports in general. Dogs were racing over in St. Petersburg, and it was around the time March Madness was coming in. I started up a conversation with him one day about college basketball—and remember, I was the maven of college basketball. But he knew more about college basketball than I will ever know. He knew all the teams. The University of Cincinnati was probably his favorite because that was his hometown; the "Big O" played there, and they won a couple of national championships. He knew everything about all the games—and I suppose there was reason for that.

Then we came back home to Philadelphia. After the regular season started, *that bunch* as they have been called, usually disappeared into the players' lounge or trainer's room after the games, so there were just a few people who would talk to me or allow themselves to be interviewed in the locker room. But Pete was always there. Basically, I found him to be very easy to talk to, very knowledgeable about sports, and kind of a fun guy. The only time I interviewed him for the record was after games, although one time I did a feature on him. Before the games, he would be hanging around the batting cage, and we normally got into a conversation about the sport of the day, whatever it happened to be. Often it would be about NHL hockey or the NBA, because they were just going into their playoffs. He watched TV all the time, and his favorite teams in the NBA were the Sixers and the Boston Celtics.

When we were looking at batting practice, of course, we talked about baseball. Pete knew exactly what was going on with anyone who happened to be at the plate hitting at the time—what he was doing right, what he was doing wrong, and inside stuff. Again, it was just conversation. I usually didn't have a microphone with me. There was nothing said that I would run home to the station to broadcast, but he probably studied hitting the baseball more than anyone except my all-time hero, Ted Williams. I was always impressed with Pete's knowledge. I got the impression he knew all that he did because he had worked at it; he had studied it. If, in fact—and I think it is a fact—he bet on games, maybe even baseball games, hopefully it wasn't on his own team. That I'll never know. The fact that Pete Rose is not in the Hall of Fame is one of the great tragedies of the game of baseball. His critics may be right, I don't know, but I just wish that someday he will get into Cooperstown.

Although he will probably never be considered for Cooperstown, a true Hall of Famer in the eyes of many Philadelphia fans is my old friend

Dallas Green, who came off the bench, so to speak, reluctantly to lead the Phillies to their first World Series championship in 1980. Now he's the team's senior advisor to the general manager. I had a chance recently to reminisce with Dallas, who was his usual outspoken self ("I'm a screamer, a yeller and a cusser. I never hold back," he used to say) in discussing a variety of hot-button topics including:

- why he never wanted to manage the Phillies;
- how many of those feisty Phillies virtually hated him and, in at least one instance, almost came to blows with him;
- how he helped convince the Chicago city fathers that the only chance of the Cubs getting to a World Series was by installing lights in Wrigley Field;
- how he was fired for the only time in his career by (you guessed it) George Steinbrenner, the owner of the New York Yankees;
- what's wrong with the game today and why the current Phillies are the best team in the franchise's history;
- why he would never want the baseball commissioner's job.

Dallas attended the University of Delaware where former Phillies owner Robert R.M. Carpenter helped him to get a basketball scholarship. "I loved the game of basketball," he recalled. "I could shoot and I could rebound. I didn't have great speed, but I could get the job done. And I loved to play. Obviously, I went to school on a basketball scholarship, but Mr. Carpenter knew why I was there. I was there to pitch." Dallas says that he had a pretty good won-loss record with the Blue Hens and held the school record for earned run average for a while. Although he was elected basketball captain for the following season, he signed to play for the Phillies for a small bonus after his junior year.

Green spent 13 years in the major leagues—five of them as a player with the Phillies, Washington Senators, and New York Mets—and probably would have lasted longer had it not been for the brutal weather in upstate New York. "I was recognized as one of the top prospects all through my minor league career, and I probably threw harder than anybody we had, even Dick Farrell. But when I was with Buffalo, a triple-A team, I pitched five straight complete game wins even though the lake was still frozen over. It was cold as Hell, Al. About the sixth or seventh inning of about the third game, I started feeling stiff, but back in those days you rubbed some hot stuff tucked in your shirt and went out and pitched. In my sixth game, I couldn't reach home plate. And back then nobody knew how to treat these things—there weren't any doctors, no sports specialists at all."

At Buffalo, Dallas pitched against future Phillies like Jim Owens, Jack Meyer, and Jack Sanford in Syracuse, and was on the last team to go to Havana to play the Sugar Kings. "We were the last team in there before Fidel Castro took over. All those stories were true. Machine guns all over the place. I didn't know what they were back in those days, but there were lots of automatic weapons. We walked the streets, but we didn't go too far out of the hotel."

After his playing days ended, Green joined the Phillies front office and gradually moved up the ladder. "I always thought I wanted to be a general manager, that was my path," he recalled. The Pope [Paul Owens] was obviously my mentor and my friend, and helped lead me there. He made me do the right things to learn the trade and prepare myself by doing the minor league work, by going out and managing a rookie club, and then coming in to the front office to run the scouting and development departments.

"Even when we were talking about firing Danny Ozark, I didn't have any thoughts about manager. Hughie Alexander brought it up, and a couple of other guys in the room were popping pretty good and yakking and kind of think-tanking, and my name came up a couple of times and the Pope kept saying, 'Well, you know....' He really didn't want me to do it, but he knew it made sense because we were only going to do it for a month or two—only August and September of the '79 season. He said, 'Dallas, all I want is you to go down there, find out who really wants to play for the Phillies and who wants to be part of what we're doing, because we're getting a little long in the tooth and we're going to have to make some changes if we can't win here.'

"Because we had done so well in '76, '77, and '78, the 1979 season was a disaster. In '77, we were the best team in the country, and we should have won in '78. But in '76, we weren't prepared. I mean, the Big Red Machine, they just killed us. And even though we didn't go to the dance in those years, we showed that we had some good baseball players. I was director of minor league scouting at the time, and I wasn't jumping up and down saying, *Yeah, I'm going to go down...I'll do it...I'll do it...I'll do it,* because it wasn't my shtick. But I was driving home at three or four or five in the morning after all these sessions were done, and I'm thinking to myself, *Well, you know it kind of makes sense—I know the organization, I know the kids, I know our team pretty well, and all Pope wants is some information. And I can get that, I can do that.* I knew the coaching staff very well, and I knew everything there was to know about being a manager—except front-hand information. I called him back about four or five in the morning when I got home and said, 'Hey, I'll do it!' And he said, 'Okay, here's what we're going to do....'"

Asked if these players were a tough bunch to manage, Dallas said diplomatically, "Well, they all grew up together, so they were a clique. I mean, they were strong personalities. Bowa and Boonie were heavily into the Players Union; Pete was kind of the outsider, but Schmitty and Maddox and Bowa all grew up together, came into the big leagues at about the same time, and played together for seven or eight years. They really ran the roost. Danny was the manager, but they said when they wanted to play and when they didn't want to play, and what they wanted to do, and the Pope and I were so frustrated. We knew we had good individual people, but they never came together totally as a team. And that was our whole shtick. We were going to give them one last shot to be a team, and we kinda had a game plan. And I was the guy who had to go down there and sell the game plan. It wasn't a helluva easy job."

Green, who had managed Manny Trio and Greg Luzinski in the minor leagues, quickly found out what "The Clique" thought about him. They also wasted little time in testing him:

"Hate's a strong word, but it came pretty close to that. They loved Danny. They really did. All of them. And I told them right from the beginning, 'You guys got Danny fired. You guys are the reason I'm here and Danny's not.' I put the onus on them, and they didn't like that at all. Basically, to a man, they didn't like me at all from the very beginning, because now we were going to do certain things my way. Oh, man! I mean, we had some knock-down drag-outs. I knew the feelings in the room, but Al, I've never been one to worry about what other people think. The leaders of the guys who understood were Carlton, Pete, Trio, and Bake [McBride]. Tug was also on my side, but he had gotten hurt in Spring Training, so he was kind of sidelined until July. Bowa hated me to a degree. Hate is a strong word, but it came close to that. I mean, he had his own radio show, and he was banging me every day he could. Bull called me 'Hitler.' I was determined that they weren't going to rule the roost. The Pope had my back. Ruly Carpenter, the owner, could waive, but he was with us. He loved the players, obviously. He knew we had to do something strong to get it done."

In the middle of August, the Phillies were swept in a four-game series in Pittsburgh, leaving them in third place, six games behind Montreal and the Pirates. In between games of a doubleheader loss to Pittsburgh, Green exploded and his obscenities reverberated throughout the corridors of Three Rivers Stadium.

"It was a long battle, although I knew that the coaching staff and certain guys were with me. John Vukovich was a big supporter and would jump all over Bowa—that's why he was on my team. He was my 25th guy, and he was my hammer. He did as much work for me as anybody. But yeah, Al, we battled all five months. After I blasted them unbelievably in Pittsburgh and we went on the road out to the West Coast, the Pope was irate. He said, 'Dallas, I want to talk to them.' I said, 'Do you want all the kids in? Because we call the kids up from the minors on September 1.' And he said, 'I want everybody!' And he went down the line—Bowa, Boonie, Bull, Schmitty. He didn't miss a guy, and he tore them a new asshole, I'm telling you—individually and as a team."

"I wasn't that close to the Pope," I admitted, *"but I always thought he was kind of a laid-back guy."*

"No, no, no, no, you misread him, Al, oh my God. I mean he had an unbelievable temper. Eddie Ferenz [the team's traveling secretary] and I were his best buddies, and we were with him all the time. I can't tell you how many fights or near fights, or near disasters we had with him because, you know, he'd drink some of that firewater and get after it pretty good. But he was a helluva baseball guy and knew the game. He could feel the temperature of what was going on. He knew I was right all along, and yet he let me go through it to handle it the best I could."

"Did things ever get physical?" I asked.

"No. The closest was Ronnie Reed at that doubleheader in Pittsburgh. I ordered Ronnie to walk a guy, and he gives me one of these—you know, stomping around the mound—and Boonie couldn't get him started again, and then he walked a guy, and then the next guy got a big hit or something. Reed comes storming in and he's challenging me. We're going chin-to-chin. I mean, we were very close to being physical, and it would have been my mistake because Ronnie was a pretty big guy. But it was the same old thing. If I'm telling him to walk a guy, he's got to walk the guy. I'm the manager; he's not the manager. So we got through that. I had probably a handful of blistering meetings, because I was a cusser and a screamer, and I didn't spare anybody's feelings about it. I knew that it could go either way with those kinds of things. But I was so anti-Ozark in my way of doing things, I probably went a little heavy along the other way. But it worked. We had the first ring and the first trophy."

After managing the Phillies to a third-place finish in 1981, Green accepted an offer to go to Chicago as the Cubs' general manager. Two things stand out in my mind about his time in the Midwest, one of them something that Phillies fans would rather forget. Remember *that* trade—the one that sent Larry Bowa and Ryne Sandberg to the Cubbies for Ivan DeJesus? Dallas was the brains behind that deal, and all I'll say is: *Hall of Fame—Ryne Sandberg—2005!* Green also brought the city of Chicago into the modern age of sports. Well, at least he brightened things up.

"I told them right from the very beginning, the reason they lost in 1969—they blew it right at the end like our '64 team did—was because *you didn't have lights.* I said, 'Your guys wore out. Day baseball wears you out as a player! You can't compete. We can't compete if we don't have lights. It's that simple!' Al, I'm telling you, I did a lot of homework. I went to a big community gathering when we first started talking about lights. They got irate and I told them, 'What other general manager has ever come to you, faced you eye-to-eye, and told you how you're supposed to win the game? Isn't that why the franchise is here? Isn't that why we're here? We're here to win, and you can't win without lights.' And they proved it in 1984. We won the National League championship but we lost the extra game, the home game, because we didn't have the lights."

In 1988, the Chicago City Council and Mayor Harold Washington (who died a week later) approved a change to the city ordinance, allowing the Cubs to install lights in Wrigley Field.

The following year, Green returned to the managerial ranks with the New York Yankees. He lasted less than a season. The Yankees had finished nine games over .500 the previous year, but fell nine games under the break-even point at 56-65 with Dallas in charge. For the first time in his career, he was fired.

"It's not a pleasant deal," Dallas recalled. "Everybody was taking bets when that was going to happen. I mean, Mr. Carpenter was selling chances on *when Dallas was going to get fired.* We talked about that a lot. But you know what? George [Steinbrenner] and I got along super. To his credit, he allowed me to do the job the way I wanted. I hired the first all non-Yankee coaching staff ever. I had four guys that had really been big league managers on that staff. And we had a pretty good team until George took over. He traded our number-one pitcher, Rick Rhoden. Dave Winfield broke down and had a back operation in Spring Training. I lost Ron Guidry immediately to an arm operation. And we ended up having just a lousy team. And yet still, when I got fired, we were only about six or eight games out of first place, and they ended up 23 out. But to George's credit, Al, he's a wonderful man. If he'd come in this room now, he'd charm the hell out of you. He just was an ogre when he came to the ballpark, that's all."

"Dallas," I went on, *"what do you think of the salaries that are being paid to major league players today?"*

"Well, being an ex-general manager, I never have begrudged guys money that puts asses into seats. That has always been my way of doing it. My gripe about our system today is that we are paying mediocre players—and a lot of players that don't even belong in the big leagues—entirely too much money. The strength of the Players Union has become paramount in the game, and almost to the point where they're running the game. Agents are running the game. The worst job in baseball today is the general manager's job. No question about it. It's a terrible job! Ruben Amaro Jr., who was my batboy in 1980, is prepared as well as anyone, but he'll have his ups and downs. He'll disappoint at times, but he's got a great nucleus and great ownership to work with, and that's a big plus. No question about that!

"Al, what is happening in baseball here the last couple of years is absolutely awesome. This is the best team I've seen in Philadelphia ever. I'm retired, so I really don't know them, but I love this team. They play hard, the fans have caught on, and I've never seen anything like this before. I knew the '50 team pretty well because I was back in that era. Of course, I'm somewhat prejudiced about my '80 team, but this team has grit, determination, gamesmanship. They slide on their bellies and play the game hard. They come to play every single day. They don't care what the score is; they're going to battle you until the last out of the ninth inning. They don't make a ruckus and they just play the baseball game the way it's supposed to be played. Obviously, they have great God-given talent, but a lot of teams have great God-given talent but don't make it work. Charlie [Manuel] really gets a big credit for that, he really does. He's done a wonderful job. If he had been managing when Danny

[Ozark] was around, he would have won a couple of rings, no question about that.

"The philosophy really started with Pope, and the philosophy has never really changed. We believe strongly that scouting and development have to be the backbone of your entire system and particularly your major league. It is proven out there. A lot of those kids are home-grown kids, and we want to continue that way. Obviously, baseball has changed. It's become big money and it's become free agents, and we didn't have to deal with that before. So ownership has become much more involved than it was back in Pope's day and my day, and we've had to make adjustments because of that. And the adjustments mainly are the ownerships' willingness to spend money. And once they got to the new ballpark era, yes, they were more than willing to continue the philosophy of developing our own kids, but we were willing to go to Jim Thome, and we were willing to go to David Bell, and we were willing to go to some of the pieces of the puzzle that we didn't have, and that has evolved even more so in David Montgomery's time."

"If you received a phone call tonight saying you have been selected to become the Commissioner of Baseball," I asked, *"would you take the job?"*

"Oh, no. That might be the second worst job. Again, you really can't decide your own destiny in baseball anymore. Even though the manager is the closest to the players where you can have a game plan and you can do your thing in the minor leagues, you still get interference, but not too much. But as you come up the ladder, the interference increases—from ownership, from the league offices in New York, from everybody else involved. The group of owners today—it has always amazed me, and George Steinbrenner was a perfect example of this—they can be so successful in their own businesses and screw up baseball as well as they have."

I also have memories of *two* Steve Carltons—the winning pitcher in Game 2 and the deciding Game 6 of the '80 World Series—and he was quite an enigma. I recall that day three years later in 1983, when most of the Phillies were celebrating their surprising pennant-clinching win in a cramped locker room in Chicago's Wrigley Field. Steve, though, was in the trainer's room with a few of his buddies like Tim McCarver, Larry Bowa, and Mike Schmidt—drinking Dom Perignon while his teammates and the news guys outside were drinking $5-a-bottle bubbly.

I met Carlton the first time I went to Spring Training in Clearwater in 1972. He had just joined the team after being traded to Philadelphia for

Rick Wise. It was getaway day and he was packing up and getting ready to leave camp and head north. I had a microphone and I asked him if he had a couple of minutes. That couple of minutes turned into about a quarter of an hour, just talking baseball—about the season coming up and about pitching. Steve was very nice to me. Up to that point, he had always been available to the media, not your buddy-buddy, mind you, but cooperative. Then later in his career, of course, came about two years of silence. Whatever generated it, I don't know for sure; I think it was something about Steve's family, something that he didn't want to see in print.

Mike Schmidt was another enigma. He was a great baseball player, certainly the best the Phillies ever had at third base, and perhaps the best third baseman to ever play the game. He definitely deserves to be in the Hall of Fame. But he always left the impression with everybody that he was cool—you know, he took it all in stride. Mike never overreacted. He was never emotional about whatever he did. His famous line was: *There's nothing like the joy of winning and the agony of reading about it the next day,* or something like that. And, of course, there was that incident in 1985 when he came out of the dugout wearing a wig and sunglasses and for a brief spell rendered the boo-birds silent. Underneath it all, the fans really wanted to embrace Mike, but he never threw out the vibes that a lot of athletes do like, *Hey, I enjoy it. I like the fans, and I'm having a wonderful time.*

At one time, we were both members of the White Manor Country Club—he belonged there for a couple of years. From what I understood, Mike would come out very early in the morning, tee it up and go out alone. He never played golf with anybody else. He would just hit balls by himself. He was a pretty good player who was very serious about the game and, like many others, had dreams of maybe playing someday on the Senior Tour.

I remember sitting down and talking to Mike and his wife, Donna, a lovely lady, shortly after that famous wig episode, and I asked, "Why don't you let the fans know that you really like them? No matter what the media says, you're playing for the fans." And Donna said, "See, Mike?" She agreed with me. And he said, "Well, you know, I'll try." But it just wasn't in him.

Mike Schmidt was a great athlete, but he just didn't have the close association that he could have had with the fans, who really love you in this town if you show any affection in return. I don't think his standoff-ish attitude hurt his game, but it would have helped his public relations if he had been friendlier. People certainly would have remembered him differently than they do now.

Another one of my favorite (and most notorious) moments covering the Phillies occurred on September 28, the day they clinched the 1983 National League pennant by beating the Chicago Cubs, 13-6. I had a cameraman who was standing on a Coke box in the corner of the smallest locker room in the major leagues—the visiting team's dressing room at Chicago's Wrigley Field. I had him elevated so he could shoot me as I waded into the crowd of media people—it was such a mob scene that you could hardly move. I was holding a microphone, but I couldn't get it up high enough for relief pitcher Al Holland to see that it was a microphone or that it had a Channel 10 logo. I tapped him on the back and he turned around. I said, "How do you feel?" To which he answered—and I was on live television—"I feel fucking great!"

Something registered in my brain: *He just said that on the air and we're live.* And I knew that they were having a great time in the control room back in Philadelphia, jumping up and down and hollering. There are some things that you didn't do in television in those days, and using the F-bomb stands at the top of the list. In all fairness, Holland didn't know he was on live TV, because I didn't have the mike in his face. I had brain-freeze after that—I had no idea what I asked him or what else I said. When I got back to Philly and arrived at the station, I was treated like a returning hero. Those were the days!

The Phillies weren't in the World Series in 1986, but the New York Mets were, and since we were part of CBS at Channel 10, the network honchos assigned us to help cover the event. The first thing I did when I arrived at Fenway Park in Boston was to walk out to left field and touch *the wall,* the fabled Green Monster! In those days, I had a portable phone that weighed about 20 pounds. So we'd sit in the Red Sox dugout and order dinner and other fun stuff.

Then, when we got to New York, we couldn't find a room because we hadn't planned on covering the Series until the last minute. Jeff Asch and I ended up near Grand Central Station in what now would be called dilapidated housing. When immigrants came across the Atlantic Ocean for the first time, this would be the place they'd stay because they didn't have any money. My door didn't have a lock on it, so I had to put a chair and a headboard against the door. In order to shave, I had to sit on the bed, because there wasn't enough room in the bathroom. The TV in the room looked like one of those 10-inch, black-and-white jobs from the 1950s and carried *four* stations.

Everything was going along pretty well until Game 6, when Billy Buckner let the ball go through his legs, with two outs in the ninth inning, to allow the Mets to tie the game. New York won to tie the Series, and I don't have to tell you what happened in Game 7.

For me, it was personal. I wasn't just a reporter, although I've forgiven Billy B for that immortal Red Sox blunder. I had accepted an invitation to attend my high school reunion, which was scheduled during the Series. After Buckner's error, I thought to myself, *Wait a minute. If this thing goes seven games, I'm going to miss my high school reunion.* And I hadn't seen the guys in a long time. So there I was, up in the press box, rooting for the Red Sox, but hoping that the thing didn't go seven games.

It turned out to be one of those weeks when nothing seemed to jell. After Game 7, I was waiting for a late-night shot underneath the stands at Fenway Park. I was going to go live to Philadelphia, and a dude was sitting as high as he could possibly be behind home plate. Suddenly, he dropped a full cup of beer. If he were a bombardier in a B-17, he couldn't have been more accurate. I thought to myself, *I can't take this anymore.* We didn't have any press seats, so we had to sit wherever we could, and a lot of times we found ourselves sitting behind a pillar or something in the press box where we couldn't even see the game. We had to watch it on television—something that I could have done in the comfort of my own living room.

Not only that, but when the whole thing was over, I caught a terrible cold. I was really sick, and I went home for about three days. I was mad at the world and I swore, *Never again am I going to cover a World Series unless the Phillies are in it!*

(((CHAPTER 14)))

A Cameo with *Rocky* and a Final Fling at Comcast

In 1990, when it was announced that *Rocky V* was going to be filmed in Philadelphia, I was invited to audition for a role as a sportscaster. The first audition was held upstairs at Channel 10 with some other people from the station participating. I ended up having three or four additional auditions as the group gradually got smaller. Finally, I found myself auditioning with the director of the film in the back yard of a house in South Philadelphia that hadn't been cleaned in 25 years. Then the filmmakers told me that I was the one chosen for the part and that they would notify me about a week before about where to go and what to do.

I was still working at WCAU-TV, of course, so five minutes before I was to go into the studio for the 11 o'clock show, I got a telephone call: "We're shooting at 5:30 tomorrow morning. Be in the basement of Convention Hall. We'll feed you breakfast." I arrived at 5:30, and Stan Hochman was already there with his *Philadelphia Daily News* colleague Elmer Smith. So was Stu Nahan, the former sportscaster at Channel 48 who was now working in California. He had done all of the previous *Rocky* movies. A lot of other people were there who were going to be extras. The crew was going to shoot a press conference in a room in the front of the building, so they filled it up with all the extras and placed us as the reporters.

Stan and I both were given some lines. At first, I had four lines in my script and, finally, three lines. The press conference was held with the new heavyweight champion of the world, Tommy "Machine" Gunn. He would eventually lose his title to Sylvester Stallone, who regained his crown with a furious rally. The role of Machine Gunn was played by a real fighter, Tommy Morrison, who had been personally selected for the part by Stallone. Morrison later defeated George Foreman in a unanimous 12-round decision for the World Boxing Association heavyweight crown.

We were assigned to ask questions. Sylvester was there, and it got to be noontime. We had been in the basement for almost seven hours when we were given a break, and then we came back and went on for another three hours. There was a reason for the length of time. If Stallone didn't like a scene, we did it over again. He really was on top of things. That's the way he worked. He ran the whole show. And it wasn't so much that he complained that something didn't look good or wasn't shot well, because it was videotaped before filming. But Stallone had a lot to say about the lines that were being said, where the people were sitting, and how they were shot. We'd frequently hear him say things like, "Change that line" or "Why don't we try something else?"

I did my lines like all the other actors. By now it was early evening, and there must have been about 50 background guys on the set who never said anything. Most of them were getting ready to hop on the train, because these guys had another gig in New York or Washington or Baltimore. That's how they made their living—they were extras, which fascinated me because I was in showbiz now, and I was one of them.

As time went by, I started to get phone calls from people that I hadn't seen in years: "I see you're in *Rocky V*. And I'm thinking to myself, *How do they know that?* Well, I didn't find out until the last minute that I had two lines in the preview, which was about a half of what I did in the actual filming. I was excited, so I sent my wife and daughter down to the Wayne Theatre near our home to check out the preview. Later, I went and watched it myself. Now I was really excited.

The premiere was held in Philadelphia and a large crowd was there, along with my wife and daughter. There was no traditional red carpet, but I sat right across from W. Wilson Goode, and the mayor and I had popcorn together. Everybody that I knew, including all the sports people, and all the politicians that I didn't know, filled up the place. It was wonderful. Then the movie began and I couldn't wait because I didn't know what happened prior to *my part,* as I called it. Then my time came on the big screen and I said to Tommy: "You may be the champion of the world, but you're no Rocky!" The audience stood up and cheered. For a second I thought to myself: *Well, they appreciate the work I've done.* It occurred to me that I had just uttered *my line,* but for one brief moment I was the star. And then came the realization that the only true star was Rocky. To this day, I still get royalties three times a year, because every time *Rocky V* plays on TV, is rented, or makes money in any way, the revenue all goes to Hollywood and the production company distributes everyone's share. My last check was for $45.

I've been blessed to be honored a number of times by the good people of Philadelphia, and it's really difficult to single out one particular award that stands out above the others. So I'm going to be diplomatic about this and mention some cherished distinctions alphabetically.

I had been the regular master of ceremonies for the annual Big 5 Hall of Fame luncheons for a number of years, but nothing prepared me for the day when I walked into the Palestra in 1993 to find out that one more presentation had been added to the ceremony. It was for me! I was the first media person to be so honored, which was just an incredible thrill. These coaches, players, and writers were my friends and colleagues. I don't think my eyes were dry for long. Knowing the significance of such an award to a Big 5 player made it even more meaningful. I knew that I had succeeded among people that I cherished and held in great respect. If you walk around the Palestra, take a look at the mural on one of the walls with a big picture of me in the background with other broadcasters. You'll notice that I can't help grinning from ear to ear.

The Broadcast Pioneers are composed of talented people who have spent many years in the business. When I was voted into their Hall of Fame in 2009 at the Bala Golf Club, I guess I qualified because I had been in the business for 50 years, more than four decades of that time in Philadelphia. As I told the crowd, "When I got here in 1964, I rode a covered wagon up Conestoga Road and that qualified me as a pioneer."

My good friend Mort Crim was also honored that night. And the reason was because I really politicked—something I otherwise never do. I kept saying, "Vince Leonard is in; we got Bill Custer in" (which, of course, was posthumously). And then I said, "I don't want to go in unless Mort's in with me." Jessica Savitch had also been inducted after she had passed away. As you know by now, our Eyewitness News group was very close. In concluding my short remarks (which is itself something remarkable), I compared this day to a moment in sports history. Back in 1974, when I walked into the Flyers' locker room, I saw on the blackboard a message from Coach Fred Shero before Game 6 of the Stanley

Cup Finals: "Win Tonight and We'll Walk Together Forever!" So I said, "The circle is now complete forever, and I'd like to think as of tonight, the five of us will walk together again."

I got all choked up that night because I meant it. This wasn't a *me;* this was a *we.* It wasn't the fact that we were good on the air, but that we were extremely close. I could have taken up an hour just talking about the adventures that we had. I told them about flying down to Louisville for the Kentucky Derby with Vince and Mort, and staying overnight with the Colonel. We had meetings like that all the time. We'd go out on picnics, we went on trips, we went out to Denver to see Bill. We went to Vail, Colorado and had a reunion there, and before Bill passed away, we were planning to have another one on Mackinac Island in Upper Michigan. But we always stayed in touch. It was the only time in my life when I worked with people that I was truly close to. We were family, and I wanted everyone to know that. I was extremely grateful that the Broadcast Pioneers recognized us, and I thanked them.

I was nominated 20 times for prestigious Emmy Awards presented by the Mid-Atlantic Chapter of the National Academy of Television Arts and Sciences, and was fortunate enough to win ten of them. The first one was absolutely the best, but they were all extremely gratifying. Jessica Savitch, who by then had become a big star and an anchor at NBC in New York, awarded the first one to me for Outstanding Sports Reporting as sports director in 1983. This was the chapter's first awards gala at the Adams Mark Hotel on City Avenue, across from WCAU and WPVI. I jumped out of the chair, completely forgot to kiss my wife (not too smart!), ran up, and accepted the award. It felt great to be honored by my friends. Later I won for other features that I'd done on the air or for one of the other half-dozen categories in sports.

At the beginning, the awards were pretty much concentrated in Philadelphia, but the competition has since been expanded to include some 650 industry professionals throughout Pennsylvania. Stations enter tapes that they consider worthy—they are sent to judges working at undisclosed stations out of town by NATAS, the National Academy of Television Arts and Sciences. But you don't know if you've won until the night of the dinner. I have been asked occasionally to evaluate tape from other cities.

Locally, I was really flattered when a 1979 *Philadelphia Daily News* poll named me the "Best Sportscaster in Philadelphia," and, after I retired, when *Daily News* sportswriter Kevin Mulligan wrote that I was

"Arguably, Philly's most recognizable, most popular and best sports anchor ever."

Another local thrill came in 2011 when I was elected to the Philadelphia Sports Hall of Fame. After 50 years of covering games from the bleachers, I was selected to enter the playing field with some of the greatest athletes and coaches who represented the City of Brotherly Love. I'm honored to be with them.

In 2001, I was inducted into the Philadelphia Jewish Sports Hall of Fame. Temple's longtime sports publicist Al Shrier, a Hall of Famer himself, was instrumental in getting that organization off the ground. Temple's venerable basketball coach Harry Litwack was there and hit the wall with a sledgehammer, a tradition that symbolized the new addition. I served as master of ceremonies for a number of their events at the beginning and presented one of my Emmys to the group's display room as a token of my affection.

To cap it all off, on September 25, 2010, the Mid-Atlantic Chapter of NATAS presented me with its prestigious Board of Governors Award, recognizing my career longevity, lifetime achievements, and significant contributions to the television industry. The good news is that the presentation was made during the 28th annual Emmy Awards ceremony, a swanky black-tie event at the Loews Hotel in Philadelphia. The bad news is that I wasn't there to receive the award, and never even saw the video showing various stages of my career that people tell me was one of the highlights of the very moving ceremony.

And why wasn't I there? Let me explain, my friends.

Before the event, I pulled off something that only I can do. I was having some medical problems, including a bad hip, and had to make sure that I didn't overdo it. But I arrived at the cocktail reception feeling just great. I wasn't drinking because I was on medication, and didn't even think to take some water to stay hydrated. I was overwhelmed with the number of people there that I hadn't seen in years and, apparently, I didn't sit down for almost an hour. Just before going in for the dinner, I got dizzy and fainted. They called the medics and I was taken to Pennsylvania Hospital. The doctors there decided that it wasn't serious, but they told me to check with my physician on Monday. He said that I was fine, but just a little dehydrated. My phone never stopped ringing for an entire week afterward. Michael Klein, the *Philadelphia Inquirer* columnist, asked me what I would have said at the dinner. I gave him the short version: *My career started in December 1954, and it ended three times—in*

1998 at Channel 10, five years later at Comcast, and tonight—the official end of a long and wonderful career.

Even though I wasn't there for all the festivities, it turned out to be a moment in my life that I will never forget. My friend Bill Baldini accepted the special Emmy for me, and he said that it was followed by damned near a one-minute standing ovation. Believe me, I was extremely humbled, especially when I think of the long line of distinguished recipients that preceded me, starting with Walter Annenberg, who built Triangle Publications into a world-class organization and later became Ambassador to Great Britain. This award was certainly the exclamation point to my 50 years of broadcasting.

Speaking of Bill Baldini, I have to tell you that he was the best TV news reporter in the city. On several occasions, he was my sixth-man designated hitter. He went to the big stories out of town when major sports stories crossed over to news. Bill was with me in London for the American Bowl, in Kansas City for the 1980 World Series, in Buffalo and Edmonton for the Stanley Club Finals, and in Phoenix where Penn State won the national title. But he wasn't going to New Orleans for Super Bowl XV when the Eagles played the Raiders. The reason was that another reporter had complained that she never went on these trips. A cameraman passed the story on to Jim Murray, the general manager of the Eagles. Murray then called the station and told them that if Bill didn't go, WCAU TV would lose its access to the team. Bill was added to the traveling party.

When it comes to great memories, I'll never forget the day that I retired from Channel 10. Mayor Rendell gave me a Liberty Bell and named a day just for me. Eagles coach Ray Rhodes presented me with a football jersey with my name and number (10) on the back. Paul Owens gave me a Phillies jersey. The Flyers gave me autographed hockey sticks; I kept Bobby Clarke's and distributed the others to friends.

My final night on the air was special, and I know that Dave Coskey, who was then the 76ers' promotions guru, had a hand in setting it up. Coach Maurice Cheeks and World B Free came in and gave me a Sixers jersey with my name and number on it. It really got emotional. I have no memory of what I said when I saw them. Cheeks had tears in his eyes and I did, too, because I had no idea that they were coming.

And speaking of Dave Coskey, who has been a great friend ever since his younger days in Villanova's sports information office, he was the guy responsible for adding a few years to my career two weeks after I retired from Channel 10. He asked me to do something for Comcast SportsNet—the exciting, new, all-sports all-the-time TV venture in town—and host a show called *Where Are They Now?* We did profiles of such former Philadelphia sports celebrities as Roman Gabriel of the Eagles and Bobby Jones of the 76ers. One thing led to another. I didn't have a contract and I just got paid for what I did, but eventually I ended up doing a daily 30-minute interview show called *Spotlight* half an hour before *Daily News Live.* In addition there were some monthly *Sports Classics* shows and other pre- and postgame shows, including locker room interviews after all the Eagles home games.

After Robin Roberts died in May 2010, I got phone calls from all over the place: "I saw your interview with Robin Roberts." The Comcast people made a copy for me and after I watched it again, I understood why the Phillies Hall of Fame pitcher was the most respected man in baseball.

Working at Comcast was a lot of fun. Not only did it give me the distinction of being the only sportscaster ever to work at *five* stations in the same market, but I was traveling and I was doing nothing but sports once again. And I thought, *This is what ESPN must be like!* Now we had the sports angle at Channel 17 many years go, but we also had a whole lot of other programming there, like Wee Willie Webber doing his show for kids.

When I began working for Comcast, I was told by some of my colleagues there that they heard that the station didn't want to hire me. They knew that I had already retired, and when someone said, "Let's bring Al in," one of the bosses commented, "I thought that this is going to be a young organization." Anyway, I ended up working there for five years, and I loved every minute of it. I had a lot of friends there, really good people. I wasn't making a lot of money—that wasn't the object—I just loved working. When I retired in 2004, I did so because I thought it was time. I was 76 years old and I had spent more than 45 years in the business in the City of Brotherly Love.

And besides, Comcast gave me the opportunity to conduct my all-time favorite interview!

((((CHAPTER 15))))

Wilt Chamberlain Tells All...for the Final Time

D ave Coskey, the former Vice President of Marketing and Opera-
tions of the 76ers, told me that Wilt Chamberlain was always elusive anytime the subject of an interview came up. But when Dave mentioned my name to him, suddenly everything was okay.

The phone rang in my house. My wife answered and excitedly said
to me, "WILT CHAMBERLAIN'S ON THE PHONE! WHAT IS WILT
CHAMBERLAIN DOING ON THE PHONE TALKING TO YOU?" I
hadn't filled her in yet, but she was extremely impressed and told everybody, "Do you know who called Al?"

So on April 29, 1999, we went out to Los Angeles where I spent almost the whole afternoon with the Big Dipper, taping an interview that
lasted for two and a half hours. Then he took us on a tour of his house.
Afterward, the two of us talked in the kitchen for about an hour about
everything—not just about basketball or the NBA—but about anything
that came to our minds. I left there with a great feeling that after all these
years he had come to understand that he was *Wilt Chamberlain*. There
was nothing he could do about it. He finally accepted that fact and was
content and at peace. Then less than six months later, on October 14,
1999, he passed away at the age of 63.

Here are the highlights of my interview, short segments of which ran
on WCAU-TV and Comcast SportsNet. Wilt opened the conversation
by emphasizing how fortunate he was to be financially able to do

anything he desired. "Before I was so greedy," he explained. "Now when I make a deal, it's for charity."

Explaining how he generated considerable income during his days in the NBA, Wilt said: "I was lucky. I had good business friends—all the way back to [76ers owners] Ike Richman and Eddie Gottlieb, the Kutchers [entrepreneurs in New York's Catskill Mountains], and a whole bunch of other people who passed on their business skills to me. I was bright enough to realize that they were always trying to help me, but while I was playing, I owned nightclubs, which was somewhat frowned upon. One time a league official said to me, 'Wilt, we don't like the idea that you own Small's Paradise in Harlem.' 'Well, I could understand that some bad people come to these places and so forth, and there are sometimes issues with guns and things like that,' I replied. And there is the question, *Who has the gun and who's using the gun?* I ran some businesses—jazz clubs and music clubs—and I love music. And then I said to them, 'You also must understand something else: I make about five times a year there more than what you are giving me. If I'm going to give up anything, unfortunately it has to be basketball.' But in the end, they made me give up this club.

"I was asked once at a press conference in Milan, Italy, 'If you weren't Wilt Chamberlain, what would you have been?' I looked out the window and saw there was an exhibit outside about Leonardo da Vinci, and I said that I would have liked to be like him. Well, if you know anything about Leonardo da Vinci, he was an architect, a builder, a sculptor, a painter. He wrote books. I mean, how he could possibly do all the things he did is beyond me. No 20 guys could have done what Leonardo da Vinci did.

"But in the real sense of the world, I've gone out and done a lot of land developing. I do a lot of architectural types of things and designing—even to building and interior designing. I would probably have done two things—either gotten into being an architect or a builder or ventured into commercials, because I can see that commercials run the little world out there—as can be proven by guys like Michael Jordan. So owning some commercial entity of some kind where I could write and distribute them would be ideal, because it still stokes me to see a great commercial. I watch TV sometimes just to see the great ones."

Wilt admitted that he still watches TV "24 hours a day," is still an insomniac, and consumes an "unreal" amount of liquids. "I'm afraid that I am an insomniac, and that's a curse that came from basketball. When I played basketball in the evenings, even at the time when I was a kid, you'd play a seven o'clock game or a nine o'clock game. And then after the game you're starving, but also you're a little nervous in the stomach. So you eat a little later on, and even later on. I mean, what I could eat even back in those days was unbelievable. So I'd even go to bed on two turkeys, ten hamburgers, four hoagies, and a couple of steak sandwiches. I've refined my drinking, though. I no longer drink two quarts of 7-Up every day. Now I drink a gallon of lemonade or a gallon of orange juice or a gallon of tangerine juice. I still drink 7-Up or I mix it with just about everything I drink. I am a liquid person. The amount of liquid I can consume is unreal.

"I weigh less now than my last two or three years while playing in the NBA. I'm weighing about 310 right now. I weighed about 320 or 330 last year. I work out every day—run and do all these machines. What I have given up: About two years ago, I'd go down to the beaches of Santa Monica, and I'd challenge all the great volleyball players down there. We had four-man games. Some of the guys you see playing now in the Olympics, I played against them every day. And they loved to play against me. They loved to kick my butt. They liked the idea of beating old Wilt. I'm in two Halls of Fame, which I'm very proud of. I was one of 20 people inducted into the International Volleyball Hall of Fame last year [1998] for beach volleyball.

"I also played tennis and paddle tennis. There's almost nothing I don't play, although I don't play golf. That little golf ball is too far from my eyes to focus on and much too small, and I have too many friends like Bill Russell who are consumed by it. And most of them fib about it. I haven't got an honest word out of Bill Russell yet about how good a golfer he is. But I ask his friends and they shake their heads and say, 'No!' It's just degrees of lies. I hope people won't take this personally wrong, but even Michael Jordan has been lying to a degree about just how good he is. I go to all the tennis matches, and some of the CBS hierarchy tell me that they've seen Jordan play and that he may make a little mistake on the card here, and a little this and a little that. But he isn't as good as he has led people to believe he is."

Wilt said that he loves having his "dance card" full. "I had one lull period," he explained. "I moved to Hawaii because we were going to try to build a major arena in the hopes that one day we could bring an NBA franchise there, and we did something that had never been done before.

One of my friends said to me, 'You know, Wilt, we can file for the air rights over the bus station downtown, because no one owns the air rights. As we build up top, we can have underground parking, whatever.' The mayor told us that this was correct, so we got the air rights to build this wonderful arena with hotels and everything. But the Honolulu city administration changed and it never happened. But it was a clever idea.

"I got a little lax while I was in Hawaii. All I did was play racquetball. I got involved in a couple of music clubs. But all of a sudden, after a couple of years, I said to myself, *What am I doing here?* I was working on my tan. Most people thought I was Samoan because I was walking around barefoot all the time. So I thought it was time for me to get back to things that I had been doing."

Asked if he was still a huge sports fan, Wilt replied, "I would say there's no one bigger. I was sitting here the other day talking to a guy about boxing, about my younger days in Philadelphia when my father would take me to matches and I'd be naming this fight and this boxer, and this guy said, 'I can't believe you know that much about boxing.' The point is I am still a tennis junkie—I know everyone in tennis, and I go to the U.S. Open almost every year. I missed one recently because I was on business in Argentina. I'm still a basketball junkie. I watch five or six games. There are three satellites in my house right here and three satellites in my restaurants. I'll watch everything. I'll watch football, Australian rules football, regular football, or European football. I'm also a baseball guy, and sports are just what's happening in my life. I attend mainly high school and very few college games, some track and field meets. Almost never go to pro games."

Wilt said that his "biggest single regret" is not having participated in the Olympics, perhaps in track and field. "But that was because of logistics. If I had been raised in California, there's no doubt in my mind that I would have been in the Olympics—maybe as a quarter-miler or high jumper or shot-putter or triple-jumper or something of that nature, because the weather was more conducive to those kinds of things than in the East. But I was raised in the great city of Philadelphia where they had the greatest basketball players in the world, and I grew these long, long legs, and they said, 'Hey, man, you should be playing basketball.' My brother, who is older than I, played basketball, and they talked me into a game that at the time I was not very fond of. I was fond of anything where you could run. Just like Jim Thorpe—just get out there and run. I always thought basketball was for, you know, a little softer people who played the game. I used to tease my brother about that. He wanted to beat me up for saying he was a softie. But I wasn't really very much in love with basketball.

"But then we had a group of guys—Vince Miller, Howard Johnson, Marty Hughes and others—we all got together in seventh grade. Several of us came at the same time. We had this thing going that we all wanted to be some time on the starting team at Overbrook High School, because great players like Jackie Moore and Hal Lear were there before us. We had all these incredible guys to look up to. And then we had the Philadelphia Warriors with Jack George and Joe Fulks scoring 60 or so points, and Paul Arizin, who was everybody's dream. Everybody wanted to have a jump shot like Paul Arizin. Then you had Tom Gola at La Salle, and Villanova had two All-Americans, Bob Schafer and Jack Devine, on their team. One of the great stories in high school on our team was that Villanova asked us to have some scrimmages against them where no scores were kept. So we went and scrimmaged these two All-Americans and a school that was ranked two or three in the nation in college basketball. And yes, *we* kept the score."

Asked if the nickname *Wilt the Stilt* bothers him, he replied, "Yes, but it was appropriate. I was this long, angular, skinny guy, who was totally all legs. It was Jack Ryan who thought of that name in the Philadelphia *Bulletin*, and I never liked it. When I go out and sign things for charities, some people ask me to sign it *Wilt the Stilt*, and I kind look at them and think, *Well, they're paying $75 or so for the autograph*, and I say, 'Okay, I'll sign Wilt the Stilt. I can't even remember how to spell Stilt. How do you spell Stilt?'

"When I was a little guy, they called me *Dippy*, and I turned it into the *Big Dipper*. We had a guy in the neighborhood who gave everyone nicknames. A lot of people thought it was because I dipped under doors, but it was really because I looked a little 'dippy' when I was six or seven years old. It wasn't anything flattering. But it became a term of endearment with all my high school buddies and all the people who came to see me play. The only person who called me *Wilt* was my mother. Later, a few people called me *Norman*, because Wally Jones always called me that. But even my nieces and nephews call me *Uncle Dippy*.

"I started to grow at a rather early age. One summer in fourth grade, I grew about six and a half inches and when I was 14 years old, I was six-eleven and a half. I was a bashful, somewhat reticent type of person. I stuttered a lot and was not very secure. I had these long, skinny legs. I remember that when we started playing basketball, I had to wear these shorts, and I would try to wear these high socks with a rubber band around them. That was only to try to make the legs look a little fatter with the high socks. Because my legs were so skinny for a guy my size, I was embarrassed by them. But then after I got somewhat good, I realized that people weren't looking at my legs—they were looking at what I was doing. Then it wasn't so bad. But I really wasn't a pretty picture when I was young, not until basketball."

Wilt explained why he, the greatest player in the city's history, didn't stay in Philadelphia and go to a local college. "There are several reasons. The only one negative one is that I remember them asking coach Ken Loeffler if he was going to recruit me for La Salle. And Ken said, 'No. I like six-six or six-seven guys who are really mobile and can do it all.' I always wanted to ask him, *Well, what is mobility? I think I got a little mobility.* But that was his choice. I always remember that hurt me when I read about that. But my second choice of all the schools to go to was the University of Pennsylvania, because I was a track lover and the Penn Relays and the way that the U. of P. treated track and field was to my liking.

"But Red Auerbach was coaching me at Kutcher's Country Club up in the Catskills then. I knew that the NBA had a thing called the territorial draft, and he said to me, 'How would you like to go to Harvard?' I knew that Harvard was prestigious and all that, but I never even dreamed about going there to college. And he said, 'I can get you a Governor's grant.' Then he said, 'How are your grades?' I always had great grades. Red and I weren't really on the best of terms most of the time, and needless to say, I didn't wind up at Harvard. [Had Wilt done so, the Celtics would have had territorial rights to select him in the player draft.] But Eddie Gottlieb beat him to the punch, though. In 1955, Eddie drafted me out of high school, because I was still in his territory and Harry Litwack had heard up in the mountains that Red was going to have me go to Harvard and make me the territorial draft. So Eddie heard that and took me in the draft. Red had trouble with me most of the time, anyway. He had trouble getting me to go to practice when I wanted to make money. He had trouble with me about a whole lot of other things."

Wilt claimed that he once blocked 27 shots in a game at Phoenix, and said that the one thing in basketball that he regretted was that the

NBA didn't keep blocked shots as an official statistic. "That's because every time I see a shot blocked now, I hear, 'Oh that's how Bill Russell used to block them.' One time Bill came to me and asked, 'Wilt, have you played against this guy [Walt] Bellamy yet?' I said, 'Yeah, I was just in a game against him a couple of days ago in Fort Wayne, Indiana. The first 14 shots he took, I blocked 13.' Bill said, 'That boy is going to kill us because, when he plays, he's going to make blocking shots look so easy. People are going to think that blockings shots is nothing if you can block that many shots in a game.' I said, 'He'll learn,' and sure enough he did—he learned to take jump shots from the corner.

"They talk now about my shot-blocking expertise, but when I was a young kid in high school and a young kid in college, it was my defense they talked about much more than my offense. Al, I know you're old enough to remember my first game as a pro. In my first game in New York, I had something like 41 points and 34 rebounds. The *New York Post* and Jack Kiser in the *Philadelphia Daily News* wrote about the game, and they said that the real Wilt Chamberlain wasn't about the points or rebounds, it was how I destroyed them defensively and took them completely out of the rhythm and so forth. What I want to know—and I'll ask you, Al, because you've been around as long as anybody, why do they never talk about my heroics on defense or shot blocking?"

"*You once scored 100 points in a game and averaged 50 points a game in the NBA,*" I explained. "*You averaged better than 48 minutes a game, including playoffs and overtime games, and NBA games are only 48 minutes long. You scored an innumerable number of points, and that's what sports are all about. They never look at the other end of basketball. They do now a little bit, but basically you earn your money hitting home runs in baseball and scoring in basketball.*"

"All right. I get what you're saying," Wilt replied. "But I want to ask the public another question. There are records that I'm proud of. The ones that come to mind the most to me are averaging 27.5 rebounds a game, or a lifetime of averaging almost 23 points. But just go for one year right now—averaging 27.5 rebounds a game or playing 48.4 minutes a game, averaging 50.5 points a game for a whole season, or getting 55 rebounds in a game. Which one of those records is the most meaningful and would be the hardest to break?"

"*Rebounding, probably because they didn't keep offensive rebounding statistics, just cumulative stats,*" I said. "*In order to average that many rebounds a game, you can't just have ten in one game. The trouble with your numbers, Wilt, is that they're overwhelming and they're tough to digest. But those of us who saw you play, we understand. But if no one saw you play, they couldn't relate to it, like I can't relate to the number of years it takes to get to another galaxy. You were unique. You were the first seven-foot basketball player who could play the game at both ends of the floor and you were 'normal-sized.' You could run like a deer. You weren't big and slow like George Mikan, and you weren't fat and cumbersome like Bob Kurland and those kinds of guys. And you still are unique today. Those of us that are old enough to know can only say that the two greatest athletes maybe in our lifetime are you and Ali. Now in all deference to Bill Russell and certainly Kareem and everyone else, someone had to set the standard—and you set the standard."*

Asked about pressure he experienced as a youngster because expectations were so high, Wilt said, "I remember Phog Allen, when he came to visit my mother, he said to her, 'Your son is a rare talent and I could take two Phi Beta Kappa's and two coeds and we will definitely win the national championship at Kansas.' That's just a highlight of what people expected of me. So when we didn't win the national championship, people said we didn't do what we were expected to do. We played against a team that was number one in the nation in North Carolina. We lost in triple overtime by one point and we were number two. That's when people started to term me a loser, because I didn't do what some people thought was just the natural thing—win championships.

"In 1953, my sophomore year, I lost my first major high school game to a very good team called West Catholic for the Philadelphia city championship. They beat us, 54-42, by triple-teaming me the entire game, but I still scored 29 points. Now I go to the University of Kansas, and we lost that game by one point in triple overtime to North Carolina. Then I'm in the pro's, and I'll guarantee you, Al Meltzer, because I love numbers—if you can give me 10 points in all those seven games that we played against the Boston Celtics, instead of Bill Russell having 11 rings, I would have eight or nine. It was just a matter of 10 points in all those games. We lost more games by one point, by two points, by one point, by two points. I mean, Don Nelson takes a shot. It hits the back of the rim and bounces up to the Big Dipper where it kisses the stars, bounces back and goes in. Later I'm called for a goaltending by Mendy Rudolph in the corner on a shot that I take out of the air from Tom Heinshon. I've never forgotten those games that we lost by one or two points.

"I got into a very heated argument with one of my favorite people—my coach Alex Hannum—because he said, 'You know the only thing in sports that matters is winning.' I said, 'Alex, to me what matters is to give it the best that you've got!' He said, 'No. It's all about winning.' And he and I would go into tirades over this issue. I've lost so many games by one or two points that could have changed my career. My disappointment is that some people view me as a loser and other guys as winners because players like Michael Jordan won the gold ring more that I did.

"Meanwhile, other things were going wrong that affected my career. They were changing rules to stop me from doing this or from doing that. I didn't really mind. I remember they widened the lane for two years in a row. That started with George Mikan because he was so good. They widened it for George and they widened it twice for me. After my third year, after I got 50 points a game, they knew that widening the lane was not going to be the answer. When I was in college, my coach Phog Allen was an exponent for the 12-foot basket. Now he was a very bright man, but he was totally wrong there, because if you have a 12-foot basket, that means all the trajectory of the shots coming off of there will be higher. But who does that give the advantage to? The big man. Once he got me, he stopped doing that, but he used to have a 12-foot basket in the gym. What people don't realize, 77 percent of rebounds taken in a given game are taken below the rim, not above the rim. So it isn't how big you are.

"When I'm bragging about myself, I say to people, 'You can take Kareem Abdul-Jabbar. You take Olajuwon. You take Patrick Ewing and David Robinson—four guys who have over 60 or 70 years of experience in the NBA. How many rebound championships did it bring for those athletes who are all going to be in the Hall of Fame? Kareem with his agility. The smartness of the Admiral and how he's built. Olajuwon, quick and fast with great feet and so forth. Patrick with his talent. They're still playing. People like Wes Unseld and Charles Barkley, who aren't that big, have won titles. I think Kareem and Robinson each won one, but we're talking 60 years, and eras aren't as competitive today as then.'"

"Wilt, you set standards and changed the rules for people making money in the NBA," I said. "No one in any other sport ever had as much influence. I remember Chicago Bulls coach Johnny Kerr telling a player once in an airport, 'Do you know how much you owe that guy? He has set the standard for what kind of money you're making. If it wasn't for him, you wouldn't be making anywhere near the kind of money you're making.' I'll never forgot that because it wasn't millions in those days. You changed

the game. You set the pay scale. You changed the rules, and no one else in any sport has ever done that. They may have scored more points or won more titles, but no one had as much influence. Does this register with you?"

"Well, one personal thing that registered with me, I played for 13-14 years. From the year I came in until the year I left, I made more money than anyone else in the league. I don't know if any other athlete can say that, whether it be Babe Ruth or Wayne Gretzky or Michael Jordan. I know Jordan left making the most money, but I came in making the most money. Haskell Cohen, who handled publicity for the NBA at the time, was a good friend of mine who gave me the job at Kutcher's. I said to him, 'One day, I want to make six figures in the NBA.' And he said to me, 'Wilton, that's impossible!' He said basketball does not have that type of thing going for it, and guys like Bob Petit and Bob Cousy both were making $22,500. So I said to him, 'I will never play for that. I'll go out there and become a carpenter or a painter. I can make some money.' Haskell laughed at me. 'That's never going to happen,' he said. The first time it happened, I went to him and said I was making six figures, and you said it was never going to happen. He looked at me and said, 'Well, you got me there.'

"Back in the late '50s and early '60s, there was a great camaraderie among guys of color, or black, or whatever you wanted to call them at that time, because they knew that they were pioneering something. They knew that more was being asked of them than their counterparts. They had a respect for each other. I had to do an article recently to set the record straight, because Jerry West said that he thought that I was jealous of Elgin Baylor or Elgin Baylor was jealous of me—similar to what's now going on in the Lakers organization between Kobe Bryant and Shaquille O'Neal.

"I took offense to that, and Elgin took even more offense to it than I did. So I called the paper and explained to them that I knew Elgin ever since I was in high school. He would invite me down to Washington to play. We played against each other out of respect for one another. He used to say, 'Come on down to Washington so I can kick your butt.' And I'd say, 'I'll be right down.' I'd go down to Washington and unfortunately for me most of the time, he did just that. He kicked our butts and we'd be back the next week. But there was never any personal jealousy, but I was jealous of the moves that he made that no one else could do. I was jealous of Oscar Robertson, who could make a game of basketball look like sitting in a rocking chair. But that doesn't mean that you're going to take that jealousy out on the floor and maybe not give the ball to him.

"I came to the LA Lakers averaging about 34 or 35 points a career, and I ended up averaging 11 or 12 points. There were times when I took no shots in a game—none. From taking 63 shots in a 100-point game to taking none. I thought this was the best thing for me to do for the team—even though there were times when my teammates were asking me to take the shots. Look at that 33-game winning streak that we had. There were times I scored 33, 34, 35 points, but some games I scored eight, nine, seven, six—whatever it took. Sometimes, I feel a little bit dismayed because people maybe didn't fully appreciate that, because you hear this phrase all the time—*He's unselfish*—as the guy passes the ball to a guy driving through traffic. There is no such thing as *unselfish* basketball. Either you play correctly or incorrectly. Either that was a good play or a bad play. It's not unselfish, because if I give you the ball and you score, do I get an assist? And isn't an assist as big as anything else out there?

"If they want to talk about being unselfish, I was unselfish. I was the greatest scorer in the history of the game, and I was giving the ball to Keith Erickson, to Gail Goodrich, to anybody. Jerry West was averaging 25-26 points a game before I got there, and he was averaging the same thing when I played there. Gail Goodrich wasn't averaging anything, and he ended up averaging 26. Elgin was averaging about the same. I took away from none of those guys' averages but my own. But people said, 'Well, he was playing a different kind of game.' Well, yeah, it was a different kind of game where I didn't see myself scoring, but that's the way I think basketball is really supposed to be played.

"Billy Cunningham once talked to me about my shooting while we were walking down the tunnel to a game. He said to me, 'Wilt, you know you have a penchant for doing something no one else can do. Why give that up? Nobody in the history of the game can score like you. And that's your signature. If you stop doing that, you're doing something that's demeaning to yourself. You're also not allowing the fans to see something that you can do better than anybody else. I think you should never give up shooting—shoot your 35 shots a game and remember that!'

"*Wilt,*" I said, "*you played on the greatest team in the history of the NBA, the 1966-67 Philadelphia 76ers. When you won your first championship with that team, you were the happiest man in America. But a little over a year later, you were traded to the Los Angeles Lakers. Is there a story there?*"

"Yes, there are two stories. One, I had become very compassionate and truly respectful and friendly with Alex Hannum. Jack Ramsay and

Irv Kosloff called me into the office and offered me the coaching job. It had been a great regular season. We had just moved into the Spectrum, had the league's best record [62-20], and I won my third straight MVP award. But we ended up losing another heartbreaker to the Celtics in the seventh game of the Eastern Finals after being up three games to one. For some odd reason, I thought to myself that Alex also wanted to be a general manager along with being the coach, because he wanted to bring in who he wanted to bring in—and you had the other guy [Ramsay], who was a great basketball mind. So anyway, they offered me the coaching job and the coaching job was hinging on: We want you to coach if Hal Greer agrees. And I thought to myself, *What does that have to do with it?* And I asked, 'So what happens to Alex?'

'Well, we're going to get rid of Alex.'

"I was not about to step into someone's job who I thought should be there, and so I said, 'Well, thank you, but no thanks. Thank you, but I really can't do that.'

"I realized that Alex was not going to be there because they already fired him. So I came back out here to California where we were living. Soon afterwards, my father died from cancer, and I was really a little angry after losing that heartbreaking series to Boston. Martin Luther King had gotten killed—and I had asked that we stop playing so they could get some solidarity from the situation. I was really very distraught about that whole situation, especially about my father and about the fact that they fired the guy that got us there. And so that was it for me. I came out here and I just told my family, 'I've had enough of basketball. I'm going to give it up.'

"While I was out in LA, I bought a travel agency for my brother. The agency was run by a guy named Bloomingdale, who was a friend of Jack Kent Cooke. We got to talking and he said, 'Well, what about next year?' I said I don't know because I'm going to give up basketball. He told Jack Kent Cooke, 'Wilt is here and he's unhappy and would like to give up basketball.' But at the same time, I met a guy, Sam Schulman, the owner of the Seattle SuperSonics, and he had some friends who lived in Vancouver, Canada. I fell very much in love with Vancouver, and Schulman got wind that I didn't want to play anymore—period. Then he tried to talk me into coming to play for Seattle.

"But Cooke said, 'If you're going to play anywhere, this is where you need to be.' Jack was like my coach from Kansas—he could talk anybody

out of anything. And since my father was here—and I thought these were
the last days he was going to be around—I chose the Lakers over Seattle.
And when I told people back in Philly that I basically was going to retire,
they had no choice but either to try to trade me or get nothing for me. I
had already convinced myself that I was totally gone. I had already played
for nine or ten years. When I came into the league, the average guy
played for three or four years and the good guys played for six or seven.
So that was a long time. I had already had my career. I was ready to move
on to something else. It wasn't like I was jumping out of the game after
one or two years. I'd had it. I was up to here with the losses. I was up to
here with what was going on.

"Kosloff and I had somewhat like a bittersweet relationship. That's
because my man, of course, was Ike Richman, and before Ike died, he got
me to come from San Francisco to Philadelphia during the 1964-65 season, because I didn't want to leave San Francisco at that time. I enjoyed
where I was, and I was going to go back and play with the Globetrotters at
the time. So he said, 'Wilt, I own half of the team, and I'll tell you what—if
you come to us, I will give you one half of my half.' I've got physical proof
that this definitely happened and he definitely made this offer. But you
didn't write those kinds of things down, because you weren't allowed to
have that in the bylaws at that time—a player owning any part of a particular team. Unfortunately for us, a year later, Ike had a heart attack and
died. But I always thought that Kosloff knew what it was all about. And
yet, I mean, he had a wonderful family, he was wonderful man. But he got
me for a quarter of something that belonged to me, you understand? So
there was no real love lost with Kosloff. Not that I hated him or anything.
And I said to myself, *You know, Ike was so good to me throughout the
years. I don't care that I'm not going to pick up some other money for whatever. Just knowing Ike was enough, and he did a number of things for me.*

"My leaving Philadelphia was to go out in this world and make a life
on my own. I am rooted in Philadelphia. I tell people that almost everything I owe—my financial situation, my good upbringing and incredible
memories, which may be the biggest part of my life—is to Philadelphia,
where I was raised. I have so many friends and family that are still there.
Would I love to have a hoagie right now! Do you understand? I was born
at the University of Pennsylvania Hospital at 37th and Spruce, and I'm
totally happy about it. Do you understand? A lot of times, just because
you are not at a place, it doesn't mean in your soul and your heart that

your feelings are not there. I love Philadelphia. Just because you don't see me there every day, it's still very much a part of me. I've tried sometimes to think about buying a ranch and becoming a gentleman rancher, but I'm a city boy. At one time, it was the third largest city in America. Its historic value is beyond doubt, and I'm a history buff and all those kinds of things.

"I made a statement in the paper the other day that I don't root for the Lakers, I don't root for Philadelphia and the Golden State Warriors—the three teams that I played for—because right now the way the NBA is, they trade guys so fast. So I follow individual players. For example, I may like this guy and the next day they trade him to Boston. Am I now supposed to be a Boston fan? I do follow Philadelphia closely, but the ownership has changed so very much, the only person I know there is their longtime PR man, Harvey Pollack.

"Bill Russell and I have dinner quite frequently. We talk about the game as professionals, remembering how the game ought to be played. We see a lot of things that we don't like. And that isn't to say that what we see is altogether correct or what's actually happening, because the league requires people to be more specific in their duties today. Bill Russell is known as a defensive player, but yet he got all those rebounds and he averaged almost 16 points a game for his whole career—16 points a game! So he's not like Dennis Rodman, who gets 16 rebounds and only one point a game. Plus, Bill Russell was a great assist guy—I think he averaged four or so assists a game for his career. So that makes him a great all-around player. Maybe up there with anybody else."

"I consider the greatest rivalry in sports—team or individual—was Wilt Chamberlain against Bill Russell," I said to him. *"For 15 or 20 years, including playoffs, you would go man-to-man. What were the feelings in those days between you two?"*

"Bill Russell is a very very proud man. I thought his game of basketball was as good as anybody's who ever played the game. He might not tell you that, but that's how I feel. All of the rings he won proved it to that degree. But he knew that playing against me was another story. He really had to get himself ready to play those games. They tell me when the games were over, he would throw up and get sick in the bathroom, and sometimes he would throw up before the games.

"But surprisingly, even though you called it the greatest rivalry, and I respect him greater than any other player that I've ever seen or ever played against, I didn't see him as my personal confrontation. I saw the

Boston Celtics as my great personal confrontation. Every time I stepped on that court, I knew that it was not only going to be Bill Russell behind me to block a shot or steal the ball or impede my progress. It was going to be KC Jones coming from the weak side to slap the ball out of my hand when I put it down; Tom Heinshon coming over there, hoping that I would run smack into him. Heinsohn used to set picks on me in the frontcourt. As I was coming up the court, he would send Bill Russell running so he could get the ball to him. That's why I look at all of it maybe a little bit more as a challenge with the greatest team *and* the greatest player I ever could face, not just the greatest player."

"But there was always that respect that brought out the best in him and the best in you," I remarked.

"Oh, God! As I said to people, being of color back in those days there was camaraderie. There was a feeling of what's going on. And we also knew that we were the best. That's how we got to be there, because they weren't bringing anyone of color into the game unless they were the best. The challenge was always there. Whether we said it or didn't say it, it was always there!

"Elgin [Baylor] and Oscar [Robertson] and I were also good friends. We were walking down the street in New York one day after doing *The Ed Sullivan Show* or whatever, and Elgin looked at Oscar and said, 'Hey, Oscar, how can you score so many points and be so slow?' And Oscar looked at Elgin and said, 'Slow? I can beat any one of you guys out here running.' And Elgin set him up because Elgin knew how fast I was. So Elgin said, 'If you beat Wilt, then I'll race you.' Now we were right on 7th Avenue and Broadway. So he said, 'Just race Wilt to the corner.' And I was ready for it, understand? So I raced him to the corner and I beat him easy. And he came back and Elgin said, 'And you're going to beat me? You can't even beat a seven-footer and you're going to beat me?'

"But that's the kind of challenges we bestowed on each other all the time—some of them with a lot of verbiage, some of them very quietly. We were definitely opponents on the basketball court. The thing I liked about Russell more than anybody I ever played against was that he gave no quarter. He tried to play me with all the finesse and talent he had in his character and body. He wasn't worried about trying to make some dirty move or whatever. He said, 'I want to beat him at the game of basketball and not anything else.' Understand?

"Although I thought I was taking a more wholesome approach of trying to beat their whole team, I knew that Bill was really the pivot of that team. He was really the captain. I think his rebounding was even superior to his defense, because he always got the ball for them. But I always thought my numbers were good against Russ. Even in my first year, I scored more against Russell and Boston than I did against anybody else.

"So what I'm trying to say is that we had this very strong respect for each other. Not just Bill Russell, but Elgin and Oscar and myself and whoever it may be. Russell had this train set, and he would invite us over to his house to listen to records and watch his trains. And his wife at that time was Rose, and she would cook us stuff and whatever.

"Every Thanksgiving, the Celtics would play the 76ers in Philly, so I would have KC and Sam Jones and Russell to my house. Bill would eat dinner and then he would giggle and say, 'Oh, I'm really tired.' And my mother would say, 'Why don't you go upstairs and sleep and rest in Wilt's bed?' And we would be downstairs talking. Meanwhile, Russell would be resting for a couple of hours, getting ready for the game. Later, I would come home and my mother would say, 'You all lost!' And I'd say, 'Well, Mom, you gave him all that good food and then you gave him my bed.'

"How all-around was a guy named Michael Jordan? His basic thing was that he was a great defensive player, but it was about scoring. His assists were lousy. For a guy known as Sky Jordan, he averaged about five rebounds a game. What kind of a *Sky* is that? And yet Russell was a great all-around player. So I talk about things like that to him—about the fact that I don't know how they pick the best player and all that. Then I say, 'Bill, lend me a ring or two.' I tell him, 'What a lot of people don't understand is that they only talk about you defensively. They always talk about me offensively, and I resent that. You don't have to resent it because you have all those rings and you can sit back and say, Oh, ha ha!' Bill has been bitter about some things, which makes me feel like, *Well, you see it's not about race,* because in some ways I'm much more relaxed and feel better about life today than he feels about life, and he seemingly has everything going for him."

"*I was there on the train coming back from New York during the 1966-67 season,*" I said, "*when Alex Hannum told Jack Kiser and George Kiseda that no center has won the assist title in the NBA, and the next year, guess who led the league in assists with 6.8 a game?*"

"I took some heat from friends of mine like Billy Cunningham in the middle of that year when I was leading the league in scoring. A couple of guys like Hal Greer got hurt, and our scoring situation was not quite as balanced as it should be, and Alex goes to Jack Kiser and says, 'Jack, I've got to get Wilt to score a few more points. He's passing off too much, and I really need him to score a few more points. But how do I tell him? I got him into this mode of passing all the time; how do I tell the big fella that I need him to score more points?' Jack said, 'Don't worry, I'll take care of it.' So the next day Jack wrote this great article in the *Philadelphia Daily News*, saying that *Wilt can get 30 rebounds when he's 62 years old. Unfortunately, his scoring ability has really decreased a lot. He just can't go for two years and not use those tools. He says, it's a shame we can't have the old Wilt of two, three years ago on this team, blah, blah, blah.*

"So the next day, I'm on the stage at Convention Hall, watching the pregame, and Jack comes up to me and I say, 'What is this BS that I can't shoot the ball anymore?' And he says, 'Oh, I didn't say it like that. But there's no way you can go for a year or two years and just think you're going to score anytime you want.' So you know me and how I react. I went out that night and got 60 points. Then the next game I got 55, and the game after that I scored 58. And I saw him after the third game in the dressing room and I said, 'What was that you said about my scoring?' And he said, 'I was wrong, big fella.' Then he turned and looked at Alex and when I saw Alex's reaction, only then did I know I was set up. I had been had."

"Let's talk about one of your favorite topics," I interjected, *"foul shooting."*

"Okay, but let me backtrack for a minute. When I was real young, I ran track and field in the Penn Relays. We were one of the first sports events ever shown on television back in 1946. I ran this 30-yard shuttle, and I was extremely fast. You have to understand that some things are such a gift, to have a guy my size who was so fast. I was also quite skinny, but I was throwing the shot put 12, and 14, and 20 feet further than all of these big, bulky guys, and they were saying, 'Oh, well, we can't win nothing when Wilt's here.' And I would wear my little cap, my little beanie with my long, skinny, knobby knees, and they'd say, 'This guy's a shot-putter? How's a giraffe going to be a shot-putter?' So it wasn't like I was this great hulk of a guy who I later became—my legs were still skinny. The shot put helped build muscularity to my frame, but that additional muscularity was the one single thing that impaired my foul shooting. And I really believe that for sure, Al, because you can ask anybody who knew me back in those days: I could shoot good fouls.

"When I got bigger, I was in a shot-put ring in Kansas. Somebody threw the shot and it bounced off the board and hit me on the knee. My knee was sore for a while, and I couldn't take that deep bend. So I changed my stance and just started standing up straight and throwing free throws that way, and that was the beginning of the end. I think I shot free throws in the '70s in college and 51 [percent] in the NBA."

"People I asked were all of the same mind that you didn't really want to work on your free-throw shooting in the NBA. Is that pretty accurate?" I wanted to know.

"By that time, I was tired of all the attention I was getting in a negative way—*If you don't shoot your fouls*—and that wasn't altogether true. Remember, I had a coach by the name of Dolph Shayes who was as good as it comes in shooting fouls. His first comment after my first year in the NBA when I shot about 61 percent—which is not horrible compared to some of the things that you see today—was, 'Wilt should be ashamed of himself.' He said there should not be a pro without some practice who can't shoot 75 percent. Every day in practice, I made 85-90 percent, but I had the worst foul-shooting season of my life—37.5 percent for the year under Dolph Shayes. I laughed about that for two weeks. I said to myself: *I wonder, is my mind that messed up? Subconsciously, I'm going to show Dolph that it ain't all about practice. I'm just really terrible.*

"I remember Ike Richman said, 'Wilt, we've got to do something about your foul shooting.' He said he was going to send me to a psychiatrist. He said, 'I'm going to pay for it, $50 an hour.' I said, 'All right, you pay for it, I'll go!' I went to eight or nine different sessions. My foul shooting didn't improve a thing. I said, 'Ike, forget about a psychiatrist. Right now I haven't learned anything.'"

I broke in once again: *"I remember one time in Boston Garden, it was two hours before the game, the lights were on, and I heard this ball bouncing. It was you. You were at the free-throw line. I heard that you could make free-throw shots when there's nobody around. So I came over and watched. You made nine out of ten."*

"One time, Calvin Murphy was here at my restaurant, and I took him inside where I have a basketball court and we played Horse. And I was beating him. So Calvin goes to the foul line. And he makes five or six in a row. I go make five or six in a row. And then he misses. So when he misses, I go to the foul line and I make my seventh one and I win the game on a foul shot. Then I said, 'Calvin, don't believe all those stories that I can't shoot fouls.' And Calvin was so mad, he replied, 'I don't know how I missed those two foul shots in a row; I can make 25 in a row any time I want.' So I said, 'Calvin, if you can make 25 on these baskets, I'll give you my doggone place.' Calvin then gets to the foul line and he's up to 19, 20, 21. When he gets to 23, I said, 'Calvin, now here's when the pressure really counts.' And sure enough, he misses the 24th. So my claim to fame was that I beat him on the line shooting Horse."

"But," I added, *"not on television in front of all those people."*

"Hey, you can't be perfect at everything. I always said, 'Maybe I was leaving room for improvement.' I left it too long, that's what happened."

CHAPTER 16

Wilt Chamberlain Tells More… for the Final Time

"*C*ertainly *not a lot of people in this world have been able to go through life as you have,*" I said to Wilt. "*There are pluses and minuses to all of it. Being who you are, I suppose even today it carries with it a burden—you can't be a private person. Let me ask you also: Do you think now what it would be like to have eight little kids running around?*"

"Well, I do think about that. Maybe that's one of the reasons why I've gotten involved with a lot of youth programs. It gives me the chance to interact with kids and things like that. Remember, I came from a large family. I always say I owe everything to basketball, but that's a far second to what I owe to my mother and father, who worked diligently and raised me as correctly as you possibly can. And I think that there's a fear syndrome there, and the fear syndrome is that I could not duplicate as a husband and as a father what my father and my mother were able to do—meaning that I'm out on the road a lot with the temptations of chasing women and, just maybe, not being a good enough father. My mother and father had been married for 50 years before my father died, and I have a great deal of respect for the institution of marriage. So since I have that, maybe it's kept me away from trying to get married. When I was young, my mother—God bless her—would always ask, 'When are you going to get married?' when I'd call her. But then I noticed, when I was in my 30s, that she noticed seemingly different types of women out there who were gravitating toward athletes simply because they had money and those kinds of things. And I think that she was fearful that I was going to get caught up in one of those types of situations. And then she stopped asking me when I was going to get married. She saw that as long as I was happy as a single man, that kind of sufficed for her. I'm not laying those excuses on people, but I think I had a fear of really making that commitment and being able to keep it. So I feel good that I won't have to lie to ladies and lie to people, because I've gotta tell you, Al, you've been out there on that road and you've seen a few guys who are not where they're supposed to be."

I decided to interject a famously notorious question: *"I asked you this once before when I was interviewing you and I was working at Channel 10—that 20,000 figure. How in the hell did that come about?"*

"First of all, I was hoping you'd ask that because it's a misnomer itself in some ways. We are all fascinated by numbers, and when I see fathers now in a grocery store with their kids, they'll point to their kids and say, 'He scored 100 points in one game.' So I'm writing a book called *A View from Above* with a chapter called 'Sex Rules the World.' And I'd say, well, sex does rule the world because I've had many, many encounters. As a writer, how do I let people know what *many* is? *Many* might mean four to this person, five to you, 100 to somebody else. So how do I get into this without being graphic? Without calling names? And right away, being a numbers person, I said a number is what will do it. So I thought of a number that was a round number and may be close, whatever, and I used that number. Now, of course, to the average person, that number is so preposterous that I can understand them not believing it. Believe me, I can fully understand people saying, *Oh, Wilt is so full of it.* But people who know me, they know that number may be less than what it is. But the point of using a number first of all was to show people that sex was a great part of my life, as basketball was a great part of my life, and that's one reason why I was single.

"But two things bother me. I was incorrect by not telling people at that particular time that this is a different era—this is an era of many diseases that can be fatal. And I'm not giving you guys a number to go out there and try to be another Wilt Chamberlain, or whatever. But I should have been a little more in-depth about being descriptive in explaining that this is not the same time, because I came along in the '60s when women discovered the pill and all of a sudden became very much more active out there, too. It was a different sexual situation going on in those days than it became later, and I did a very poor job of describing that. But in the last two sentences of that chapter, I said that for all of you men out there who think that having a thousand different ladies is really cool, I have learned in my life that having one lady a thousand different times is much more satisfying. And no one ever picked up on that. It wouldn't sell the book."

"This surprised me," I admitted. *"Not the number, but the fact that you talked about it, because in all the times we traveled together in the NBA, you never mentioned anything about that."*

"Never. That's out of character for me. I had already sold the book to Random House, and they were going to make it their number-one book of the Christmas season, which was really a feather in my cap. I had sold it without that statement in it, and they wanted me to talk a little bit more about politics and a little bit more about some of my sexual exploits, whatever. But the book had already been sold and I thought, I'm not going to be naming names or anything like that. So I just thought a number would be better. What happens, Al, if I had said 50,000? What happens if I had said 100,000? Would that have been taken lighter? But I must say that I am a very private person that way, and I had to apologize—and I'll continue to apologize—for all the ladies that I have known, that I was not using them as a number. That's what makes it sad to me, because I had some wonderful relationships. I should have told them then I was not trying to use women as a number, especially because I come from a family of six wonderful sisters. It was not the thing to do. So every now and then in life, you know, a pitfall or something happens that you wish you could take back. I would be more than happy if I could have said it in another way.

"I proved one thing, though, Al. I said sex does rule the world. And, therefore, the only thing to get out of that great book of mine, which I happen to love, was all about that one sentence about 20,000 women. Because sex does rule the world. And if you read that chapter, you will see some things that I am saying where they even had little boys 11-12 years old drinking milk, and this wonderful, buxom girl walks by in this commercial with her boyfriend, and she kind of winks at them and she says to them, 'Keep drinking your milk and one day you will grow up.' What she's saying is that you can grow up and have a girl like me. I mean, that was a *milk commercial!* But if you are writing a book, you've got to be honest about the book, and you have to reveal some things. And whenever you reveal some things, people are going to look at it any way they want. So now you're writing this book, and you know that sex is a part of your life—you don't tell people about it at all? I mean, you just leave it out? The whole time I played professional basketball, I never gave a ticket to a young woman to come and watch a game. And I'm saying this because basketball was my love and my work, and it wasn't a way for me to show off for people."

"I've always wondered," I asked him, *"what's it like being Wilt. One time I told people, 'Walking with Wilt through an airport was like walking with the Washington Monument.' People were in awe of you."*

"The way I started looking at it later in life—a lot of guys came along who are taller than me. I was in Heathrow Airport in London one day, and I was talking to a good-looking young lady who was on a flight with me from New York. She was waiting for a flight to Zurich, and I was waiting to go to Vienna. She said, 'You are the tallest guy I've ever seen. Are you the tallest guy in the world?' I said, 'Yeah, I'm the tallest guy in the world'—anything to keep her attention. And just as I'm saying, 'Yeah, I'm the tallest guy in the world,' who walks by me but Kareem. I see Kareem out of the corner of my eye and I quickly said, 'Would you believe the second tallest guy in the world?' without even missing a beat. And she looked at Kareem and he was gone, rushing to catch a plane to Paris. And she didn't know what to make of that.

"But you know what? Being seven-foot tall and being of color and being of note, and being outspoken and being all of the things that I am, really makes me a unique package. And I've told people there are a lot of great-looking guys—the Clark Gables of the world—a lot of rich people in the world, and so forth. But if you've got to have one thing going for you, be different. Understand? And I think Dennis Rodman has kind of proven that as he has done his thing in the league over the past four or five years—about being different—that gets him all that attention. But my difference comes a littler more naturally.

"I owe almost everything I have to people who have rooted for me, who have stood by me, and have believed in me. And I'll tell you what I mean. When I used to go out and play in the NBA and I'd have 55 or 60 points in a game, I always was very, very happy about that, and I'd go home, grab a couple of sandwiches and watch myself on TV, and really feel good about myself. But for a different reason, because I knew that the next morning, my father was going to read about it in the *Inquirer.* And my mother and my sisters and brothers were going to see it, and they could go to work with their chests stuck out a little bit about what their son or brother had done the night before. And when I had a bad game, I always felt embarrassed because they were going to have to deal with that aspect of it. But for me, I loved having bad games—of course, I didn't have that many of them—because that was the time I would go out and mingle with some guys at a bar or the club, and the guys would say, 'Hey, you had a good game,' and I would say, 'Oh no, I had a terrible game.' But I didn't mind talking about having a terrible game, because I always felt if I went out and had 55 or 60 points, they would think I was out to boast about my 55 or 60. If I went out and only had 20, they would feel a little more kindly toward me and realize, he didn't have a good game, but he's out here talking about it."

"One time," I recalled, *"some writers and a few of the guys came out of 30th Street Station after a game with the New York Knicks and went across the street to that restaurant. The name Ali comes up and you say something like, 'Hey, maybe I'll take him on.' What's that all about?"*

"Ali's advisor, Cus D'Amato, was a good friend of mine. And as I told you, my father was a huge boxing fan, and he used to take me to matches as a kid. I got to know D'Amato, and I used to work out with him a little bit and work on some things that he taught me. One day, he said to me, 'Wilt, I want to teach you how to fight one guy. With the things that you've got going for you, I want to set up a fight with you and Muhammad Ali. I think that basketball players are best suited to be boxers, because of things like footwork and legwork that they've got going for them. I can have you beat Muhammad Ali. I'm not going to teach you the fight game. I'm going to teach you how to fight just one guy, because we know everything there is that he can do, and he will not know anything that you can do.' So I remember saying, 'That makes sense to me. But what happens if he hits me one time?' He said, 'We'll see about that. That's why I know I want you, because if you're not afraid of being hit, then you might do something foolish. You want to be fearful of him.' And so he got me really thinking about fighting Muhammad Ali. And then Herbert Muhammad said, 'Sure, we can do that, and we can make a lot of money.' So, sure enough, they offered me five million dollars to fight in the Houston Astrodome. And I remember leaving my place in LA, and I said to my father, a big fight fan, 'Dad, I've got a couple of days off, and I'm getting ready to go to Houston to sign to fight Muhammad Ali.'

"Now I know my father is a Muhammad Ali fan like you cannot believe. So my father, who's five feet, eight and a half and had never said anything negative about my game, looked at me and said, 'You know what? Instead of going to Houston, I think I know what you should do. Why don't you go to that gym down on the corner and work on your foul shooting?' That statement created a lot of embarrassment in a whole lot of ways. So I looked at my dad and said, 'Well, Dad, you're probably right.' We were that close to signing. The only reason we didn't sign was because of ancillary rights. Herbert Muhammad wanted them all and my faction, which was just my lawyer and my accountant, decided that we were not going to give it all to them. And Muhammad Ali said, 'Give them half!' But Herbert didn't want to do it. But the truth of the matter was—and Herbert said it later on—he did not want Muhammad to fight me. He said, 'Champ, you don't know what this man might be able to do. There's no sense going out there and losing a fight to a basketball player. And he may be able to take you down.' Of course, Muhammad didn't believe that. But Herbert was a little bit afraid of that. So he weaseled out on this ancillary rights thing, so he knew that we weren't going to sign. And that was the end of it—which may have been the best thing for me. My father's advice was probably the best advice.

I had what I thought was an interesting question: *"Is it true that you wanted to be a pro football wide receiver?"*

"Yes. Hank Stram, who won a couple of championships as coach of the Kansas City Chiefs in the American Football League, had a camp up in the Catskills right next to me. So one day he saw me walking across the field, and he threw a ball at me and I caught it. And he threw me another pass, and I caught it and he said, 'Are you fast?' And I love it when people ask me if I'm fast. I love it! So I said, 'Fast? What's fast?' And he said, 'Have you ever run a 40 before?' So I said, 'Not a 40, but I've run a 50 and a 100 at times.' So he said, 'Do you mind if I time you in the 40?' So he times me—and this is in 1962 or '63—and I run a 4.4 or 4.5 in bare feet. And he goes, 'Would you like to be a receiver? I can use you.' I said, 'Hey, the football season goes into the basketball season. What kind of money are you talking about?' And he said, 'I can get you as much money as you want.' And I replied, 'My knees are not quite ready for that right now.' But Hank tried for a long time to try to get me to play football.

"I used to get some offers that would blow my mind away. One time I was coming from Europe on a Globetrotter tour, and three guys meet me at the airport. They said, 'Excuse me, can we talk to you for a second?' One of them said, 'We own your contract.' I said, 'Contract for what?' He said, 'You were drafted number one by the Georgia soccer team.' I had to sit down and laugh. 'The Georgia soccer team?' He said, 'Yes, but they sold your contract to the Cosmos in New York'—and Pele was playing for the Cosmos at the time. 'We think you would make the greatest goalie ever to play the game, and we are prepared to give you a million dollars to come and play with the Cosmos.' I said, 'Give me your card,' and I'm thinking, *Are you kidding me?* And sure enough, I was drafted to play a game that I hadn't played a day in my life."

"We skipped a very important part of your life," I inserted, *"which people are vaguely familiar with—that year between Kansas and being eligible for the NBA. In those years, you couldn't play until your college class graduated, and you joined the Harlem Globetrotters."*

"Most people don't know that for almost 17 years I've played on and off for the Harlem Globetrotters. But the year when I started with them almost caused a problem, because after that season I liked them so well I did not want to come back and play in the NBA. Abe Saperstein and Eddie Gottleib were very close friends. And it was Abe Saperstein's Harlem Globetrotters which may be the biggest reason for the NBA ever making it, because they used to play these doubleheaders and the Globies would play the first game, and people would come to watch the Globies and stay to watch the NBA. It was just so much fun. I had a chance to go to Europe, trying to speak a little French, a little Italian, a little German, and playing with a dream team. You have to understand that as a kid of color back in those days, the Harlem Globetrotters were like being a movie star. I mean that's what you dreamed about—being able to handle the ball like Meadowlark Lemon, who showboated all the time, or Goose Tatum or Marcus Haynes.

"I always remember sitting on the bus with these guys who I idolized—they gave me the back seat—and we would be traveling 600 or 700 miles every day, sometimes playing two or three game a day. And I can remember getting back on the bus at night sometimes and saying, 'You remember, fellas, I used to dream about this.' Can you imagine how dumb I was bouncing around and playing in the same stinking suit for three games? I mean, I've never seen anyone being so versatile, getting the most out of two suitcases. One had your Globetrotter paraphernalia and one you carried around with your clothes, because you'd dress up for three and a half months on the road. You would press your own clothes by turning the hot water on in the bathroom and steaming your stuff. Guys would trade things. But, hey, they all looked so fresh, like they were coming from a photo shoot somewhere. I don't know how they ever did it, yet the guys looked like they were on the cover of *GQ* with those two suitcases."

"How good were the Globetrotters?" I asked.

"At that time, they were legitimately the best and they could beat any team. They were definitely *it*. Meadowlark was just the most sensational, awesome, incredible basketball player I've ever seen. Dr. J or Jordan for me would be Meadowlark Lemon. He would bet you money that he could make a shot that looked like one in a million, and it always went in. I played guard on the Globies. Every big guy fancied himself playing guard. I had a pretty good two-hand shot, not like Dolph Shayes or anything, but I could shoot from 40 feet out, a one-hand stab and jump shots. I loved that. That was like heaven. I liked being out there on that floor. The only problem was that Abe, who was an incredible businessman, thought that every game I should score 100 points. So he would implore the guys to keep giving me the ball. I'd say, 'Abe, people are not coming out to watch me score 100 points. They want to see Meadowlark doing his thing and stuff like that.'"

"When you were growing up, did you know of Josh Gibson and the Negro Baseball Leagues?" I asked.

"Absolutely! Baseball was not my game, but we had a guy named Parnell Woods who was our road manager, who played for the Birmingham Bears in the Negro League. One time, I asked him, 'How did they pick Jackie Robinson?' He knew Jackie and he said, 'They tell you they picked Jackie Robinson because of his temperament and because he would be the guy who would handle adversity, and so forth. That may have been true, but they wanted a couple of other guys because if they had got Josh Gibson'—and he named some other guy who could run really fast, and he named Satchel Paige, the pitcher. 'Those players would have embarrassed white baseball with their superior talent. Josh Gibson would have been hitting the ball out of Yankee Stadium, over the flag, into the Bronx, and they didn't want that. So they picked somebody who was good but by far not even close to being the greatest.'

"Baseball was one sport that I never tried, but guess what, I was drafted by the Baltimore Orioles coming out of college as a baseball player. They admired me as a pitcher. Baseball was a game I enjoyed to watch, but I never thought about playing."

"Did you ever pitch?" I wondered.

"Hell, no. I fooled around and I could throw some curves and whatever. But I was so bad, I was the only guy who would strike myself out. I would throw the ball up and try to hit the ball to the outfield and couldn't figure out how to do it. Maybe they just wanted to see me come off that mound and scare somebody to death.

"There's one question that you didn't ask me. Because if you came into my house about 30 years ago, you would have seen a number of trophies—about 40 or 50—the only trophies I ever had in my house. And guess what those trophies were for? Bowling! I was a bowling nut, and I won two bowling championships at Kansas. I averaged 209 for one and 206 for another. I won the all-around event. I still have a letter that my roommate's mother wrote congratulating me for winning one of those championships. Billy Welu, a great bowler back in the old days, saw me bowl one time and I got to meet him. He said, 'You're a good bowler, I watched you one day.' And I was so in awe that Billy Welu had watched me bowl."

"I used to think," I commented, *"that Jim Brown was the greatest all-around athlete I ever saw. I just changed my mind."*

"Jim Brown and I used to challenge each other in everything—it was that black thing I was telling you about. One night we started bowling. I bowled 10 strikes in a row and as I'm getting ready to bowl my 11th strike in a row—Jim had bowled about 100—all of a sudden the lights go out in the place. I looked around and said, 'I'm bowling a perfect game. Turn the lights back on!' And the guy who's running the place said, 'I'm sorry, we've got to close the lanes because the league's starting in five minutes.' So I'm putting my shoes on and I look up and there's a sign: WE GIVE $1,000 FOR ANYONE BOWLING A 300 GAME. And Jim said, 'It's the only time my hands are up. You got me in bowling.' I don't know why but they were the only trophies I kept. I was a pin boy when I was a kid. I used to handle two or three lanes at a time."

"On the cover of the Sixers' '98-'99 brochure, there's a picture of a guy holding up a card which says '100' on it. The game against the New York Knicks was never televised. It was played in Hershey, so no one will ever see it. There was some audio. Bill Campbell had somebody send copy of the tape. But it's a monumental moment, not only in basketball but in all of sports. What do you remember about it?" I asked Wilt.

"Strangely enough, that 100-point sign might have been the only camera in the whole arena at that particular time. I remember that morning we took a bus from Gotty's office and we drove to Hershey three or four hours before the game, because we were saving money by not staying in a hotel room. So we had three or four hours to kill, and I remember going down to this penny arcade that we had in this arena. And I remember grabbing this rifle, shooting it, and just annihilating the marks that these guys had previously made as the highest. And along comes my friend and lawyer, Ike, and he goes to the guy who works at the arena and asks what the highest score was. The guy tells him and Ike comes to me and says, 'Wilt, I bet you that you can't shoot, say, 9,050 points.' So I shot like 1,000 points higher. Now Ike didn't know what to do. I was in a zone shooting this rifle, and we didn't even give it a thought.

"But I do remember in the first half of the game, I usually stayed in the post, shooting turnaround jump shots. But I was shooting jump shots from the top of the key, and I was hitting very, very well. I ended up with 40, 41 points at halftime. But that wasn't anything startling because I was averaging 50 that year, and there was a lot of times I'd have 37 or 38 by halftime, so there was nothing really magical about that.

"The magic only started to happen when I got into the 70s. And when I got into the 70s, everybody in the stands—which was about 4,000 people, a lot of people back in those days in that arena—started chanting, 'We want 100!' Well, Al, I've got to be honest with you, I had had a rather soft night the night before with no sleep at all getting into Philadelphia. I hadn't slept in two nights and two days, and I was really tired. Now the Knicks were becoming humiliated and really angry that I was trying to get a record on them. They didn't really care for that at all, and they did everything possible to keep me from getting the record. I heard that Fuzzy [Levane] called time out and says, 'If anybody shoots the ball before 23 seconds, I'm taking you out of the game...,' and 'I want you to foul anyone who attempts to get the ball...,' and 'Don't let Wilt get the ball...,' and all sorts of things that just didn't make any sense. I found this out later from Willie Naulls. So now my team is giving me the ball in the backcourt so they can't get fouled. Now why would I want the ball in the backcourt? I'm tired of being fouled in the frontcourt.

"So for the next quarter and a half, as you will see, my shooting went down terribly percentage-wise because I was really tired and people are chanting, '100! 100!' And I'm thinking, *If I get 100 this week, next week they'll want 200! I'm not going to worry about any 100!* And I'm becoming really annoyed about this chant for 100. The good thing was that I was making my foul shots—I had made 25 out of my first 26. Then I remember going to the foul line and missing two in a row, and I said to myself, *Not this old crap again.* And I knew then that I was really mentally out of it. So I lost all concentration, but I was really close with 92 or 93 points, so I felt like I might as well go ahead and go for it. When it was done, I didn't see it as the miraculous thing that other people thought it to be because, first of all, I was far too tired to appreciate it. Secondly, I remember saying to someone, 'Man, 100 points, that's just twice my average; what's the big deal about that?' I said, 'Al Attles got 16 or 17—that's three times his average.' I was not trying to downplay it, I was just telling it like it was.

"As you may have heard, I drove home that night in a car with some Knicks players, because I was living in New York at the time and I was commuting. Willie Naulls was driving, so I sat in the front seat with him. The guy who guarded me for a while was sitting in the back seat, and I immediately fell asleep. When we hit a toll road stop, I would wake up and I could hear them saying, 'Can you believe that SOB got 100 points against us?' And the whole conversation for two and a half hours was them calling me names. So finally they dropped me off at my house. I got out of the car first and said, 'Hey, fellas, thanks for the lift,' and then I said, 'You know, I'm so sorry about that 100 points. I really didn't mean to be an SOB, but what the hell!'"

CHAPTER 17

A Look Back and
a Look Ahead

One night years ago when I was still at Channel 3, I was covering a Flyers game in the very crowded Spectrum press box. At the time we were still shooting film, by the way. My friend Tom Brookshier was there with a technician, and next to the technician was something that I had not seen before. It looked like a camera, but not a regular camera, so I asked the technician, "Whatcha doing? What is this?" He said, "This is a *live* camera. It's called a *mini-cam*. CBS has a few of them which they send around to the CBS-owned-and-operated stations for the local people to try out to see how they work."

When I got back to work at the station that night, I said, "I've seen the future and it's not going to be great!" And as it turned out, that's what would have happened had we all stayed at Channel 3. They brought in a new news director near the end of our tenure, and he wasn't satisfied having the best news team, not only in this town, but maybe in the country. He and the people who owned Channel 3 weren't particularly happy with the way things had gone for the past five or six years, because they were not comfortable with the professional talent. Sometimes we asked questions and sometimes there weren't any answers. But that's another story.

Management decided that the way to avoid all of that would be to have news gathering go electronic with the mini-cams: live news all the time from everywhere. That's when we started to see mini-cams from all of the stations around town with a reporter and cameraman doing "live remotes," as we called them. And that's what eventually took over local news. The problem is that much of what they call news today is actually manufactured. It isn't real news.

For example, if you were working on a daytime story from Citizens Bank Park, because the Phillies were scheduled to play a game there that night, you would do a live shot from the empty stadium, looking for any kind of angle: *Hey, guess what happened here this afternoon with the Philadelphia Phillies?* It was just an excuse to be live from anywhere, and the whole process has just grown exponentially ever since Tom Brookshier first went live with that little mini-cam when we were all still shooting tape from the Spectrum at a Flyers hockey game.

It's really discouraging how the local TV stations have been ignoring sports on their news shows more and more for the past 30 years. (I'm not talking about Comcast SportsNet, which continues to do a thoroughly professional job in this regard.) I covered the Phillies when they won their first World Series in 1980. As I mentioned earlier, I interviewed everybody who was at the Vet that night—the manager, coaches, every player and team official. I had literally hours of tape. But most of it never saw your TV screens. Do you know why? My station had live cameras pointed at all the major bars, clubs, and street corners in the city, and they went to them immediately after the game. They never came to me because the news director said, "This is not really a sports town." I can't begin to tell you how frustrating that was.

During our nightly newscasts, the people at Channel 10 never would mention that I was coming up at the end of the telecast by saying something like, Stay tuned for sports! They never announced anything about sports until 25 minutes after the hour, when the rating machines were turned off for the final five minutes at the end of the half hour. The anchors would cut my time constantly by ad-libbing and making small talk at the end of the show—and hey, that was *my* air time they were taking. My friend and producer Bill Werndl and I literally had to fight every day with the news department for a few extra seconds for an important sports story.

Not only was there a significant philosophical gap between news and sports people in the TV newsroom, but for many years a wall existed between members of the print and electronic media. Back in the day, as they say, the newspaper guys thought that the TV types were overpaid airheads with fancy hairdos and makeup. I challenge that vociferously: I never wore makeup.

The problem was that members of the print media ran the press boxes because they had rigid deadlines and had to write their stories during the games. What the hell was a 6:00 p.m. or an 11:00 p.m. deadline for us "airheads" who didn't have to go *live* until after the game? As a result, the writers got preferential seating. During a Phillies World Series game at Veterans Stadium, for example, I had to sit in a restaurant in right field. In most arenas around the country, we were assigned seats with the fans during NBA and NHL playoffs.

But all of this has changed because many of the print guys (and gals) have themselves become airheads. Just tune in to your TV or radio and see how many of them now have their own shows. All is well now. We are all considered just *media,* and I have many friends in the print business.

And while we're on the subject of friends, when the Eagles were run by Leonard Tose, Dick Vermeil, and Jim Murray, they were the most cooperative, accessible team in the National Football League, without question. And that's what bothers me about the club today. I'm not talking about their PR department because I love those guys—it's the CIA attitude of the front office. Andy Reid is the winningest coach in their history, and he plays the game because he is both coach and general manager. But when you're working on the other side as a writer, sportscaster, or talk show host, it makes it very difficult to cover that team. I got the feeling from the very beginning that the Eagles brain trust didn't really want to talk that much. I figured they just bought the franchise and had never been in football before. But it didn't change. All I wanted to do was be able to stand up and ask a question during the press conference and get an honest answer. That's all! I wasn't trying to make news. I was just trying to find out what was happening, put my show together, and be done with it. But the feeling was: *We're up front; you're there; you're the enemy.*

I understand that it is difficult to be a person who is prominent politically or athletically. The guy that owns the NFL franchise is the number-one guy in every city in the National Football League—the biggest man in town. That's the way it is, and you have to act accordingly. Not that you have to be a great guy and shake hands with everybody, but you should be a little more cooperative with the people who are trying to make your football team a little better in the eyes of the fans. They're doing their job. They're not out there to roast you all the time, but after a while you get to the point where you think, *Well, I wasn't going to say anything, but they're not telling me anything, and it's about time I said something*—which is not a good relationship.

Professional football is played only once a week. The stadiums are full and television is saturated with NFL games and features five, six, seven days a week. There are shows all over the place, and they have their own NFL network. Frankly, the Eagles don't really need the love and affection from the fans as much as the Phillies do, because people are going to buy tickets to their games no matter what their record is. I don't think there will ever come a time when there will be empty seats in Lincoln Financial Field. Football still rules the roost in Philadelphia, although the Phillies have been catching up in the past few years. The Eagles have made a deep dent in the community, but that can only last as long as they keep winning or staying competitive. But I don't think that it will ever get to the point where they're not going to fill up the house with a team that can make the playoffs.

Personally, I must say that it wasn't great fun for me to cover the Flyers. When they started in 1967, I was doing Big 5 basketball and the 76ers as they captivated the city by winning the NBA championship. That's the team that was voted the best in the first 50 years of the NBA. From day one, I was considered the *basketball* guy in town, not the *hockey* guy, even though I graduated from a great hockey school, St. Lawrence University, a Division I institution that produced Mike Keenan and Ray Shero. The Flyers players and coaches couldn't have been more cooperative; my problem was with the ownership—even though I had demonstrated that I knew the game and what it took to play it.

Compounding the problem was the fact that Ed Snider never liked basketball from the day the Flyers and Sixers moved into the Spectrum. When "Mister Ed" became president of the Sixers, all of the talk about being a basketball fan was pure baloney.

One of the joys of covering the Flyers and 76ers, however, was developing a friendship with Pat Croce, who served as trainer for both teams before starting a chain of physical therapy centers. Pat eventually sold them for $40 million and then talked 76ers owner Harold Katz into selling the team to him and Ed Snider. Pat was the premier promoter but left the club after a disagreement with Snider, whom he thought was going to retire. In 2005, Pat opened a $10 million Pirates Museum in Key West, Florida. Five years later, he founded the St. Augustine Pirate and Treasury Museum. You meet a lot of people in my business and a few stand out. Pat Croce is one of them.

I'm not saying that the media is perfect or infallible, and it is certainly not beyond reproach. Even Big Al has his flaws, like my colleagues and competitors who, on occasion, have been known to go too far in search of the "Big Story."

Okay, that's enough of my problems. Let's take a look into Big Al's crystal ball and see what's ahead for the world of sports. Two things are going to happen. First, sports on television will get nothing but bigger. Television, of course, has exploded because of cable, sophisticated satellites, and other new technology in the past several years. Just look at the millions of people who watched the World Cup in 2010. Moreover, planes will soon fly twice as fast, meaning that teams that go from New York to Los Angeles in five hours will go from New York to London in three hours. As long as you can cut down on travel time, league officials in all professional sports will be able to put a franchise in any city in the world. You will be able to see NHL hockey in countries like Russia and Sweden where many players are being drafted annually by U.S. teams; Major League Soccer in Spain, NBA and WNBA basketball in London, Paris, Rome, and Tel-Aviv; and Major League Baseball in Korea. It's conceivable that overseas franchises in Latin America, Europe, Asia, and Africa will someday join with U.S. franchises to form international professional leagues. And when we call it the World Series, by God, it's going to be a real World Series, because it could be Japan against the Philadelphia Phillies.

We're talking down the road, but I think all this will happen sooner than a lot of people expect—maybe in 20 to 25 years. But as travel time decreases and more international television coverage is added, worldwide interest in sports can only get bigger. TV will introduce events to fans in the United States that most Americans don't pay too much attention to right now. I remember people became captivated by bullfighting when I was at Channel 17 some 45 years ago. It was our most-watched show until we went to color.

If you asked me back in 1954 what I expected from the broadcasting profession, it would have been like taking a trip to Mars for me. As I look back on my half-century in the business, I never could have come up with the ideas that have now become reality. But television and the electronics industry did it. TV has made sports successful, there's no question about that, and TV will widen its world appeal exponentially. I see television sets getting bigger and I see them going 3D. And every home will have one. I have no knowledge of electronics, but technology is moving at speeds it has never achieved before. We may not be doing any ballgames on the moon, but one day Mars may have a franchise.

As many others do, I see the population increasing in the United States and all over the world. The more people there are, the more viewers there will be. Sports are the common denominator because every country has them, and people crave as much of this type of entertainment as they can find. We introduced baseball and basketball to the world, and the rest of the world has tried to teach us soccer. We haven't done very much with soccer yet, but once the game is opened up by shortening the playing field and increasing the scoring, the rest of the world's football will probably catch on. If the success of the Philadelphia Union in its new 18,500-seat stadium in Chester is any indication, it looks like the sport finally has traction here after 50 years of trying. Fans want scoring, right? No matter what game it is, the more action and scoring provided, the more popular the game becomes.

And speaking of Philadelphia, I see either Temple or Villanova University continuing its ascendency into big-time, Division I, Bowl Championship Series–eligible football by being accepted into the Big East Conference. Elsewhere in the Delaware Valley area, look for professional golf to return with a major PGA tournament making a regular tour stop. The success of the recent AT&T Tournament helped to seal that deal.

The recent sale of the 76ers to billionaire Joshua Harris, a Penn graduate, for a reported $300 million, was not a last-second deal. Ed Snider had been president of both the Flyers and 76ers, and it had been known for a while that the NBA team was being shopped around. When the Flyers and the NHL came to Philadelphia in 1967, it became obvious that Snider's attention would be on the hockey team 99 percent of the time. Why would a multi-billion-dollar company like Comcast want to give up a local basketball team for chump change? I rest my case!

As far as the immediate future goes for local television news and particularly sports, there's no question where everything is headed. TV news has pretty much married itself to weather and local news. Finally, way down at the bottom of the list, we find sports. The fun-and-games department is getting maybe three minutes on the air, if that, at the very end of the newscast. Sports departments will eventually disappear from local stations. You may still get three minutes of sports, but stations will be getting it packaged and won't have to produce it themselves. This could easily happen within the next five years.

Comcast, for example, will have the capability to deliver neat packages because it is now setting up sports channels all over the country. I see Comcast taking over a major share of TV sports. The company already owns 51 percent of NBC as well as the Golf Channel (the source of most professional golf programming), the Versus Cable network that carries NHL hockey, as well as USA and Bravo—and these sources are expanding as we speak. As I mentioned before, in Philadelphia, Comcast still owns the Flyers and the Wells Fargo Center. That will make it easy for the company to package whatever local stations want for their newscasts, including a menu offering choices for video clips, sound bites, and interviews. This will allow local news anchors to do their own voice-overs, or Comcast will supply it as part of the package. Look for more acquisitions of sports teams in the future.

Television is at the point now where it must cut costs. Not only that, but we're seeing already that the professional baseball, basketball, and football leagues are producing their own shows on their own networks, which means that someday soon they'll own the rights to their products and will sell them individually to every city. Therefore, you may get the NFL on ABC in one city and on CBS in another city. They'll put everything up for bid. They'll have their own sales staff and their own TV operation.

Do you know about the setup that ESPN is now operating up in Bristol, Connecticut? How about the sophisticated NFL Films organization over in Mt. Laurel, New Jersey, or the NFL Network in Los Angeles? That network is an enormous operation for just *one* professional sport. So instead of sending out bids, major league sports producers will sell their own product individually in each market—which means there will be no more middlemen handling the money that they're making now. Which is going to hurt the big networks like ABC, CBS, NBC, and FOX. Professional sports operators can increase their revenue by a tremendous amount of money if they don't have to pay a network to carry their games when someone will pay them to carry the games. That, I think, is going to happen fairly soon—not 25 years from now, but in the foreseeable future. It's inevitable.

Look, we now have a football franchise in Philadelphia that first sold back in 1940 for $165,000 and went for $5.5 million in 1963. That same franchise in 2010 was valued at $1.1 billion. We're talking big-time money. As TV grew, the money grew—not just in football, but for all sports. As the money grew, the teams got much more of it, and now you've got a great baseball player in Philadelphia—Ryan Howard—who signed a $125 million contract not too long ago.

However, I see the National Football League soon running into a lot of problems, because the players don't have guaranteed contracts like all of the other professional sports. Still, now that its labor problems seem settled for the foreseeable future, I predict that the NFL will move into Canada very soon, starting with Toronto. All it needs to expand farther north is two things—first money, and second more money!

Now don't quote me on these predictions in some distant year, but that's the way I see it at this point. That's based on a half-century of experience in the business. And as I've said many times, it's been a wonderful ride!

One of the things that differentiated me from a lot of guys in broadcasting, especially in Philadelphia, was that I did the sports on the news in the TV studio, but also handled play-by-play. That combination led to a tremendous amount of credibility, and that credibility led to unprecedented acceptance by the public, who understood that I clearly knew what I was talking about.

I've often said that I was a child of broadcasting. My career has been like bookends of local television sportscasting. It promised unlimited possibilities when I started, and it's succumbing to larger forces 50 years later. I was there back in the Stone Age, when radio was king, television was in its infancy, and videotape hadn't even been invented. And now my watch is over. I'm most proud that we went from 0 to 100 miles an hour—from radio to cable to satellite TV. And I had the best job. I actually got paid to watch games and experience the Golden Age of Sports in Philly in the early 1980s when the Phillies won their first World Series, the 76ers took the NBA championship, the Eagles went to the Super Bowl, and the Flyers reached the Stanley Cup Finals!

After 50 years in TV sports, 40 of them in Philadelphia, I'm most proud of the years here because this is one of the toughest television markets in the country. Lasting this long means that what I did on the air was give the viewers something to think about.

For me, the people who watched were like family and friends. Hardly a day goes by, in my retirement, when someone doesn't come up to me to say hello and talk sports. As I look back on it, I came to Philadelphia in 1964 and did Big 5 basketball on TV 17. It gave me a big start, and because of you, my viewers, 40 years later I can say, "It's been my pleasure!"